This Year in Barcelona

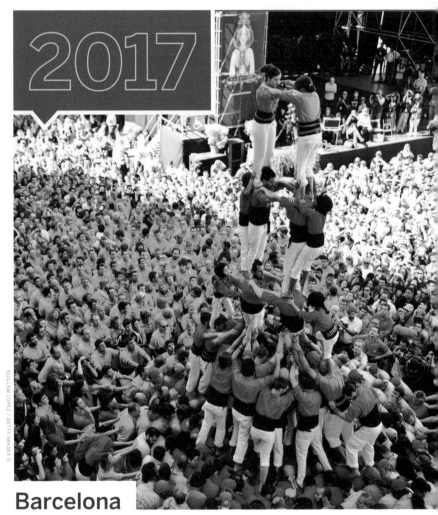

Barcelona

There's always something going on in buzzing Barcelona. Numerous concerts and festivals keep the cultural side of things busy, while traditional fiestas are a heady blend of religion, curious customs and riotous revelry. Clockwise from above: A *castell* (human castle) at Festes de la Mercè (p14); Diada Nacional de Catalunya (p14); *Correfoc* (fire runs) at Festes de la Mercè (p14)

Top Festivals & Events

Festes de Santa Eulàlia – 12 February (p7)

Festival Pedralbes – June (p11)

Festival del Grec – July (p12)

Festa Major de Gràcia – August (p13)

Festes de la Mercè – 18–24 September (p14)

Plan Your Trip
This Year in Barcelona

January

Barcelonins head to the Pyrenees for action on the ski slopes, while others simply enjoy a bit of post-holiday downtime (school holidays go to 8 January).

5 January

☆ Cavalcada dels Reis Mags

On the day before Epifanía (Epiphany), children delight in the Cavalcada dels Reis Mags (Parade of the Three Kings), a colourful parade of floats and music, spreading bonhomie and boiled sweets in equal measure.

Throughout January

☆ Festival Mil·leni

Running from November to May each year, this festival (www.festival-millenni.com) consists of a series of high-profile concerts in various venues around town.

1–29 January

⊙ Brick by Brick: Ceramics Applied to Architecture

In a city known for its mind-boggling buildings, it's apt that Museu del Disseny de Barcelona (p40) is holding an exhibition focusing on the use of ceramics in architecture. *Brick by Brick: Ceramics Applied to Architecture* features pieces from ancient Mesopotamia right up to contemporary works.

DAMIEN SIMONS / GETTY IMAGES ©

17 January

☆ Festes dels Tres Tombs

In addition to live music and *gegants* (papier-mâché giants worn over the shoulders of processionists), the festival dedicated to Sant Antoni features a parade of horse-drawn carts in the neighbourhood of Sant Antoni (near the Mercat de Sant Antoni).

February

Often the coldest month in Barcelona, February sees few visitors. Nonetheless, some of the first big festivals kick off, with abundant Catalan merriment amid the wintry gloom.

1, 3 & 4 February

☆ A Night at the Theatre
Take a guided tour of the magnificent Gran Teatre del Liceu (p194) between 10am and 1pm (20/80min €5.50/11.50) and return at night to see Massenet's opera *Werther*.

12 February

🎭 Festes de Santa Eulàlia
This big winter fest (http://lameva.barcelona.cat/santaeulalia) celebrates Barcelona's first patron saint with a week of cultural events, including parades of *gegants* (papier-mâché giants), open-air art installations, theatre, *correfocs* (fire runs) and *castells* (human castles).

25–28 February

🎭 Carnestoltes (Carnaval)
This pre-Lent festival (http://lameva.barcelona.cat/carnaval) involves several days of fancy-dress balls, merrymaking and fireworks, ending on the Tuesday before Ash Wednesday. Over 30 parades happen around town on the weekend.

Every Friday & Saturday

☉ Dancing Fountain
For a fun way to kick off your evening, head to the gorgeously kitsch Font Màgica (Magic Fountain) in Montjuïc for a sound and light show. It's open year-round, with February performances on Friday and Saturday at 7pm, 7.30pm and 8pm.

SHUTTERSTOCK/NATURSPORTS ©

Catalan Festivals

Catalonia's best celebrations tend to revolve around religious holidays. Festivals dedicated to Nostra Senyora de la Mercè (Our Lady of Mercy) and Santa Eulàlia – Barcelona's two patron saints – are the city's biggest bashes. You'll see plenty of *sardana* (Catalonia's national folk dance) and *castellers* (human-castle builders) there. You'll also see *gegants* (huge papier-mâché giants) and *capgrossos* (oversized heads worn by costumed actors).

Another feature of these Catalan fiestas is the *correfoc* (fire run), where horned devils brandishing firework-spouting pitchforks wreak mayhem in the streets. They are sometimes accompanied by firework-spouting dragons, or even wooden carts that are set alight. Full coverings (hats, gloves, goggles) are highly recommended for anyone who wants to get close.

Plan Your Trip
This Year in Barcelona

March

After the chillier days of winter, March brings longer, sunnier days, though the nights are still cool. There are relatively few tourists and fair hotel prices.

3 March

✿ Festa de Sant Medir

This characterful religious procession in the Gràcia *barrio* (district) includes the throwing of tons of candy to the sweet-toothed masses.

Early March

🍷 Barcelona Beer Festival

Craft beer has hit the scene in full force in Barcelona. Come see the latest tastemakers in action at this three-day beer and food fest (www.barcelonabeer festival.com), with over 300 craft beers on hand. So many beers, so little time!

12 March

🏃 Barcelona Marathon

Runners converge on Barcelona every March for a marathon (www.zurichmarato barcelona.com) that usually starts and ends at Plaça d'Espanya, passing such places as Camp Nou and La Sagrada Família.

12–15 March

☆ Beethoven Extravaganza

The Palau de la Música Catalana (www.palaumusica.cat) is putting on all nine of Beethoven's symphonies in a four-day stretch, conducted by Venezuelan Gustavo Dudamel.

Palau de la Música Catalana (p98)

04

April

Spring arrives, complete with wildflowers blooming in the countryside, Easter revelry and school holidays, although showers can dampen spirits. Book well ahead if coming around Easter.

23 April

🎎 Día de Sant Jordi
Catalonia honours its patron saint, Sant Jordi (St George), on 23 April. Traditionally, men and women exchange roses and books – and La Rambla and Plaça de Sant Jaume fill with flower and book stalls.

24–30 April

☆ Barcelona Open
The city's premier tennis tournament, and an important fixture of the international clay-court season, sees some top names slug it out.

Late April

☆ Festival Internacional de Cinema d'Autor (D'A)
This well-curated film festival (www. cinemadautor.cat) presents a selection of contemporary art-house cinematic work over a few days in late April. The festival usually focuses on one main director.

Late April

✖ Alimentaria
Though it's a serious trade fair (www. alimentaria-bcn.com) rather than a food festival, this is well worth visiting for foodies. A highlight is the show cooking area, where top chefs demonstrate their skills.

29 April–7 May

🎎 Feria de Abril de Catalunya
Andalucía comes to the Parc del Fòrum with this week-long southern festival featuring flamenco, a funfair, and plenty of food and drink stalls.

SHUTTERSTOCK/MAXISPORT ©

9–16 April

🎎 Semana Santa (Easter Week)
On Palm Sunday people line up to have their palm branches blessed outside the cathedral, while on Good Friday you can follow the floats and hooded penitents in processions from El Raval's Església de Sant Agustí (Plaça de Sant Agustí 2).

This Year in Barcelona

May

With sunny days and clear skies, May can be one of the best times to visit Barcelona. The city slowly gears up for summer with the opening of the chiringuitos (beach bars).

Early May

☆ **Barcelona International Comic Fair**
Spain's biggest comics event (www.ficomic. com) takes place over three days in early May at the Fira Montjuïc trade fair venue.

Mid-May

☆ **Spanish Grand Prix**
One of the fixtures of the motor-racing calendar, the Spanish Grand Prix (www. formula1.com) is held at the Circuit de Barcelona-Catalunya, northeast of the city.

Mid-May

👁 **La Nit dels Museus**
The 'Night of the Museums' is a Saturday event (http://lameva.barcelona.cat/lanit delsmuseus) when all the city's museums throw open their doors, offering free entry and a range of entertainment. Museums are free the day after, too, to celebrate International Museum Day.

Late May or Early June

☆ **Primavera Sound**
For one week in late May or early June, the open-air Parc del Fòrum stages an all-star line-up of international bands and DJs (www.primaverasound.com). There are also associated concerts around town, including free open-air events at the Parc de la Ciutadella and the Passeig Lluís.

Late May or Early June

☆ **LOOP Barcelona**
This multiday fest features video art and avant-garde films shown in museums, theatres and nontraditional spaces (such as food markets) around the city.

CHRISTIAN BERTRAND /SHUTTERSTOCK ©

Mid-May

☆ **Ciutat Flamenco**
One of the best occasions to see great flamenco in Barcelona, this concentrated festival (www.ciutatflamenco. com) is held over four days in May at the Teatre Mercat De Les Flors.

June

Tourist numbers are well on the rise as Barcelona plunges into summer. Live music festivals and open-air events give the month a celebratory air.

Early June

🏠 Vintage a Barcelona

Taking place at Els Encants Vells (p160) flea market, this two-day fair is a must for lovers of vintage and retro. Food trucks, DJs and concerts provide a festive background.

Early June

☆ MotoGP de Catalunya

Spaniards are crazy about motorcycle Grand Prix (www.motogp.com), and their riders have been very successful in recent years. This is one of the most popular races, and livens up the city for a weekend in early June.

Mid-June–Early July

☆ Festival Pedralbes

This summertime fest (www.festivalped ralbes.com) takes place in lovely gardens and stages big-name performers (think the Pet Shop Boys, Kool & the Gang and Carla Bruni).

Mid-June

☆ Sónar

Sónar (www.sonar.es) is Barcelona's massive celebration of electronic music, with DJs, exhibitions, sound labs, record fairs and urban art. Locations change each year.

23 June

✿ La Revetlla de Sant Joan

Locals hit the streets or hold parties at home to celebrate 'St John's Night', which involves drinking, dancing, bonfires and fireworks (http://lameva.barcelona.cat/culturapopular/en/festivals-and-traditions/nit-de-sant-joan). In Spanish, it's called 'Verbenas de Sant Joan'.

Late June or Early July

✿ Pride Barcelona

The Barcelona Gay Pride festival (www.pridebarcelona.org) is a week of celebrations, culture and concerts, along with the traditional Gay Pride march on Sunday.

Late June or Early July

🏠 080 Barcelona Fashion

A well-regarded fashion fair (www.080bar celonafashion.com) displaying the season's innovative summer wear.

15 June

✿ L'Ou Com Balla

On Corpus Christi, L'Ou com Balla (the Dancing Egg) bobs on top of flower-festooned fountains around the city. There's also an early evening procession from La Catedral, and traditional Catalan folk dancing.

Plan Your Trip
This Year in Barcelona

July

Prices are high and it's peak tourist season, but it's a lively time to be in the city with sun-filled beach days, open-air dining and outdoor concerts.

30 June–9 July
✦ Mediterranean Games

This athletics and sports tournament includes 31 events and participants from 24 countries from right around the Mediterranean. Though they are being hosted by Tarragona, several events will be held in Barcelona.

Early July
☆ Crüilla

This well-attended music festival (www. cruillabarcelona.com) runs over three days in early July and features an eclectic line-up covering everything from rock to flamenco.

Mid-July
☆ Rockfest Barcelona

This three-day summer festival (www.rock festbarcelona.com) pulls some very big names indeed from the hard rock and metal end of the spectrum.

Throughout July
☆ Festival del Grec

The major cultural event of the summer is this month-long festival (http://lameva. barcelona.cat/grec) with dozens of theatre, dance and music performances held around town, including at the Teatre Grec amphitheatre on Montjuïc, from which the festival takes its name.

July–August
☆ Sala Montjuic

Picnic under the stars while watching a movie at this open-air cinema (salamont juic.org/en), which also features concerts and is usually held throughout July and into the first week of August.

June–August
⁂ Music in the Parks

From June to August, the city hosts Música als Parcs (Music in the Parks), a series of open-air concerts held in different parks and green spaces around the city. Over 40 different concerts feature classical, blues and jazz groups.

August

The heat index soars; barcelonins leave the city in droves for summer holidays, as huge numbers of tourists arrive. It's a great time to hit the beach.

Early August

✿ Circuit Festival

Running for about two weeks, this is a major gay fiesta (www.circuitfestival.net) with numerous party nights, including an epic final all-day all-night bash in a water park. There's a parallel lesbian event, Girlie Circuit (www.girliecircuit.net).

5, 12, 19 & 26 August

☆ Festival Piknic Electronik

Every Sunday from late June through September, you can enjoy a day of electronic music (www.piknicelectronik.es) at an outdoor space on Montjuïc. It attracts a mix of young families and party people.

Mid-August

✿ Festa Major de Gràcia

Locals compete for the most elaborately decorated street in this popular week-long Gràcia festival (www.festamajordegracia. cat) held around 15 August. The fest also features free outdoor concerts, street fairs and other events.

16–19 August

✿ Festes de Sant Roc

For four days in mid-August, Plaça Nova in the Barri Gòtic becomes the scene of parades, *correfoc* (fire runs), a market, traditional music, and magic shows for kids.

IAKOV FILIMONOV/GETTY IMAGES ©

Street parade, Festa Major de Gràcia

Plan Your Trip
This Year in Barcelona

September

After a month off, barcelonins return to work, although several major festivals provide ample amusement. Temperatures stay warm through September, making for fine beach days.

Late August or Early September

🎉 **Festa Major de Sants**
The district of Sants hosts a five-day festa (www.festamajordesants.net) with concerts, outdoor dance parties, *correfocs* and elaborately decorated streets.

11 September

🎉 **Diada Nacional de Catalunya**
Catalonia's national day curiously commemorates Barcelona's surrender on 11 September 1714 to the Bourbon monarchy of Spain, at the conclusion of the War of the Spanish Succession.

Late September

🍷 **Mostra de Vins i Caves de Catalunya**
At this wine and *cava* (sparkling wine) event, you can taste your way through some of the top wines of Catalunya. It's usually held on Passeig Lluís Campanys near the Arc de Triomf over four days toward the end of September.

29 September

🎉 **Festa Major de la Barceloneta**
This big September celebration in Barcelona honours the local patron saint, Sant Miquel, on 29 September. It lasts about a week and involves plenty of dancing and drinking, especially on the beach.

FERNANDO VAZQUEZ MIRAS/GETTY IMAGES ©

18–24 September

🎉 **Festes de la Mercè**
Barcelona's co-patron saint is celebrated with fervour in this massive five-day festival (http://lameva. barcelona.cat/merce). The city stages sporting events, free concerts, dance performances, human towers of *castellers*, parades of *gegants* and a fiery *correfoc*.

October

While northern Europe shivers, Barcelona enjoys mild temperatures and sunny days. With the summer crowds gone and lower accommodation prices, this is an excellent time to visit.

Throughout October

☆ Festival Internacional de Jazz de Barcelona

With an excellent program of high-quality concerts throughout the month, this long-standing festival (www.barcelona jazzfestival.com) is a musical highlight.

October

☆ Flamenco

For those who think the passion of flamenco is the preserve of the south, think again; some of the big names of the genre come from Catalonia. See a perfomance on Friday nights at the Jazz Sí Club (p196); also watch out for big-name performers at the Palau de la Música Catalana (p197).

Mid-October

✘ Mercat de Mercats

The 'market of markets' is a celebration of Catalan cooking and the wonderful locally sourced ingredients that have made Barcelona such a foodie destination. Over one weekend in October, this food fair features great foods, wines and workshops. Held in front of La Catedral.

Throughout October

☆ Symphony for the Senses

With amazing acoustics in a modern building, seeing a show at L'Auditori (p198) is a must for music lovers. Visit www.auditori. cat to see the program and buy tickets. If you arrive early, check out the Museu de la Música, on the 2nd floor of the administration building, where some 500 instruments are on display.

VOLANTHEVIST/GETTY IMAGES ©

Human Castles

One of the highlights of a traditional Catalan festival is the building of human *castells* (castles). Teams from across the region compete to build towers up to 10 'storeys' tall. To successfully complete the castle, a young child, called the *anxaneta*, must reach the top and signal with her or his hand.

Plan Your Trip
This Year in Barcelona

November

Cooler days and nights arrive, along with occasional days of rain and overcast skies. For beating the crowds (and higher summer prices), though, it's an excellent month to visit.

1 November

✤ Día de Todos los Santos

All Saint's Day is traditionally when locals visit the tombs of family members, then get together for the Castanyada, when roasted chestnuts and other winter foods are eaten.

Throughout November

✗ Tapas Crawl

Tapas, those bite-sized morsels of joy, are an essential pillar in Barcelona's culinary scene. Tapas bars are found all across the city, but La Ribera hosts some of the liveliest; hit several in a bar crawl around El Born, where locals go for an authentic Barcelona night out.

Mid-November

✤ L'Alternativa – Barcelona Independent Film Festival

Showcasing feature-length and short films, plus premieres by new directors, this film festival (www.alternativa.cccb.org) includes free and ticketed events.

Throughout November

⊙ Camp Nou

See a football match at Camp Nou (p70), hallowed ground for football fans across the globe. Or take a self-guided tour of the stadium and learn about the sport's most famous players at FC Barcelona's museum.

Barcelona FC vs Inter Milan

December

As winter returns, Christmas draws near, and the city is festooned with colourful decorations. Relatively few visitors arrive until Christmas, when the city fills with holidaying out-of-towners.

Late November– Christmas

🎁 **Fira de Santa Llúcia**
Held from late November to Christmas, this holiday market (www.firadesantallucia.cat) has hundreds of stalls selling all manner of Christmas decorations and gifts – including the infamous Catalan Nativity scene character, the *caganer* (the crapper).

24 December–6 Jaunary

🎊 **Navidad**
Christmas in Spain is a two-week affair, with the major family meals on the night of Christmas Eve, New Year's Eve and 6 January.

31 December

🎊 **New Year's Eve**
On New Year's Eve, the fountains of Montjuïc (Font Màgica) take centre stage for the biggest celebration in town. Crowds line up along Avinguda Reina Maria Cristina to watch a theatrical procession and audiovisual performance (plus *castells*), followed by fireworks at midnight.

NITO/SHUTTERSTOCK ©

Christmas Crappers

At Christmas some rather unusual Catalan characters appear. The *caganer* (crapper) is a chap with dropped pants who balances over his unsightly offering (a symbol of fertility for the coming year). There's also the *caga tío* (poop log), which on Christmas Day is supposed to *cagar* (crap) out gifts.

Plan Your Trip
Need to Know

Daily Costs

Budget:
Less than €60

- Dorm bed: €17–28
- Set lunch: from €10
- Bicycle hire per hour: €5

Midrange:
€60–200

- Standard double room: €80–140
- Two-course dinner with wine for two: €50
- Walking and guided tours: €15–25

Top End:
More than €200

- Boutique and luxury hotels: €200 and up
- Multicourse meal at top restaurants per person: €80
- Concert tickets to Palau de la Música Catalana: around €50

Advance Planning

Three months before Book hotel and reserve a table at a top restaurant.

One month before Check out reviews for theatre and live music, and book tickets.

One week before Browse the latest nightlife listings, art exhibitions and other events to attend while in town. Reserve spa visits and organised tours.

Useful Websites

Barcelona (www.bcn.cat) Town hall's official site with plenty of links.

Barcelona Turisme (www. barcelonaturisme.com) City's official tourism website.

BCN Mes (www.bcnmes.com) Trilingual monthly mag of culture, food, art and more.

Lonely Planet (www.lonely planet.com/spain/barcelona) Destination information, hotel bookings, traveller forum and more.

Spotted by Locals (www.spot tedbylocals.com/barcelona) Insider tips.

Arriving in Barcelona

El Prat airport Frequent *aerobuses* make the 35-minute run into town (€5.90) from 6am to 1am. Taxis cost around €25.

Estació Sants Long-distance trains arrive at this big station near the centre of town, which is linked by metro to other parts of the city.

Estació del Nord Barcelona's long-haul bus station is located in L'Eixample, about 1.5km northeast of Plaça de Catalunya, and is a short walk from several metro stations.

Girona-Costa Brava airport The 'Barcelona Bus' operated by Sagalés (one way/return €16/25, 90 minutes) is timed with Ryanair flights and goes direct to Barcelona's Estació del Nord.

Currency

Euro (€)

Languages

Spanish, Catalan

Visas

Generally not required for stays of up to 90 days. Some nationalities need a Schengen visa.

Money

ATMs are widely available (La Rambla has many). Credit cards are accepted in most hotels, shops and restaurants, but few bars.

Mobile Phones

Local SIM cards can be used in unlocked European and Australian phones. Other phones must be set to roaming. With an EU phone, you'll pay normal call costs.

Time

Central European Time (GMT/UTC plus one hour).

Tourist Information

Oficina d'Informació de Turisme de Barcelona (p238) provides maps, sights information, tours, concert and events tickets, and last-minute accommodation bookings.

When to Go

The sweltering summer (July and August) is peak tourist season. For pleasant weather, but without the ocean dips, come in late spring (May).

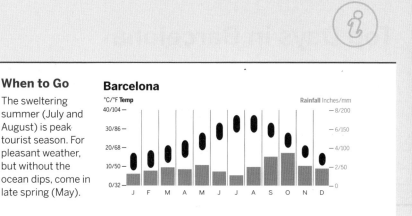

Barcelona

Reus airport Buses operated by Hispano-Igualadina (one way/return €16/25, 90 minutes) are timed with Ryanair flights and go direct to Barcelona's Estació Sants.

Getting Around

Barcelona has abundant options for getting around town. The excellent metro can get you most places, with buses and trams filling in the gaps. Taxis are the best option late at night.

Metro The most convenient option. Runs 5am to midnight Sunday to Thursday, till 2am on Friday and 24 hours on Saturday. Targeta T-10 (10-ride passes; €10.30) are the best value; otherwise, it's €2.15 per ride.

Bus A hop-on, hop-off Bus Turístic, from Plaça de Catalunya, is handy for those wanting to see the city's highlights in one or two days.

Taxi You can hail taxis on the street (try La Rambla, Via Laietana, Plaça de Catalunya and Passeig de Gràcia) or at taxi stands.

On foot To explore the old city, all you need is a good pair of walking shoes.

Sleeping

Barcelona has a wide range of sleeping options, from inexpensive hostels hidden in the old quarter to luxury hotels overlooking the waterfront. The small-scale B&B-style apartment rentals scattered around the city are a good-value choice.

Wherever you stay it's wise to book well ahead. If you plan to travel around holidays such as Easter, Christmas or New Year's Eve, or in summer, reserve a room three or four months ahead of time.

Useful Websites

○ **Airbnb** (www.airbnb.com) Apartment and room rentals.

○ **Booking.com** The most comprehensive hotel booking engine for Barcelona.

○ **Lonely Planet** (www.lonelyplanet.com/spain/barcelona/hotels) Huge range of hotels, hostels, guesthouses, B&Bs and apartments.

○ **Oh-Barcelona** (www.oh-barcelona.com) Good-value selection of hotels, hostels and apartment rentals.

For more, see the Survival Guide, p236

Plan Your Trip
Top Days in Barcelona

MARK AVELLINO/GETTY IMAGES ©

Barcelona's Must-Sees

On your first day in Barcelona, visit the city's major highlights: stroll La Rambla, explore the atmospheric lanes of the Barri Gòtic and linger over the stunning artistry of La Sagrada Família. History, great architecture and a celebrated food market are all part of this sensory-rich experience.

❶ La Rambla (p44)

Start with La Rambla. Don't miss the human statues, the Miró mosaic, and key buildings facing La Rambla, including the 18th-century Palau de la Virreina.

➲ La Rambla to Mercat de la Boqueria

🏃 Find the market's entrance on La Rambla's west side.

❷ Mercat de la Boqueria (p90)

Packed with culinary riches, this staggering food market is the favoured stomping ground for chefs and conjurers, weekend cooks and hungry-looking tourists. Don't leave without having a few snacks – perhaps from one of the delectable tapas bars in the back.

➲ Mercat de la Boqueria to Barri Gòtic

🏃 Head back down La Rambla, then turn left into Plaça Reial after passing Carrer de Ferran.

Day 01

❸ Barri Gòtic

Delve into Barcelona's old city. Cross picturesque Plaça Reial (p48) before wandering narrow lanes that date back to at least the Middle Ages. Make your way to the magnificent Catedral (p62), then visit the Temple Romà d'August (p65).

➲ Barri Gòtic to Cafè de l'Acadèmia

🚶 Cross Plaça de Sant Jaume, walk along Carrer de la Ciutat and take the first left.

❹ Lunch at Cafè de l'Acadèmia (p133)

Arrive early to get a seat at this small, atmospheric restaurant serving excellent Catalan cuisine. The multicourse lunch special is fantastic value.

➲ Cafè de l'Acadèmia to La Sagrada Família

Ⓜ Take Line 4 north from Jaume I; transfer at Passeig de Gràcia for Line 2 to Sagrada Família.

❺ La Sagrada Família (p36)

Roll the drums, turn on the stage lights and get ready for Spain's most visited church. This one-of-a-kind religious monument is as unique as the Giza pyramids and as beautiful as the Taj Mahal.

➲ La Sagrada Família to Tapas 24

Ⓜ Take Line 2 back to Passeig de Gràcia. Walk southeast down the street of the same name, then take your second left.

❻ Evening Bites at Tapas 24 (p140)

This great basement spot does a smart line in innovative takes on traditional tapas. It's a top place for a light bite or a full meal.

From left: Tapas at Mercat de la Boqueria; Miró mosaic, La Rambla

Plan Your Trip
Top Days in Barcelona

Mar i Muntanya (Sea & Mountain)

This itinerary takes you along the promenade that skirts the Mediterranean, then into the old fishing quarter of Barceloneta before whisking you up to the heights of Montjuïc for fine views, fragrant gardens and superb art galleries – including two of the city's top museums.

❶ Barcelona's Beaches (p122)

Start the morning with a waterfront stroll; Barceloneta Beach is scenic but once derelict area that experienced a dramatic make-over around the 1992 Olympics. Look north and you'll see Frank Gehry's shimmering fish sculpture, while to the south rises the spinnaker-shaped tower of the W Hotel.

➲ Barceloneta Beach to Can Ros

🚶 Look for Carrer del Almirall Aixada just north of the rectangular beach sculpture. Can Ros is about 350m back from the beach on this road.

❷ Lunch at Can Ros (p139)

Take your pick of the seaside restaurants if you want the view, but otherwise head back a few streets to this family-run gem, which has been dishing up excellent seafood for generations.

➲ Can Ros to Teleférico del Puerto

🚶 Walk to the southern end of Barceloneta and you'll see the cable car to your right.

Day
02

❸ Teleférico del Puerto (p241)

After lunch take a scenic ride on this aerial cable car for fantastic views over the port and the dazzling city beyond. At the top, you'll arrive in Montjuïc, a mini-mountain that's packed with gardens as well as hosting a few first-rate museums.

⊙ Teleférico del Puerto to Fundació Joan Miró

🚡 Take the cable car up to Montjuïc, disembark and follow the main road 800m west.

❹ Fundació Joan Miró (p58)

You can see a full range of works by one of the giants of the art world at this impressive museum. Paintings, sculptures and drawings by the prolific Catalan artist are displayed along with photos and other media. Outside is a peaceful sculpture garden with views over Poble Sec.

⊙ Fundació Joan Miró to Museu Nacional d'Art de Catalunya

🚶 Follow the path through the sculpture gardens east, take the steps up to the main road and continue east to the museum.

❺ Museu Nacional d'Art de Catalunya (p54)

Not to be missed is the incomparable collection of artwork inside the enormous Museu Nacional d'Art de Catalunya. The highlight is the impressive Romanesque collection – rescued from 900-year-old churches in the Pyrenees. Other halls showcase Catalan works from the Middle Ages up to the early 20th century.

⊙ Museu Nacional d'Art de Catalunya to Tickets

🚶 Descend toward Plaça d'Espanya. Turn right before the fountain, left on Carrer de Lleida and right on Avinguda del Paral·lel.

❻ Dinner at Tickets (p145)

You'll need to book weeks in advance to score a table at Tickets, but it's worth it, The celebrated restaurant run by the Adrià brothers showcases an ever-changing menu of molecular gastronomy.

From left: Barceloneta Beach; Teleférico del Puerto

Plan Your Trip
Top Days in Barcelona

La Ribera

Like adjacent Barri Gòtic, La Ribera has narrow cobblestone streets and medieval architecture galore. Yet it's also home to high-end shopping, a brilliant Modernista concert hall and a treasure trove of artwork by Picasso. Great restaurants and a fanciful green space complete the Ribera ramble.

Day

03

❶ Museu Picasso (p76)

Picasso spent his formative years in Barcelona; you can see his early masterpieces inside this inspiring museum.

○ Museu Picasso to El Born

🏃 Stroll southeast along Carrer de Montcada.

❷ Window Shopping in El Born

The medieval streets of El Born hide an abundance of shopping intrigue. For unique, beautifully made men's and women's clothing, stop in the Barcelona-born boutique Custo Barcelona (p158).

○ El Born to Cal Pep

🏃 Walk across Plaça de les Olles.

❸ Lunch at Cal Pep (p137)

For lunch, belly up to the bar at this bustling eatery for tasty seafood tapas.

○ Cal Pep to Basílica de Santa Maria del Mar

🏃 Stroll northwest along Carrer de la Vidriería and turn left on Carrer de Santa Maria.

LEMON TREE IMAGES/SHUTTERSTOCK ©

❹ Basílica de Santa Maria del Mar (p112)

A few blocks away, this captivating church is built in the style of Catalan Gothic. The 14th-century masterpiece soars above the medina-like streets surrounding it.

❍ Basílica de Santa Maria del Mar to Parc de la Ciutadella

🚶 Walk northeast on Carrer de Santa Maria and continue around the former Mercat del Born site to the park.

❺ Parc de la Ciutadella (p79)

After the compact streets of La Ribera, catch your breath and stroll through the open green expanse of this manicured park. You'll find sculptures, a small zoo, the Parlament de Catalunya, and the centrepiece, a dramatic if utterly artificial waterfall dating from the 19th century.

❍ Parc de la Ciutadella to Palau de la Música Catalana

🚶 Take Carrer de la Princesa back into El Born and turn right after 200m, making your way northwest.

❻ Palau de la Música Catalana (p98)

Designed by Domènech i Montaner in the early 1900s, this intimate concert hall is a Modernista masterpiece, with luminescent stained glass and elaborately sculpted details throughout. Come for a concert (p197), but it's also worth returning by day for a guided tour.

❍ Palau de la Música Catalana to El Xampanyet

🚶 Make your way back (southeast) to Carrer de Montcada.

❼ El Xampanyet (p178)

Just up the road, El Xampanyet is a festive spot to end the night. You can sample mouth-watering bites and let your cup brim with ever-flowing *cava* (Catalan sparkling wine). It's usually crowded but friendly, just politely elbow your way in for a bit of refreshment.

From left: Parc de la Ciutadella; El Born

Plan Your Trip
Top Days in Barcelona

RACHEL LEWIS/GETTY IMAGES ©

Art & Architecture

This tour takes you up to the enchanting (if accidental) park Gaudí designed overlooking the city, down the elegant architectural show-piece avenue of Passeig de Gràcia and into El Raval. There you'll find the city's top contemporary art museum anchoring Barcelona's most bohemian neighbourhood.

❶ Park Güell (p66)

Go early to Park Güell to beat the crowds and see the early morning rays over Barcelona and the Mediterranean beyond. Stroll the expanse of the park, ending your visit at Casa-Museu Gaudí (p69), where you can learn more about the life and work of the great Catalan architect.

◗ Park Güell to Gràcia

Ⓜ Take Line 3 from Vallcarca to Fontana.

❷ Gràcia (p110)

The village-like feel of Gràcia makes for some great exploring. Stroll from plaza to plaza along the narrow shop-lined lanes, stopping perhaps at open-air cafes along the way. Good streets for browsing include Carre de Verdi, Travessera de Gràcia and Carrer de Torrijos.

◗ Gràcia to Botafumeiro

🚶 Walk southwest along Travessera de Gràcia and turn right on Carrer Gran de Gràcia.

Day

DIEGO LEZAMA/GETTY IMAGES ©

❸ Lunch at Botafumeiro (p147)

This is one of Barcelona's best seafood restaurants. If the tables are full, ask for a spot at the bar.

○ Botafumeiro to Passeig de Gràcia

🏃 Amble southeast along Carrer Gran de Gràcia, which leads into Passeig de Gràcia after 400m.

❹ Passeig de Gràcia

Head to L'Eixample to see high-concept architecture. Passeig de Gràcia is a busy but elegant boulevard lined with exquisite Modernista buildings, including Gaudí's La Pedrera (p72) and Casa Batlló (p50).

○ Passeig de Gràcia to MACBA

🏃 Continue along Passeig de Gràcia, cross Plaça de Catalunya to La Rambla and turn right on Carrer del Bonsuccés.

❺ MACBA (p96)

A few streets away from Placa d'Espanya you'll reach the city's top contemporary art gallery, MACBA. It houses an excellent range of Catalan and European works from WWII to the present.

○ MACBA to El Raval

🏃 Walk along Carrer dels Àngels and turn left on Carrer del Carme.

❻ El Raval

Spend the early evening strolling the lively multicultural street scene of El Raval. Stop for a breather in the pretty courtyard of the Antic Hospital de la Santa Creu (p91) and check out Gaudí's Palau Güell (p88).

○ El Raval to Koy Shunka

Ⓜ Take Line 3 from Paral·lel to Catalunya.

❼ Dinner at Koy Shunka (p134)

Top off your night with a multicourse feast at Koy Shunka. This zenlike den of haute cuisine features a great marriage of Catalan creativity with Japanese tradition.

From left: Mosaic, Park Güell; El Raval

Plan Your Trip
Hotspots For...

GASTRONAUTS

⊙ **Mercat de la Boqueria** This legendary produce market, pictured above, is a cornucopia of sights and smells. (p90)

⊙ **La Ribera** Stroll this intriguing central district and browse its gourmet shops. (p100)

✕ **Cinc Sentits** Delight in the superb tasting menu at this top-notch modern restaurant. (p143)

✕ **Disfrutar** Have the meal of your trip at this superbly inventive molecular gastronomy restaurant. (p143)

⚲ **Espai Boisà** Learn to whip up some classic tapas and Catalan dishes in this excellent cooking school. (p210)

CULTURE VULTURES

⊙ **MACBA (Museu d'Art Contemporani de Barcelona)** The city's top destination for contemporary art, with top views to boot. (p96)

⊙ **Fundació Joan Miró** A comprehensive collection of this local boy's works, in an architecturally brilliant building. (p58)

✕ **Els Quatre Gats** Admire the fabulous Modernista decor in this historic restaurant, pictured below. (p95)

✕ **Tickets** If food can be art, then this is the most spectacular performance in town. (p145)

☆ **Gran Teatre del Liceu** Enjoy state-of-the-art acoustics in this marvellously atmospheric venue on La Rambla. (p194)

ROMANCE

👁 **Park Güell** Stroll the gardens and admire the views amid the Modernista fantasies of Gaudí. (p66)

👁 **Barri Gòtic** Walk around the historic centre and explore its hidden corners (p82).

✗ **La Vinateria del Call** Intimate and exquisite, this little old-town eatery is perfect for cosy dining. (p133)

🍷 **Caelum** Beautiful medieval cafe with candlelit downstairs space. (p132)

🕺 **Swing Maniacs** Learn to swing at a drop-in course, then hit the dance floor. (p210)

HISTORY BUFFS

👁 **Museu d'Història de Barcelona** A stunning walk through layers of history in the underbelly of the city. (p104)

👁 **La Catedral** A Gothic cathedral (above) with plenty of gravitas. (p62)

🍷 **Casa Almirall** This beautiful spot is unchanged (in a good way) since its 19th-century heyday. (p94)

🍷 **La Confitería** This former confectioner's shop is now a characterful bar full of historic ambience. (p176)

🕺 **My Favourite Things** Its old-town walking tour is a great way to hear about some of the city's history and legends. (p208)

CRAFTY CREATIVES

👁 **Casa Batlló** Exuberant, colourful and innovative, this building is like nothing you've seen before. (p50)

👁 **La Sagrada Família** The creative genius on display in Gaudí's masterpiece (above) is breathtaking. (p36)

✗ **Onofre** Small modern eatery in the historic centre doing delicious deli-style tapas. (p134)

🍷 **BlackLab** Terrific microbrewery in a historic building near the sea. More than a dozen beers on tap. (p180)

🕺 **Molokai SUP Center** Cut a cool figure on the Barcelona water on a stand-up paddleboard. (p209)

Plan Your Trip
What's New

STEFANO POLITI MARKOVINA/ AWL IMAGES LTD/GETTY IMAGES ©

Poble Sec & Sant Antoni

If you're looking for the newest creative spaces (cafes, eateries, clothing boutiques), head to Sant Antoni, the hipster epicentre of Barcelona. Famed chef Albert Adrià now runs five celebrated restaurants (including Tickets, p145), all within strolling distance of one another in the barrio (district); a sixth, Enigma, was scheduled to open in mid-2016. But here and in nearby Poble Sec, some of the most talked-about new restaurants aren't driven by famous names, but instead are unique, artfully designed spaces where non-celebrity chefs are creating extraordinary dishes.

The Epicentre of Design

After years in the works, the Museu del Disseny de Barcelona (p40) has opened, with four floors of beautifully lit exhibits covering graphic design, textiles, fashion and ceramics. The museum also stages thought-provoking temporary shows.

Craft Makers

At long last, microbreweries have arrived in Barcelona, bringing an abundance of craft beer bars in their wake. You're never far from a unique IPA, no matter where you roam.

Surfing with a Paddle

The increasingly popular sport for beach goers is gliding along on a stand-up paddleboard (SUP). Outfitters in Barceloneta hire out gear, and you can take a lesson if you're a beginner.

Poblenou Renaissance

This formerly industrial hood is on the make, with new galleries, colourful shops and restaurants forming the intersection for the creative tech- and design-folk who are increasingly moving here.

Above: Museu del Disseny de Barcelona (p40) and Torre Agbar (p229)

Plan Your Trip
For Free

NICOLAS KIPOURAX PAQUET/GETTY IMAGES ©

Free Barcelona

With planning, Barcelona can be a surprisingly affordable place to travel. Many museums offer free entry on certain days, and some of the best ways to experience the city don't cost a penny – hanging out on the beach, exploring fascinating neighbourhoods and parks, and drinking in the views from hilltop heights.

Festivals & Events

Barcelona has loads of free festivals and events, including the Festes de la Mercè (p14) and the Festes de Santa Eulàlia (p7). From June to August, the city hosts Música als Parcs (Music in the Parks), a series of open-air concerts held in different parks and green spaces around the city. Stop in at the tourist office or go online (www. bcn.cat) for a schedule.

Walking Tours

Numerous companies offer pay-what-you-wish walking tours. These typically take in the Barri Gòtic or the Modernista sites of L'Eixample.

Sights

Entry to some sights is free on occasion, most commonly on the first Sunday of the month, while quite a few attractions are free from 3pm to 8pm on Sundays. Others, including the Centre d'Art Santa Mònica (p49), Basílica de Santa Maria del Mar (p112), Palau del Lloctinent (p65), Temple Romà d'August (p65) and Antic Hospital de la Santa Creu (p91), are always free.

Picnics

It might not be for free, but you can eat very well on a budget if you stick to set menus at lunchtime. For even less, you can put together a picnic of fruit, cheese, smoked meats and other goodies purchased at such markets as Mercat de la Boqueria (p90), El Raval's Mercat de Sant Antoni (p164) or La Ribera's Mercat de Santa Caterina (p102).

Above: Mercat de Santa Caterina (p102)

Plan Your Trip
Family Travel

MIHAIL BULHAKOV/EYEEM/GETTY IMAGES ©

Need to Know

o **Change facilities** Not as ubiquitous as in North America, but generally good and clean.

o **Cots** Usually available in hotels (ask for '*una cuna*'); reserve ahead.

o **Health** High health-care standards. Make sure you have your child's EHIC card (see p236) before you travel within the EU.

o **Highchairs** Many restaurants have at least one.

o **Infant supplies** Nappies, dummies (pacifiers), creams and formula can be found at any of the city's many pharmacies. Nappies are cheaper in supermarkets.

o **Strollers** Bring your own (preferably a fold-away).

o **Transport** Barcelona's metro is accessible and great for families with strollers. Just be mindful of your bags, as pickpockets often target distracted parents.

Catalan Style

Going out to eat or sipping a beer on a late summer evening at a *terraza* (terrace) needn't mean leaving children with minders. Locals take their kids out all the time and don't worry about keeping them up late. To make the most of your visit, try to adjust your child's sleeping habits to 'Spanish time' early on, or else you'll miss out on much of Barcelona. Also, be prepared to look for things 'outside the box': there's the childlike creativity of Picasso and Miró (give your children paper and crayons and take them around the museums), the Harry-Potter-meets-Tolkien fantasy of Park Güell and La Pedrera, and the wild costumes, human castle-building and street food at festivals.

Babysitting

Most of the midrange and top-end hotels in Barcelona can organise babysitting services. A company that many hotels use and that you can also contact directly is Tender

STEFAN CIOATA/GETTY IMAGES ©

Loving Canguros (📞647 605989; www.tlcan guros.com), which offers English-speaking babysitters for a minimum of three hours (from €9 an hour).

Eating with Kids

Barcelona – and Spain in general – is super-friendly when it comes to eating with children. Spanish kids tend to eat the Mediterranean offerings enjoyed by their parents, but some restaurants have children's menus that offer burgers, pizzas, tomato-sauce pasta and the like. Good local – and child-proof – food commonly found on tapas menus are *tortillas de patatas* (potato omelettes) or *croquetas de jamón* (ham croquettes).

Family-Friendly Meals

Monvínic (p144) is a good choice for an off-peak lunch or quick dinner while the kids entertain themselves drawing on the glass wall. At Dos Trece (p135), you can enjoy quality food or cocktails while the younger

Top Five Experiences for Kids

CosmoCaixa (p124)

Museu d'Idees i Invents de Barcelona (p109)

L'Aquàrium (p86)

Poble Espanyol (p57)

Museu de la Xocolata (p102)

generation enjoys the playground. If you're after something sweet, La Nena (p145) is fantastic for chocolate and all manner of tasty things. There's also a play area and toys and books in a corner. And don't miss La Granja (p132). No kid will be left unimpressed – and without a good buzz! – by the thick hot chocolate here.

From left: Jellyfish at L'Aquàrium (p86); Park Güell (p66)

MARIUSZ PRUSACZYK/GETTY IMAGES ©

TOP EXPERIENCES

The very best to see & do

JASON WALTMAN/500PX ©

La Sagrada Família

If you have time for only one sight-seeing outing, this is it. Sagrada Família inspires awe by its sheer verticality, inspiring use of light and Gaudí's offbeat design elements.

Great For...

☑ **Don't Miss**

The apse, the extraordinary pillars and the stained glass.

In the manner of the medieval cathedrals La Sagrada Família emulates, it's still under construction after more than 100 years. When completed, the highest tower will be more than half as high again as those that stand today.

A Holy Mission

The Temple Expiatori de la Sagrada Família (Expiatory Temple of the Holy Family) was Antoni Gaudí's all-consuming obsession. Given the commission by a conservative society that wished to build a temple as atonement for the city's sins of moderni-ty, Gaudí saw its completion as his holy mission. As funds dried up, he contributed his own, and in the last years of his life he was never shy of pleading with anyone he thought a likely donor.

Gaudí devised a temple 95m long and 60m wide, able to seat 13,000 people,

❶ Need to Know

Map p254; 📞93 208 04 14; www.sagrada
familia.cat; Carrer de Mallorca 401; adult/
concession/under 11 €15/13/free; 🕙9am-
8pm Apr-Sep, to 6pm Oct-Mar; Ⓜ Sagrada
Família

✕ Take a Break

Michael Collins Pub (p254) across the
square is good for a beer.

★ Top Tip

Buying tickets online in advance is a
must to beat the frequently dispiriting
queues.

with a central tower 170m high above the
transept (representing Christ) and another
17 of 100m or more. The 12 along the three
facades represent the Apostles, while the
remaining five represent the Virgin Mary
and the four evangelists. With his characteristic dislike for straight lines (there
were none in nature, he said), Gaudí gave
his towers swelling outlines inspired by the
weird peaks of the holy mountain Montserrat outside Barcelona, and encrusted them
with a tangle of sculpture that seems an
outgrowth of the stone.

At Gaudí's death, only the crypt, the apse
walls, one portal and one tower had been
finished. Three more towers were added by
1930, completing the northeast (Nativity)
facade. In 1936 anarchists burned and
smashed the interior, including workshops,
plans and models. Work began again in

1952, but controversy has always clouded
progress. Opponents of the continuation
of the project claim that the computer
models based on what little of Gaudí's
plans survived the anarchists' ire have led
to the creation of a monster that has little
to do with Gaudí's plans and style. It is a
debate that appears to have little hope of
resolution. Like or hate what is being done,
the fascination it awakens is undeniable.

Guesses on when construction might
be complete range from the 2020s to the
2040s. Even before reaching that point,
some of the oldest parts of the church, especially the apse, have required restoration
work.

The Interior & the Apse

Inside, work on roofing over the church was
completed in 2010. The roof is held up by a
forest of extraordinary angled pillars. As the
pillars soar toward the ceiling, they sprout
a web of supporting branches, creating the
effect of a forest canopy. The tree image
is in no way fortuitous – Gaudí envisaged

such an effect. Everything was thought through, including the shape and placement of windows to create the mottled effect one would see with sunlight pouring through the branches of a thick forest. The pillars are made of four different types of stone. They vary in colour and load-bearing strength, from the soft Montjuïc stone pillars along the lateral aisles through to granite, dark grey basalt and finally burgundy-tinged Iranian porphyry for the key columns at the intersection of the nave and transept. The stained glass, divided in shades of red, blue, green and ochre, creates a hypnotic, magical atmosphere when the sun hits the windows. Tribunes built high above the aisles can host two choirs: the main tribune up to 1300 people and the children's tribune up to 300.

Nativity Facade

The Nativity Facade is the artistic pinnacle of the building, mostly created under Gaudí's supervision. You can climb high up inside some of the four towers by a combination of lifts and narrow spiral staircases – a vertiginous experience. Do not climb the stairs if you have cardiac or respiratory problems. The towers are destined to hold tubular bells capable of playing complex music at great volume. Their upper parts are decorated with mosaics spelling out *'Sanctus, Sanctus, Sanctus, Hosanna in Excelsis, Amen, Alleluia'*. Asked why he lavished so much care on the tops of the spires, which no one would see from close up, Gaudí answered: 'The angels will see them'.

Three sections of the portal represent, from left to right, Hope, Charity and Faith. Among the forest of sculpture on the

Facade detail

Charity portal you can see, low down, the manger surrounded by an ox, an ass, the shepherds and kings, and angel musicians. Some 30 different species of plant from around Catalonia are reproduced here, and the faces of the many figures are taken from plaster casts done of local people and the occasional one made from corpses in the local morgue.

Directly above the blue stained-glass window is the archangel Gabriel's Annunciation to Mary. At the top is a green cypress tree, a refuge in a storm for the white doves of peace dotted over it. The mosaic work at the pinnacle of the towers is made from Murano glass, from Venice.

> **❶ Did You Know?**
> La Sagrada Família attracts around 2.8 million visitors yearly and is the most visited monument in Spain.

TETRA IMAGES/GETTY IMAGES ©

To the right of the facade is the curious Claustre del Roser, a Gothic-style mini-cloister tacked on to the outside of the church (rather than the classic square enclosure of the great Gothic church monasteries). Once inside, look back to the intricately decorated entrance. On the lower right-hand side you'll notice the sculpture of a reptilian devil handing a terrorist a bomb. Barcelona was regularly rocked by political violence, and bombings were frequent in the decades prior to the civil war. The sculpture is one of several on the 'temptations of men and women'.

Passion Facade

The southwest Passion Facade, on the theme of Christ's last days and death, was built between 1954 and 1978 based on surviving drawings by Gaudí, with four towers and a large, sculpture-bedecked portal. The sculptor, Josep Subirachs, worked on its decoration from 1986 to 2006. He did not attempt to imitate Gaudí, but instead produced angular, controversial images of his own. The main series of sculptures, on three levels, are in an S-shaped sequence, starting with the Last Supper at the bottom left and ending with Christ's burial at the top right. Decorative work on the Passion Facade continues even today, as construction of the Glory Facade moves ahead.

To the right, in front of the Passion Facade, the Escoles de Gaudí is one of his simpler gems. Gaudí built this as a children's school, creating an original, undulating roof of brick that continues to charm architects to this day. Inside is a recreation of Gaudí's modest office as it was when he died, and explanations of the geometric patterns and plans at the heart of his building techniques.

> **❶ When to Go**
> There are always lots of people visiting the Sagrada Família, but if you can get there when it opens, you'll find fewer crowds.

ⓘ Did You Know?

Pope Benedict XVI consecrated the church in a huge ceremony in November 2010.

A Hidden Portrait

Careful observation of the Passion Facade will reveal a special tribute from sculptor Josep Subirachs to Gaudí. The central sculptural group (below Christ crucified) shows, from right to left, Christ bearing his cross, Veronica displaying the cloth with Christ's bloody image, a pair of soldiers and, watching it all, a man called the evangelist. Subirachs used a rare photo of Gaudí, taken a couple of years before his death, as the model for the evangelist's face.

Glory Facade

The Glory Facade is under construction and will, like the others, be crowned by four towers – the total of 12 representing the Twelve Apostles. Gaudí wanted it to be the most magnificent facade of the church. Inside will be the narthex, a kind of foyer made up of 16 'lanterns', a series of hyperboloid forms topped by cones. Further decoration will make the whole building a microcosmic symbol of the Christian church, with Christ represented by a massive 170m central tower above the transept, and the five remaining planned towers symbolising the Virgin Mary and the four evangelists.

Museu Gaudí

Open the same times as the church, the Museu Gaudí, below ground level, includes interesting material on Gaudí's life and other works, as well as models and photos of La Sagrada Família. You can see a good example of his plumb-line models that showed him the stresses and strains he could get away with in construction. A side hall towards the eastern end of the museum leads to a viewing point above the simple crypt in which the genius is buried. The crypt, where Masses are now held, can also be visited from the Carrer de Mallorca side of the church.

What's Nearby?

Església de les Saleses   Church

(Map p254; ☎93 458 76 67; www.parroquiacon cepciobcn.org; Passeig de Sant Joan 90; ⊙10am-1pm & 5-7pm Mon-Fri, 10am-2pm Sun; Ⓜ Tetuan) A singular neo-Gothic effort, this church is interesting because it was designed by Joan Martorell i Montells (1833–1906), Gaudí's architecture professor. Raised in 1878–85 with an adjacent convent (badly damaged in the civil war and now a school), it offers hints of what was to come with Modernisme, with his use of brick, mosaics and sober stained glass.

Recinte Modernista de Sant Pau   Architecture

(☎93 553 78 01; www.santpaubarcelona.org; Carrer de Sant Antoni Maria Claret 167; ⊙10am-6.30pm Mon-Sat, to 2.30pm Sun; adult/concession/under 16 €10/7/free) Domènech i Montaner – a contemporary of Gaudí – outdid himself as architect and philanthropist with the Modernista Hospital de la Santa Creu i de Sant Pau, redubbed in 2014 the 'Recinte Modernista'. It was long considered one of the city's most important hospitals, and has only recently been repurposed, its various spaces becoming cultural centres, offices and something of a monument. The complex, including 16 pavilions, is lavishly decorated and each pavilion is unique. Together, the complex and Palau de la Música Catalana (p98) are a joint World Heritage site.

Museu del Disseny de Barcelona   Museum

(☎93 256 68 00 www.museudeldisseny.cat Plaça de les Glòries Catalanes 37; ⊙10am-8pm Tue-Sun; permanent/temporary exhibition €6/4.40, combination ticket €8) Barcelona's design museum lies inside a new monolithic building with geometric facades and a rather brutalist appearance – which has already earned the nickname *la grapadora* (the stapler) by locals. Architecture aside, the museum houses a dazzling collection of ceramics, decorative arts and textiles, and is a must for anyone interested in the design world.

★ **Top Tip**

Audio guides – including some
tailored to children – are available for
an additional fee.

La Sagrada Família

A TIMELINE

1882 Francesc del Villar is commissioned to construct a neo-Gothic church.

1883 Antoni Gaudí takes over as chief architect, and plans a far more ambitious church to hold 13,000 faithful.

1926 Death of Gaudí; work continues under Domènec Sugrañes. Much of the **apse ❶** and **Nativity Facade ❷** is complete.

1930 Bell towers ❸ of the Nativity Facade completed.

1936 Construction is interrupted by Spanish Civil War; anarchists destroy Gaudí's plans.

1939-40 Architect Francesc de Paula Quintana i Vidal restores the crypt and meticulously reassembles many of Gaudí's lost models, some of which can be seen in the **museum ❹**.

1976 Completion of **Passion Facade ❺**.

1986-2006 Sculptor Josep Subirachs adds sculptural details to the Passion Facade including the panels telling the story of Christ's last days, amid much criticism for employing a style far removed from what was thought typical of Gaudí.

2000 Central nave vault ❻ completed.

2010 Church completely roofed over; Pope Benedict XVI consecrates the church; work begins on a high-speed rail tunnel that will pass beneath the church's **Glory Facade ❼**.

2020s–40s Projected completion date.

TOP TIPS

» **Light** The best light through the stained-glass windows of the Passion Facade bursts through into the heart of the church in the late afternoon.

» **Time** Visit at opening time on week-days to avoid the worst of the crowds.

» **Views** Head up the Nativity Facade bell towers for the views, as long queues generally await at the Passion Facade towers.

KRZYSZTOF DYDYNSKI/GETTY IMAGES ©

Spiral staircase

Nativity Facade
Gaudí used plaster casts of local people and even of the occasional corpse from the local morgue as models for the portraits in the Nativity scene.

Central nave vault

Apse
Built just after the crypt in mostly neo-Gothic style, it is capped by pinnacles that show a hint of the genius that Gaudí would later deploy in the rest of the church.

JASON WALTMAN/500PX ©

Bell towers

The towers (eight completed) of the three facades represent the 12 Apostles. Lifts whisk visitors up one tower of the Nativity and Passion Facades (the latter gets longer queues) for fine views.

NIKADA/GETTY IMAGES ©

Completed church

Along with the Glory Facade and its four towers, six other towers remain to be completed. They will represent the four Evangelists, the Virgin Mary and, soaring above them all over the transept, a 170m colossus symbolising Christ.

Glory Facade

This will be the most fanciful facade of all, with a narthex boasting 16 hyperboloid lanterns topped by cones that will look something like an organ made of melting ice cream.

Museu Gaudí

Jammed with old photos, drawings and restored plaster models that bring Gaudí's ambitions to life, the museum also houses an extraordinarily complex plumb-line device he used to calculate his constructions.

Escoles de Gaudí

Crypt

The first completed part of the church, the crypt is in largely neo-Gothic style and lies under the transept. Gaudí's burial place here can be seen from the Museu Gaudí.

EKATERINA NIKITINA/GETTY IMAGES ©

Passion Facade

See the story of Christ's last days from Last Supper to burial in an S-shaped sequence from bottom to top of the facade. Check out the cryptogram in which the numbers always add up to 33, Christ's age at his death.

STEPHEN SAKS/GETTY IMAGES ©

La Rambla

Barcelona's most famous street is both tourist magnet and window into Catalan culture, with arts centres, theatres and intriguing architecture. The middle is a broad pedestrian boulevard, crowded daily with a wide cross-section of society. A stroll here is pure sensory overload, with souvenir hawkers, buskers, pavement artists and living statues part of the ever-changing street scene.

Great For...

❶ Need to Know

Map p250; Ⓜ Catalunya, Liceu, Drassanes
The Rambla stroll, from Plaça de Catalunya to Plaça del Portal de la Pau, is 1.5km.

★ **Top Tip**

Take an early morning stroll and another late at night to sample La Rambla's many moods.

History

La Rambla takes its name from a seasonal stream (raml in Arabic) that once ran here. From the early Middle Ages, it was better known as the Cagalell (Stream of Shit) and lay outside the city walls until the 14th century. Monastic buildings were then built and, subsequently, mansions of the well-to-do from the 16th to the early 19th centuries. Unofficially, La Rambla is divided into five sections, which explains why many know it as Las Ramblas.

La Rambla de Canaletes

The section of La Rambla north of Plaça de Catalunya is named after the **Font de Canaletes** (Map p250; [M]Catalunya), an inconspicuous turn-of-the-20th-century drinking fountain, the water of which supposedly emerges from what were once known as the springs of Canaletes. It used to be said that barcelonins 'drank the waters of Les Canaletes'. Nowadays, people claim that anyone who drinks from the fountain will return to Barcelona, which is not such a bad prospect. Delirious football fans gather here to celebrate whenever the main home side, FC Barcelona, wins a cup or the league premiership.

La Rambla dels Estudis

La Rambla dels Estudis, from Carrer de la Canuda running south to Carrer de la Portaferrissa, was formerly home to a twittering bird market, which closed in 2010 after 150 years in operation.

Església de Betlem

Just north of Carrer del Carme, this **church** (Map p250; [☎]93 318 38 23; www.mdbetlem.net; Carrer d'en Xuclà 2; [⏱]8.30am-1.30pm & 6-9pm; [M]Liceu) was constructed in baroque style for the Jesuits in the late 17th and early 18th centuries to replace an earlier church destroyed by fire in 1671. Fire was a bit of a theme for this site: the church was once considered the most splendid of Barcelona's few baroque offerings, but leftist arsonists torched it in 1936.

Palau Moja

Looming over the eastern side of La Rambla, **Palau Moja** (Map p250; [M]Liceu) is a neoclassical building dating from the second half of the 18th century. Its clean, classical lines are best appreciated from across La Rambla. Unfortunately, interior access is limited, as it houses mostly government offices.

La Rambla de Sant Josep

From Carrer de la Portaferrissa to Plaça de la Boqueria, what is officially called La Rambla de Sant Josep (named after a now nonexistent monastery) is lined with flower stalls, which give it the alternative name La Rambla de les Flors.

Palau de la Virreina

The **Palau de la Virreina** (Map p250; [M]Liceu) is a grand 18th-century rococo mansion (with some neoclassical elements) that houses a municipal arts/entertainment information and ticket office run by the Ajuntament (town hall). Built by Manuel d'Amat i de Junyent, the corrupt captain general of Chile (a Spanish colony that included the silver mines of Potosí), it is a rare example of such a post-baroque building in Barcelona. It's home to the **Centre de la Imatge** (Map p250; [☎]93 316 10 00; www.ajuntament.barcelona.cat/lavirreina; [⏱]noon-8pm Tue-Sun; FREE), which has rotating photography exhibits.

Mosaïc de Miró

At Plaça de la Boqueria, where four side streets meet just north of Liceu metro station, you can walk all over a Miró – the colourful **mosaic** (Map p250; [M]Liceu) in the pavement, with one tile signed by the artist.

ⓘ Take a Break

While there are some decent eateries in the vicinity, the vast majority of cafes and restaurants along La Rambla are expensive, mediocre tourist traps. Instead, duck into the Mercat de la Boqueria (p90) for a snack.

Font de Canaletes, La Rambla de Canaletes

★ **Top Tip**

Things have improved in recent years, but pickpockets still prey on head-in-the-air tourists along here. Keep an eye on your valuables.

Miró chose this site as it's near the house where he was born on the Passatge del Crèdit. The mosaic's bold colours and vivid swirling forms are instantly recognisable to Miró fans, though plenty of tourists stroll right over it without realising.

La Rambla dels Caputxins

La Rambla dels Caputxins, named after a former monastery, runs from Plaça de la Boqueria to Carrer dels Escudellers. The latter street is named after the potters' guild, founded in the 13th century, the members of which lived and worked here. On the western side of La Rambla is the **Gran Teatre del Liceu** (Map p250; ☎93 485 99 00; www.liceubarcelona.cat; La Rambla 51-59; tour 50min/25min €16/6; ☺50min tour 9.30am & 10.30am, 25min tour schedule varies; ⓂLiceu); to the southeast is the entrance to the palm-shaded Plaça Reial. Below this point La Rambla gets seedier, with the occasional strip club and peep show.

La Rambla de Santa Mònica

The final stretch of La Rambla widens out to approach the Mirador de Colom overlooking Port Vell. La Rambla here is named after the Convent de Santa Mònica, which once stood on the western flank of the street and has since been converted into a cultural centre.

What's Nearby?

Església de Santa Maria del Pi   Church
(Map p250; ☎93 318 47 43; www.basilicadelpi.com; Plaça del Pi; adult/concession/under 6 €4/3/free; ☺10am-6pm; ⓂLiceu) This striking 14th-century church is a classic of Catalan Gothic, with an imposing facade, a wide interior and a single nave. The simple decor in the main sanctuary contrasts with the gilded chapels and exquisite stained-glass windows that bathe the interior in ethereal light. The beautiful rose window above its entrance is one of the world's largest. Occasional concerts are staged here (classical guitar, choral groups and chamber orchestras).

Plaça Reial   Square
(Map p250; ⓂLiceu) One of the most photogenic squares in Barcelona, the Plaça Reial is a delightful retreat from the traffic and pedestrian mobs on the nearby Rambla. Numerous eateries, bars and nightspots lie beneath the arcades of 19th-century neoclassical buildings, with a buzz of activity at all hours.

Via Sepulcral Romana   Archaeological Site
(Map p250; ☎93 256 21 00; www.museuhistoria.bcn.cat; Plaça de la Vila de Madrid; adult/child/concession/€2/free/1.50; ☺11am-2pm Tue & Thu, to 7pm Sat & Sun; ⓂCatalunya) Along Carrer de la Canuda, a block east of the top end of La Rambla, is a sunken garden where a series of Roman tombs lies

Plaça Reial

exposed. A smallish display in Spanish and Catalan by the tombs explores burial and funerary rites and customs. A few bits of pottery (including a burial amphora with the skeleton of a three-year-old Roman child) accompany the display.

Mirador de Colom · Viewpoint

(☎93 302 52 24; www.barcelonaturisme.com; Plaça del Portal de la Pau; adult/concession €6/4; ☉8.30am-8.30pm summer, 8.30am-7.30pm winter; MDrassanes) High above the swirl of traffic on the roundabout below, Columbus keeps permanent watch, pointing vaguely out to the Mediterranean. Built for the Universal Exhibition in 1888, the monument allows you to zip up 60m in a lift for bird's-eye views back up La Rambla and across the ports of Barcelona.

Centre d'Art Santa Mònica · Arts Centre

(Map p250; ☎93 567 11 10; www.artssantamonica.gencat.cat; La Rambla 7; ☉11am-9pm Tue-Sat, 11am-5pm Sun; MDrassanes) **FREE** The Convent de Santa Mònica, which once stood on the western flank of the street, has since been converted into the Centre d'Art Santa Mònica, a cultural centre that mostly exhibits modern multimedia installations.

---

❶ Did You Know?

La Rambla saw action during the civil war. In *Homage to Catalonia*, George Orwell vividly described the avenue gripped by revolutionary fervour.

☑ Don't Miss

Strolling the whole Rambla from end to end, keeping an eye on the architecture alongside.

JÖRG GREUEL/GETTY IMAGES ©

Casa Batlló's Modernista roofline

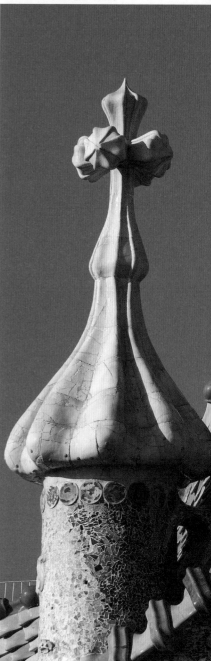

Casa Batlló

One of the strangest residential buildings in Europe, this is Gaudí at his hallucinatory best. To some, Casa Batlló appears like a mythical creature frozen in place. It has numerous intriguing design elements, both on the striking exterior and in the dreamlike, exuberant interior. It's one of three notable Modernista buildings in this landmark block.

Great For...

ℹ Need to Know

Map p254; ✆93 216 03 06; www.casabatllo. es; Passeig de Gràcia 43; adult/concession/ under 7 €22.50/19.50/free; ⊙9am-9pm (last admission 8pm); Ⓜ Passeig de Gràcia

★ **Top Tip**

A theatrical visit aimed at families has daily English departures; check the website for details.

The building is remarkable in every respect. The facade, sprinkled with bits of blue, mauve and green tiles and studded with wave-shaped window frames and balconies, rises to an uneven blue-tiled roof with a solitary tower. Casa Batlló and neighbouring Casa Amatller and Casa Lleó Morera were all renovated between 1898 and 1906, and together demonstrate Modernisme's eclecticism.

Bones & Dragons

Locals know Casa Batlló variously as the *casa dels ossos* (house of bones) or *casa del drac* (house of the dragon). It's easy enough to see why. The balconies look like the bony jaws of some strange beast and the roof represents Sant Jordi (St George) and the dragon. Even the roof was built to represent the shape of an animal's back, with shiny scales – the 'spine' changes colour as you walk around.

The Interior

When Gaudí was commissioned to re-fashion this building, he went to town inside and out. The internal light wells shimmer with tiles of deep sea blue. Gaudí eschewed the straight line, and so the staircase wafts you up to the 1st (main) floor, where the salon looks on to Passeig de Gràcia. Everything swirls: the ceiling is twisted into a vortex around its sunlike lamp; the doors, window and skylights are dreamy waves of wood and coloured glass. The attic is characterised by Gaudí's trademark hyperboloid arches. Twisting, tiled chimney pots add a surreal touch to the roof.

Facade detail

Manzana de la Discordia

Despite the Catalanisation of most Barcelona street names since 1980, the Manzana de la Discordia is still known by its Spanish name to preserve a pun on *manzana*, which means 'block' and 'apple'. In Greek mythology, the original Apple of Discord was tossed onto Mt Olympus by Eris (Discord), with orders that it be given to the most beautiful goddess, sparking jealousies that were the catalyst for the Trojan War.

☑ Don't Miss

Before going inside, take a look at the pavement. Each paving piece carries stylised images of an octopus and a starfish, designs that Gaudí originally cooked up for Casa Batlló.

CRISTINAMURACA/SHUTTERSTOCK ©

What's Nearby?

Casa Amatller   Architecture
(Map p254; ☑93 461 74 60; www.amatller. org; Passeig de Gràcia 41; adult/6-12/under 6 1hr tour €15/7.50/free, 30min tour €12/7/free; ☺11am-6pm; ⓜPasseig de Gràcia) One of Puig i Cadafalch's most striking bits of Modernista fantasy, Casa Amatller combines Gothic window frames with a stepped gable borrowed from Dutch urban architecture. But the busts and reliefs of dragons, knights and other characters dripping off the main facade are pure caprice.

Casa Lleó Morera   Architecture
(Map p254; ☑93 676 27 33; www.casalleo morera.com; Passeig de Gràcia 35; guided tour adult/concession/under 12 €15/13.50/free, express tour adult/under 12 €12/free; ☺10am-1.30pm & 3-7pm Tue-Sun; ⓜPasseig de Gràcia) Domènech i Montaner's 1905 contribution to the Manzana de la Discordia, with Modernista carving outside and a bright, tiled lobby in which floral motifs predominate, is perhaps the least odd-looking of the three main buildings on the block. Since 2014 part of the building has been open to the public (by guided tour only – a one-hour tour in English at 11am, and 'express tours' every 30 minutes), so you can appreciate the 1st floor, giddy with swirling sculptures, rich mosaics and whimsical decor.

Fundació Antoni Tàpies   Gallery
(Map p254; ☑93 487 03 15; www.fundacio tapies.org; Carrer d'Aragó 255; adult/concession €7/5.60; ☺10am-7pm Tue-Sun; ⓜPasseig de Gràcia) This is both a pioneering Modernista building (completed in 1885) and the major collection of leading 20th-century Catalan artist Antoni Tàpies. A man known for his esoteric work, Tàpies died in February 2012, aged 88; he left behind a powerful range of paintings and a foundation intended to promote contemporary artists.

✕ Take a Break
Tapas 24 (p140), a modern basement tapas joint, opens all day.

ERIK PRONSKE/500PX ©

Museu Nacional d'Art de Catalunya

From across Barcelona, the flamboyant neobaroque silhouette of the Palau Nacional can be seen on the slopes of Montjuïc. It houses a vast collection of mostly Catalan art.

Great For...

☑ Don't Miss

The fantastic assemblage of Romanesque frescoes from churches around Catalonia.

The Romanesque Masterpieces

The Romanesque art section is considered the most important concentration of early medieval art in the world. Rescued from neglected country churches across northern Catalonia in the early 20th century, the collection consists of 21 frescoes, woodcarvings and painted altar frontals (low-relief wooden panels that were the forerunners of the elaborate altarpieces that adorned later churches). The insides of several churches have been recreated and the frescoes – some cases fragmentary, in others extraordinarily complete and alive with colour – have been placed as they were when in situ.

The first of the two most striking frescoes, in Sala 7, is a magnificent image of Christ in Majesty painted around 1123. Based on the text of the Apocalypse, we

❶ Need to Know

MNAC; Map p256; ✆93 622 03 76; www.museunacional.cat; Mirador del Palau Nacional; adult/child/student €12/free/€8.40, free after 3pm Sat & 1st Sun of month; ☺10am-8pm Tue-Sat, to 3pm Sun May-Sep, to 6pm Tue-Sat Oct-Apr; ☎; Ⓜ Espanya

✕ Take a Break

On-site, there's a restaurant, cafeteria and rooftop bar with great vistas.

★ Top Tip

The collection is huge, so just pick a few sections and take your time.

see Christ enthroned with the world at his feet. He holds a book open with the words *Ego Sum Lux Mundi* (I am the Light of the World) and is surrounded by the four evangelists. The images were taken from the apse of the Església de Sant Climent de Taüll in northwest Catalonia. Nearby in Sala 9 are frescoes painted around the same time in the nearby Església de Santa Maria de Taüll. This time the central image taken from the apse is of the Virgin Mary and Christ Child. These images were not mere decoration, but tools of instruction in the basics of Christian faith for the local population – try to set yourself in the mind of the average medieval citizen: illiterate, ignorant, fearful and in most cases eking out a subsistence living. These images transmitted the basic personalities and tenets of the faith and were accepted at face value by most.

The Gothic Collection

Opposite the Romanesque collection on the ground floor is the museum's Gothic art section. In these halls you can see Catalan Gothic painting and works from other Spanish and Mediterranean regions. Look out especially for the work of Bernat Martorell in Sala 25 and Jaume Huguet in Sala 26. Among Martorell's works figure images of the martyrdom of St Vincent and St Llúcia. Huguet's *Consagració de Sant Agustí*, in which St Augustine is depicted as a bishop, is dazzling in its detail.

The Cambò Bequest & the Thyssen-Bornemisza Collection

As the Gothic collection draws to a close, you pass through two separate and equally eclectic private collections. The Cambò Bequest by Francesc Cambó spans the history of European painting between the 14th century and the beginning of the 19th century, and the Thyssen-Bornemisza collection presents a selection of European painting and sculpture produced between the 13th and the 18th centuries, on loan to MNAC by Madrid's Museo Thyssen-Bornemisza. The Thyssen-Bornemisza collection's highlight is Fra Angelico's *Madonna of Humility,* whereas the Cambò Bequest holds wonderful works by masters Veronese, Titian and Canaletto. Cranach, Titian, El Greco and Rubens also feature, but the collection's finale are the works by Francisco de Goya.

Modern Catalan Art

Up on the next floor, the collection turns to modern art, mainly but not exclusively Catalan. This collection is arranged thematically: Modernisme, Noucentisme, Art and the Civil War and so on. Among the many highlights: an early Salvador Dalí painting *(Portrait of My Father),* Juan Gris' collage-like paintings, the brilliant portraits of Marià Fortuny, and 1930s call-to-arms posters against the Francoist onslaught (nearby you'll find photos of soldiers and bombed-out city centres). There are works by Modernista painters Ramon Casas and Santiago Rusiñol, as well as Catalan luminary Antoni Tàpies.

The Fresco Strippers

Among the little known curiosities inside MNAC, you'll find a video (in Sala 3) depicting the techniques used by the 'Fresco Strippers' to preserve the great Romanesque works. The Stefanoni brothers, Italian art restorers, brought the secrets of *strappo* (stripping of frescoes from walls) to Catalonia in the early 1900s. The Stefanoni would cover frescoes with a sheet of fabric, stuck on with a glue made of cartilage. When dry, this allowed the image to be stripped off the wall and rolled up. For three years the Stefanoni roamed

---

❶ Did You Know?

An emblematic building, the Palau Nacional was built for the 1929 World Exhibition and restored in 2005.

---

the Pyrenean countryside, stripping churches and chapels and sending the rolls back to Barcelona, where they were eventually put back up on walls and inside purpose-built church apses to reflect how they had appeared in situ.

What's Nearby?

Museu d'Arqueologia de Catalunya
Museum

(MAC; Map p256; ☑93 423 21 49; www.mac.cat; Passeig de Santa Madrona 39-41; adult/student €4.50/3.50; ⊙9.30am-7pm Tue-Sat, 10am-2.30pm Sun; Ⓜ Poble Sec) This archaeology museum, housed in what was the Graphic Arts palace during the 1929 World Exhibition, covers Catalonia and cultures from elsewhere in Spain. Items range from copies of pre-Neanderthal skulls to lovely

Poble Espanyol

Carthaginian necklaces and jewel-studded Visigothic crosses.

Museu Etnològic · Museum

(Map p256; www.museuetnologic.bcn.cat; Passeig de Santa Madrona 16-22; adult/child €5/3; ⊙10am-7pm Tue-Sat, to 8pm Sun; 🚍55) Barcelona's ethnology museum presents an intriguing permanent collection that delves into the rich heritage of Catalunya. Exhibits cover origin myths, religious festivals, folklore, and the blending of the sacred and the secular (along those lines, don't miss the Nativity scene with that quirky Catalan character *el caganer*, aka 'the crapper').

Poble Espanyol · Cultural Centre

(Map p256; www.poble-espanyol.com; Avinguda de Francesc Ferrer i Guàrdia 13; adult/child €12/7; ⊙9am-8pm Mon, to midnight Tue-Thu & Sun, to 3am Fri & Sat; 🚍13, 23, 150, Ⓜ Espanya)

Welcome to Spain! All of it! This 'Spanish Village' is both a cheesy souvenir hunters' haunt and an intriguing scrapbook of Spanish architecture built for the Spanish crafts section of the 1929 World Exhibition. You can meander from Andalucía to the Balearic Islands in the space of a couple of hours, visiting surprisingly good copies of Spain's characteristic buildings.

★ Top Tip

Within the modern art collection, look for items of Modernista furniture and decoration, which include a mural by Ramon Casas (the artist and Pere Romeu on a tandem bicycle). It once adorned the legendary bar and restaurant Els Quatre Gats (p95).

Personnage, 1970, by Joan Miró

Fundació Joan Miró

Joan Miró, the city's best-known 20th-century artistic progeny, bequeathed this art foundation to his home town in 1971. Its light-filled buildings, designed by close friend and architect Josep Lluís Sert (who also built Miró's Mallorca studios), are crammed with seminal works, from Miró's earliest timid sketches to paintings from his last years.

Great For...

ℹ Need to Know

Map p256; ✆93 443 94 70; www.fmirobcn. org; Parc de Montjuïc; adult/child €12/free; ⊙10am-8pm Tue-Sat, to 9pm Thu, to 2.30pm Sun & holidays; 🛜; 🚌55, 150, 🚇Paral·lel

★ Top Tip

The Articket Barcelona (www.articketbcn.org) gives entry to several major galleries and can be bought online.

EVE LIVESEY/GETTY IMAGES ©

Sert's Temple to Miró's Art

Sert's shimmering white temple to one of Spain's artistic luminaries is considered one of the world's most outstanding museum buildings. The architect designed it after spending many of Franco's dictatorship years in the USA as the head of the School of Design at Harvard University. The foundation rests amid the greenery of the mountains and holds the greatest single collection of the artist's work, containing around 220 of his paintings, 180 sculptures, some textiles and more than 8000 drawings spanning his entire life. Only a small portion is ever on display.

The Collection

The exhibits give a broad impression of Miró's artistic development. The first couple of rooms (11 and 12) hold various works,

including a giant-tapestry in his trademark primary colours. Along the way, you'll pass *Mercury Fountain* by Alexander Calder, a rebuilt work that was originally built for the 1937 Paris Fair and represented Spain at the Spanish Republic's Pavilion. Room 13, a basement space called Espai 13, leads you downstairs to a small room for temporary exhibitions.

After visiting Room 13, climb back up the stairs and descend to two other basement rooms, 14 and 15. Together labelled Homenatge a Joan Miró (Homage to Joan Miró), this space is dedicated to photos of the artist, a 15-minute video on his life and a series of works from some of his contemporaries, including Henry Moore, Antoni Tàpies, Eduardo Chillida, Yves Tanguy, Fernand Léger and others.

Fundació Joan Miró, designed by Josep Lluís Sert

Returning to the main level, you'll find Room 16, the Sala Joan Prats, with works spanning the early years until 1919. Here, you can see how the young Miró moved away, under surrealist influence, from his relative realism (for instance his 1917 painting *Ermita de Sant Joan d'Horta*, with obvious Fauvist influences) toward his own unique style that uses primary colours and morphed shapes symbolising the moon, the female form and birds.

This theme is continued upstairs in Room 17, the Sala Pilar Juncosa (named after his wife), which covers the years 1932 to 1955, his surrealist years. Rooms 18 and 19 contain masterworks of the years 1956 to 1983, and Room 20 a series of paintings done on paper. Room 21 hosts a selection of the private Katsuta collection of Miró works from 1914 to 1974. Room 22 rounds off the permanent exhibition with some major paintings and bronzes from the 1960s and '70s.

The museum library contains Miró's personal book collection.

The Garden

On the eastern flank of the museum is the Jardí de les Esculptures, a small garden with pieces of modern sculpture. The green areas surrounding the museum, together with the garden, are ideal for a picnic.

What's Nearby?

Estadi Olímpic Lluís Companys   Stadium

(Map p256; ☑93 426 20 89; www.estadiolimpic. cat; Avinguda de l'Estadi; ◷8am-8pm May-Sep, 10am-6pm Oct-Apr; ☐150) **FREE** The Estadi Olímpic was the main stadium of Barcelona's Olympic Games. If you saw the Olympics on TV, the 65,000-capacity stadium may seem surprisingly small. So might the Olympic flame holder into which an archer spectacularly fired a flaming arrow during the opening ceremony. The stadium was opened in 1929 and restored for the 1992 Olympics.

Museu Olímpic i de l'Esport   Museum

(Map p256; ☑93 292 53 79; www.museu olimpicbcn.com; Avinguda de l'Estadi 60; adult/ student €5.10/3.20; ◷10am-8pm Tue-Sat, 10am-2.30pm Sun; ☐55, 150) This interactive, information-packed museum is dedicated to the history of sport and the Olympic Games. After picking up tickets, you wander down a ramp that snakes below ground level and is lined with displays on the history of sport, starting with the ancients.

> ☑ **Don't Miss**
> The central highlights of the collection, Miró's masterworks in Rooms 18 and 19.

ULLSTEIN BILD/GETTY IMAGES ©

> ✕ **Take a Break**
> Pack a picnic and eat it in the shady sculpture garden.

La Catedral

The richly decorated Gothic main facade of Barcelona's central place of worship, laced with gargoyles and stone intricacies, sets it quite apart from other churches in Barcelona.

The key treasure of the Barri Gòtic, the cathedral was built between 1298 and 1460, though the facade was added in 1870.

The Interior

The interior is a broad, soaring space divided into a central nave and two aisles by lines of elegant, slim pillars. The cathedral was one of the few churches in Barcelona spared by the anarchists in the civil war, so its ornamentation, never overly lavish, is intact.

The Coro

In the middle of the central nave is the late-14th-century, exquisitely sculpted timber *coro* (choir stalls). The coats of arms on the stalls belong to members of the Barcelona chapter of the Order of the Golden Fleece. Emperor Carlos V presided over the order's meeting here in 1519.

Great For...

☑ Don't Miss

The *claustre* (cloister) and its 13 geese, plus the views from the roof.

❶ Need to Know

Map p250; ✆93 342 82 62; www.catedral bcn.org; Plaça de la Seu; admission free, 'donation entrance' €7, choir admission €3, roof admission €3; ⏰8am-12.45pm & 5.15-7.30pm Mon-Fri, to 8pm Sat & Sun, 'donation entrance' 1-5pm Mon-Sat, 2-5pm Sun; Ⓜ Jaume I

✕ Take a Break

For a special Japanese meal head to nearby Koy Shunka (p134).

★ Top Tip

If you want to see the lot, it's marginally cheaper entering between 1pm and 5pm.

according to one story, six North American Indians brought to Europe by Columbus after his first voyage of accidental discovery were bathed in holy water.

Crypt

A broad staircase before the main altar leads you down to the crypt, which contains the tomb of Santa Eulàlia, one of Barcelona's two patron saints and more affectionately known as Laia. The reliefs on the alabaster sarcophagus recount some of her tortures and, along the top strip, the removal of her body to its present resting place.

Sant Crist de Lepant

In the first chapel on the right from the northwest entrance, the main Crucifixion figure above the altar is Sant Crist de Lepant. It is said Don Juan's flagship bore it into battle at Lepanto and that the figure acquired its odd stance by dodging an incoming cannonball. Left from the main entrance is the baptismal font where,

The Roof

For a bird's-eye view (mind the poo) of medieval Barcelona, visit the cathedral's roof and tower by taking the lift (€3) from the Capella de les Animes del Purgatori near the northeast transept.

The Claustre

From the southwest transept, exit by the partly Romanesque door (one of the few remnants of the present church's predecessor) to the leafy *claustre* (cloister), with its fountains and flock of 13 geese. The geese supposedly represent the age of Santa Eulàlia at the time of her martyrdom and have, generation after generation, been squawking here since medieval days. One of the cloister chapels commemorates 930 priests, monks and nuns killed during the civil war.

In the northwest corner of the cloister is the **Capella de Santa Llúcia** (Map p250; ⊘8am-7.30pm Mon-Fri, to 8pm Sat & Sun; Ⓜ Jaume I) FREE, one of the few reminders of Romanesque Barcelona (although the interior is largely Gothic).

Casa de l'Ardiaca

Upon exiting the Capella de Santa Llúcia, wander across the lane into the 16th-century **Casa de l'Ardiaca** (Arxiu Històric; Map p250; ⊘9am-9pm Mon-Fri, to 2pm Sat; Ⓜ Jaume I) FREE, which houses the city's archives. Stroll around the supremely serene courtyard, cooled by trees and a fountain; it was renovated by Lluis Domènech i Montaner in 1902, when the building was owned by the lawyers' college. Domènech i Mon-

taner also designed the postal slot, which is adorned with swallows and a tortoise, said to represent the swiftness of truth and the plodding pace of justice. You can get a good glimpse at some stout Roman wall in here. Upstairs, you can look down into the courtyard and across to La Catedral.

Palau Episcopal

Across Carrer del Bisbe is the 17th-century **Palau Episcopal** (Palau del Bisbat; Bishop's Palace; Map p250; Ⓜ Jaume I). Virtually nothing remains of the original 13th-century structure. The Roman city's northwest gate was here and you can see the lower segments of the Roman towers that stood on either side of the gate at the base of the Palau Episcopal and Casa de l'Ardiaca. In fact, the lower part of the entire northwest wall of the Casa de l'Ardiaca is of Roman origin –

View of La Catedral from the square

you can also make out part of the first arch of a Roman aqueduct.

What's Nearby?

Temple Romà d'August — Ruin

(Map p250; ☑93 256 21 22; Carrer del Paradis 10; ◷10am-2pm Mon, to 7pm Tue-Sat, to 8pm Sun; Ⓜ Jaume I) **FREE** Opposite the southeast end of La Catedral, narrow Carrer del Paradis leads towards Plaça de Sant Jaume. Inside No 10, an intriguing building with Gothic and baroque touches, are four columns and the architrave of Barcelona's main Roman temple, dedicated to Caesar Augustus and built to worship his imperial highness in the 1st century AD.

Museu Diocesà — Museum

(Casa de la Pia Almoina; Map p250; ☑93 315 22 13; www.cultura.arqbcn.cat; Plaça de la Seu 7; adult/concession/under 8 €15/12/free; ◷10am-6pm Nov-Easter, to 8pm Easter-Oct; Ⓜ Jaume I) Next to the cathedral, the Diocesan Museum has a handful of exhibits on Gaudí (including a fascinating documentary on his life and philosophy) on the upper floors. There's also a sparse collection of medieval and Romanesque religious art, usually supplemented by a temporary exhibition or two.

Palau del Lloctinent — Historic Site

(Map p250; Carrer dels Comtes; ◷10am-2pm & 4-8pm Mon-Sat; Ⓜ Jaume I) **FREE** This converted 16th-century palace has a peaceful courtyard worth wandering through. Have a look upwards from the main staircase to admire the extraordinary timber *artesonado,* a sculpted ceiling made to seem like the upturned hull of a boat. Temporary exhibitions, usually related in some way to the archives, are often held here.

Roman Walls — Ruin

(Map p250; Ⓜ Jaume I) From Plaça del Rei it's worth a detour to see the two best surviving stretches of Barcelona's Roman walls, which once boasted 78 towers (as much a matter of prestige as of defence). One section is on the southern side of Plaça de Ramon Berenguer el Gran, with the Capella Reial de Santa Àgata atop. The other is a little further south, by the northern end of Carrer del Sotstinent Navarro.

> ✕ **Take a Break**
>
> A short walk away, local favourite Cafè de l'Acadèmia (p133) serves great lunch specials and tasty traditional dishes at night.

EMRE TURAN/GETTY IMAGES ©

> ★ **Top Tip**
>
> Outside La Catedral there's always entertainment afoot, from *sardana* dancing (Catalonia's folk dance) on weekends to periodic processions and open-air markets, and street musicians are never far from the scene.

View across Barcelona from Park Güell

Park Güell

Park Güell – north of Gràcia and about 4km from Plaça de Catalunya – is where Gaudí turned his hand to landscape gardening. It's a strange, enchanting place, where this iconic Modernista's passion for natural forms really took flight, to the point where the artificial almost seems more natural than the natural.

Great For...

❶ Need to Know

Map p254; ☎93 409 18 31; www.parkguell. cat; Carrer d'Olot 7; admission to central area adult/child €8/6; ⊗8am-9.30pm May-Aug, to 8pm Sep-Apr; ᨫ24, 32, Ⓜ️Lesseps, Vallcarca

★ **Top Tip**

Access to the central area is limited by numbers; it's wise to prebook online.

A City Park

Park Güell originated in 1900, when Count Eusebi Güell bought the tree-covered hillside of El Carmel (then outside Barcelona) and hired Gaudí to create a miniature city of houses for the wealthy, surrounded by landscaped grounds. The project was a commercial flop and was abandoned in 1914, but not before Gaudí had created, in his inimitable manner, steps, a plaza, two gatehouses and 3km of roads and walks. In 1922 the city bought the estate for use as a public park. The park became a Unesco World Heritage site in 2004. The idea was based on the English 'garden cities', much admired by Güell, hence the spelling of 'Park'.

Just inside the main entrance on Carrer d'Olot, immediately recognisable by the two Hansel-and-Gretel gatehouses, is the park's newly refurbished Centre d'Interpretació, in the Pavelló de Consergeria, which is a typically curvaceous former porter's home that hosts a display on Gaudí's building methods and the history of the park. There are nice views from the top floor.

Sala Hipóstila

The steps up from the entrance, guarded by a mosaic dragon/lizard, lead to the Sala Hipóstila (aka the Doric Temple). This forest of 88 stone columns – some leaning like mighty trees bent by the weight of time – was originally intended as a market. To the left curves a gallery, the twisted stonework columns and roof of which give the effect of a cloister beneath tree roots – a motif repeated in several places in the park. On top of the Sala Hipóstila is a broad open space. Its centrepiece is the Banc de Trencadís, a tiled bench curving sinuously around

A cluster of stone columns within Park Güell

its perimeter, which was designed by one of Gaudí's closest colleagues, architect Josep Maria Jujol (1879–1949). With Gaudí, however, there is always more than meets the eye. This giant platform was designed as a kind of catchment area for rainwater washing down the hillside. The water is filtered through a layer of stone and sand, and it drains down through the columns to an underground cistern.

Casa-Museu Gaudí

The spired house above and to the right of the entrance is the Casa-Museu Gaudí (Map p254; www.casamuseugaudi.org; adult/student/child €5.50/4.50/free; ☺9am-8pm Apr-Sep,

10am-6pm Oct-Mar; 🚌24, 92, 116, Ⓜ Lesseps), where Gaudí lived for almost the last 20 years of his life (1906–26). It contains furniture he designed (including items that once lived in La Pedrera, Casa Batlló and Casa Calvet) along with other memorabilia. The house was built in 1904 by Francesc Berenguer i Mestres as a prototype for the 60 or so houses that were originally planned here.

Much of the park is still wooded, but it's laced with pathways. The best views are from the cross-topped Turó del Calvari in the southwest corner.

What's Nearby?

Gaudí Experience   Theatre

(Map p254; 📞93 285 44 40; Carrer de Larrard 41; adult/child €9/7.50; ☺10.30am-7pm Apr-Sep, to 5pm Oct-Mar; Ⓜ Lesseps, Vallcarca) This fun-filled Disney-style look at the life and work of Barcelona's favourite son is just a stone's throw from Park Güell. There are models of his buildings and interactive exhibits, but the highlight is the stomach-churning 4D presentation in its tiny screening room. Not recommended for the frail or children aged under six years.

Bunkers del Carmel   Viewpoint

(Map p254; Ⓜ El Carmel, then bus 86) For a magnificent view over the city that's well off the beaten path, head to the neighbour-hood of El Carmel and make the ascent up the hill known as Turó de la Rovira to the Bunkers del Carmel viewpoint. Above the weeds and dusty hillside, you'll find the old concrete platforms that were once part of anti-aircraft battery during the Spanish Civil War (in the post-War, it was a shanty town until the early 1990s, and has lain abandoned since then).

> ### ☑ Don't Miss
> The undulating tiled bench with views across the city.

PETER LNGER/GETTY IMAGES ©

> ### ✕ Take a Break
> **Las Delicias** (Map p254; 📞93 429 22 02; www.barrestarantedelicias.com; Carrer de Mühlberg 1; tapas €6-14, mains €8-17; ☺10am-4pm Tue-Sun & 7-10.30pm Tue-Thu, 8-11pm Fri & Sat), just east of the park, is a fine choice.

Camp Nou stadium during an FC Barcelona match

CHRISTIAN BERTRAND/SHUTTERSTOCK ©

Camp Nou

A pilgrimage site for football fans from around the world, Camp Nou, home to FC Barcelona, is one of the sport's most hallowed grounds.

Great For...

☑ **Don't Miss**

A live match, or if not, the museum's footage of the team's best goals.

Museum

The Camp Nou Experience begins in FC Barcelona's museum, which provides a high-tech view into the club. Massive touch-screens allow visitors to explore arcane aspects of the legendary team. You can also watch videos of particularly artful goals. Displays delve into the club's history, its social commitment and connection to Catalan identity, and in-depth stats of on-field action. Sound installations include the club's anthem and the match-day roar of the amped-up crowds.

You can admire the golden boots of celebrated goal scorers of the past and learn about the greats who have played for Barça over the years, including Maradona, Ronaldinho, Kubala and many others. There's even a special area devoted to

❶ Need to Know

Camp Nou Experience (☎90 218 9900; www.fcbarcelona.com; Gate 9, Avinguda de Joan XXIII; adult/child €23/18; ⏱9.30am-7.30pm daily Apr-Sep, 10am-6.30pm Mon-Sat, to 2.30pm Sun Oct-Mar; Ⓜ Palau Reial

✕ Take a Break

Just inside the gates (but outside the stadium) are a handful of open-air eating spots.

★ Top Tip

You can purchase tickets from vending machines at gate 9. No need to wait in line.

Lionel Messi, generally considered the world's greatest current footballer.

Stadium

The stadium, built in 1957 and enlarged for the 1982 World Cup, is one of the world's biggest, holding 99,000 people. The club has a world-record membership of 173,000.

The self-guided tour of the stadium takes in the team's dressing rooms, heads out through the tunnel onto the pitch and winds up in the presidential box. You'll also get to visit the television studio, the press room and the commentary boxes. Set aside about 2½ hours for the whole visit.

To make the tour, enter via Gate 9 (Avinguda de Joan XXIII near Carrer de Martí i Franquès).

Getting to a Game

Tickets to FC Barcelona matches are available at Camp Nou, online (through FC Barcelona's official website), and through various city locations. Tourist offices sell them – the branch at **Plaça de Catalunya** (Map p254; ☎93 285 38 34; Plaça de Catalunya 17-S, underground; ⏱8.30am-8.30pm; Ⓜ Catalunya) is a centrally located option – as do FC Botiga stores. Tickets can cost anything from €39 to upwards of €250, depending on the seat and match. On match day the ticket windows (at gates 9 and 15) open from 9.15am until kick off. Tickets are not usually available for matches with Real Madrid.

If you attend a game, go early so you'll have ample time to find your seat and soak up the atmosphere.

You will almost definitely find scalpers lurking near the ticket windows. They are often club members and can sometimes get you in at a significant reduction. Don't pay until you are safely seated.

La Pedrera

This undulating beast is another madcap Gaudí masterpiece, built from 1905 to 1910 as a combined apartment and office block. Formally called Casa Milà after the businessman who commissioned it, it is better known as La Pedrera (the Quarry) because of its uneven grey stone facade, which ripples around the corner of Carrer de Provença.

Great For...

ⓘ Need to Know

Casa Milà; Map p254; ☑90 220 21 38; www.lapedrera.com; Passeig de Gràcia 92; entry incl audio guide adult/concession/under 13/under 7 €20.50/16.50/10.25/free; ☺9am-8.30pm Mar-Oct, to 6.30pm Nov-Feb; Ⓜ Diagonal

★ **Top Tip**

For a few extra euros, a 'Premium' ticket means you don't have to queue.

History

Pere Milà had married the older – and far richer – Roser Guardiola, the widow of Josep Guardiola, and clearly knew how to spend his new wife's money. When commissioned to design this apartment building, Gaudí wanted to top anything else done in L'Eixample. Milà was one of the city's first car owners and Gaudí built parking space into the building, itself a first.

Top Floors

The Fundació Caixa Catalunya has opened the top-floor apartment, attic and roof, together called the Espai Gaudí (Gaudí Space), to visitors. The roof is the most extraordinary element, with its giant chimney pots looking like multicoloured medieval knights. Gaudí wanted to put a tall statue of the Virgin up here, too: when the Milà family said no, fearing it might make the building a target for anarchists, Gaudí resigned from the project in disgust.

One floor below the roof, where you can appreciate Gaudí's taste for parabolic arches, is a modest museum dedicated to his work.

Apartment

The next floor down is the apartment (El Pis de la Pedrera). It is fascinating to wander around this elegantly furnished home, done up in the style a well-to-do family might have enjoyed in the early 20th century. There are sensuous curves and unexpected touches in everything from light fittings to bedsteads, from door handles to balconies.

What's Nearby?

Casa de les Punxes   Architecture
(Casa Terrades; Map p254; Avinguda Diagonal 420; MDiagonal) Puig i Cadafalch's Casa Terrades is better known as the Casa de les Punxes (House of Spikes) because of its pointed turrets. This apartment block, completed in 1905, looks like a fairy-tale castle and has the singular attribute of being the only fully detached building in L'Eixample.

Palau del Baró Quadras   Architecture
(Map p254; 93 467 80 00; www.llull.cat; Avinguda Diagonal 373; 8am-8pm Mon-Fri; MDiagonal) FREE Puig i Cadafalch designed Palau del Baró Quadras (built 1902–06) in an exuberant Gothic-inspired style. The main facade is its most intriguing, with a soaring, glassed-in gallery. Take a closer look at the gargoyles and reliefs – the pair of toothy fish and the sword-wielding knight clearly have the same artistic signature as the architect behind Casa Amatller. Decor inside is eclectic, but dominated by Middle Eastern and East Asian themes.

✕ **Take a Break**
Stop by for a gourmet sandwich at Entrepanes Díaz (p143).

Museu Egipci   Museum

(Map p254; ☎93 488 01 88; www.museuegipci.
com; Carrer de València 284; adult/concession/
under 15 €11/8/5; ☉10am-2pm & 4-8pm Mon-
Fri, 10am-8pm Sat, to 2pm Sun; MPasseig de
Gràcia) Hotel magnate Jordi Clos has spent
much of his life collecting ancient Egyptian
artefacts, brought together in this private
museum. It's divided into different thematic areas (the pharaoh, religion, funerary
practices, mummification, crafts etc) and
boasts an interesting variety of exhibits.

Església de la Puríssima Concepció I Assumpció de Nostra Senyora   Church

(Map p254; ☎93 457 65 52; www.parroquia
concepciobcn.org; Carrer de Roger de Llúria
70; ☉7.30am-1pm & 5-9pm Mon-Fri, 7.30am-
2pm & 5-9pm Sun; MPasseig de Gràcia) One
hardly expects to run into a medieval
church on the grid-pattern streets of the
late-19th-century city extension, yet that
is just what this is. Transferred stone by
stone from the old centre in 1871–88, this
14th-century church has a pretty 16th-
century cloister with a peaceful garden.

Fundació Suñol   Gallery

(Map p254; ☎93 496 10 32; www.fundaciosunol.
org; Passeig de Gràcia 98; adult/concession
€4/3; ☉11am-2pm & 4-8pm Mon-Fri, 4-8pm
Sat; MDiagonal) Rotating exhibitions of
portions of this private collection of mostly
20th-century art (some 1200 works in
total) offer anything from Man Ray's
photography to sculptures by Alberto
Giacometti.

☑ **Don't Miss**
The marvellous roof.

JOHN ELK/GETTY IMAGES ©

Las Meninas room. Museu Picasso

Museu Picasso

*Picasso's itchy feet and his extra-
ordinary artistic output means
that his works fill several museums
in Europe. Though his best-known
works aren't here, the setting alone,
in five contiguous medieval stone
mansions, makes the Museu Picasso
unique. The pretty courtyards,
galleries and staircases preserved in
these buildings are as delightful as
the collection inside.*

Great For...

❶ Need to Know

Map p250; ☎93 256 30 00; www.museu
picasso.bcn.cat; Carrer de Montcada 15-23; all
collections adult/concession/child €14/7.50/
free, permanent collection €11/7/free, temporary exhibitions €4.50/3/free, 3-7pm Sun &
1st Sun of month free; ☺9am-7pm Tue, Wed &
Fri-Sun, to 9.30pm Thu; 🛜; Ⓜ Jaume I

★ **Top Tip**

Queues here can be very long; the people strolling to the front booked online. You should book online, too.

The permanent collection is housed in Palau Aguilar, Palau del Baró de Castellet and Palau Meca, all dating to the 14th century. The 18th-century Casa Mauri, built over medieval remains (even some Roman leftovers have been identified), and the adjacent 14th-century Palau Finestres accommodate temporary exhibitions. The first three of these buildings are particularly splendid.

History of the Museum

Allegedly it was Picasso himself who proposed the museum's creation, to his friend and personal secretary Jaume Sabartés, a Barcelona native, in 1960. Three years later, the 'Sabartés Collection' was opened, since a museum bearing Picasso's name would have been met with censorship – Picasso's opposition to the Franco regime was well known. The Museu Picasso we see today opened in 1983. It originally held only Sabartés' personal collection of Picasso's art and a handful of works hanging at the Barcelona Museum of Art, but the collection gradually expanded with donations from Salvador Dalí and Sebastià Junyer Vidal, among others, though most artworks were bequeathed by Picasso himself. His widow, Jacqueline Roque, also donated 41 ceramic pieces and the *Woman With Bonnet* painting after Picasso's death.

Sabartés' contribution and years of service are honoured with an entire room devoted to him, including Picasso's famous Blue Period portrait of him wearing a ruff.

The Collection

This collection concentrates on the artist's formative years, yet there is enough

View from one of the museum's courtyards

material from subsequent periods to give you a thorough impression of his versatility and genius. Above all, you come away feeling that Picasso was the true original, always one step ahead of himself (let alone anyone else) in his search for new forms of expression. The collection includes more than 3500 artworks, largely pre-1904, which is apt considering the artist spent his formative creative years in Barcelona.

It is important, however, not to expect a parade of his well-known works, or even works representative of his best-known periods. The holdings at the museum reflect Picasso's years in Barcelona and elsewhere in Spain, and what makes this collection truly impressive – and unique

☑ **Don't Miss**

El Foll (The Madman) and Retrato de la Tía Pepa (Portrait of Aunt Pepa).

KRZYSZTOF DYDYNSKI/GETTY IMAGES ©

among the many Picasso museums around the world – is the way in which it displays his extraordinary talent at such a young age. Faced with the technical virtuosity of a painting such as *Ciència i Caritat* (Science and Charity), for example, it is almost inconceivable that such a work could have been created by the hands of a 15-year-old. Some of his self-portraits and the portraits of his parents, which date from 1896, are also evidence of his precocious talent.

Las Meninas through the Prism of Picasso

From 1954 to 1962 Picasso was obsessed with the idea of researching and 'rediscovering' the greats, in particular Velázquez. In 1957 he created a series of renditions of the latter's masterpiece *Las Meninas,* now displayed in rooms 12–14. It is as though Picasso has looked at the original Velázquez painting through a prism reflecting all the styles he had worked through until then, creating his own masterpiece in the process. This is a wonderful opportunity to see *Las Meninas* in its entirety, in this beautiful space.

Ceramics

What is also special about the Museu Picasso is its showcasing of his work in lesser-known mediums. The last rooms contain engravings and some 40 ceramic pieces completed throughout the latter years of his unceasingly creative life. You'll see plates and bowls decorated with simple, single-line drawings of fish, owls and other animal shapes, typical of Picasso's daubing on clay.

What's Nearby?

Parc de la Ciutadella　　　Park

(Passeig de Picasso; Ⓜ Arc de Triomf) **FREE** Come for a stroll, a picnic, a visit to the zoo or to inspect Catalonia's regional parliament, but don't miss a visit to this, the

✕ **Take A Break**

Go to Euskal Etxea (p136) for authentic Basque *pintxos* (Basque tapas).

most central green lung in the city. Parc de la Ciutadella is perfect for winding down.

Museu de Cultures del Món
Museum

(Map p250; ☎93 256 23 00; http://museucul turesmon.bcn.cat; Carrer de Montcada 12; adult/ concession/child €5/3.50/free, temporary exhibition €2.20/1.50/free, 3-8pm Sun & 1st Sun of month free; ⊙10am-7pm Tue-Sat, to 8pm Sun; ☎; MJaume I) The Palau Nadal and the Palau Marquès de Lló, which once housed the Museu Barbier-Mueller and the Museu Tèxtil respectively, reopened in 2015 to the public as the site of a new museum, the Museum of World Cultures. Exhibits from private and public collections, including many from the Museu Etnològic on Montjuïc, take the visitor on a trip through the ancient cultures of Africa, Asia, the Americas and Oceania. There's a combined ticket with Museu Egipci (p75) and the Museu Etnològic (p57) for €12.

Castell dels Tres Dragons
Architecture

(MArc de Triomf) The Passeig de Picasso side of Parc de la Ciutadella is lined by several buildings constructed for, or just before, the Universal Exhibition of 1888. The medieval-looking caprice at the top end is the most engaging. Known as the Castell dels Tres Dragons (Castle of the Three Dragons), it long housed the Museu de Zoologia, which has since been transferred to the Fòrum area.

Espai Santa Caterina
Archaeological Site

(Map p250; ☎93 256 21 22; museuhistoria.bcn. cat; Carrer de Joan Capri; ⊙7.30am-3.30pm Mon, Wed & Sat, to 8pm Tue, Thu & Fri; MJaume I) FREE The Mercat de Santa Caterina's 1848 predecessor was built over the remains of the demolished 15th-century Gothic Monestir

de Santa Caterina, a powerful Dominican monastery. A small section of the church foundations is glassed over in one corner as an archaeological reminder (with explanatory panels) – the Espai Santa Caterina.

Born Centre de Cultura i Memòria
Historic Building

(Map p250; ☎93 256 68 51; http://elborn culturaimemoria.barcelona.cat; Plaça Comercial 12; centre free, exhibition spaces adult/child/ concession €6/free/4.20; ⊙10am-8pm Tue-Sun Mar-Sep, 10am-7pm Tue-Sat, to 8pm Sun Oct-Feb; MBarceloneta) Launched to great fanfare in 2013, as part of the events held for the tercentenary of the Catalan defeat in the War of the Spanish Succession, this cultural space is housed in the former Mercat del Born, a handsome 19th-century structure of slatted iron and brick. Excavation in 2001 unearthed remains of whole streets flattened to make way for the much-hated citadel (ciutadella) – these are now on show on the exposed subterranean level.

Carrer de Montcada
Street

(Map p250; MJaume I) An early example of town planning, this medieval high street was driven towards the sea from the road that in the 12th century led northeast from the city walls. It was the city's most coveted address for the merchant classes. The bulk of the great mansions that remain today mostly date to the 14th and 15th centuries.

Fundació Gaspar
Gallery

(Map p250; ☎93 887 42 48; www.fundacio gaspar.org; Carrer de Montcada 25; adult/under 12/concession €5/free/3; ⊙10am-8pm Tue, Wed, Fri-Sun, to 9.30pm Thu; ☎; MJaume I) Set in a stunning Gothic palazzo next to the Museu Picasso, the Fundació Gaspar opened in November 2015 with the intention of complementing the works of other galleries and museums around town by bringing contemporary artists who have yet to exhibit here or whose work explores new concepts and styles. The exhibitions are on the 1st floor, while the ground floor is taken up with a graceful courtyard, where you'll find the Café Gaspar and a shop specialising in edgy, arty gifts.

ⓘ Annual Pass

Though ostensibly aimed at residents, the Museu Picasso Card, valid for 12 months, is also available to visitors on presentation of ID. It's cheaper than a day pass.

AYUNTAMIENTO DE BARCELONA

MUSEO PICASSO

Museu
Picasso

Ajuntament de Barcelona

ℹ️ Did You Know?

His full name: Pablo Diego José Fran-
cisco de Paula Juan Nepomuceno
María de los Remedios Cipriano de la
Santísima Trinidad Ruiz y Picasso.

Walking Tour: Barri Gòtic

This scenic walk through the Barri Gòtic will take you back in time, from the early days of Roman-era Barcino through to the medieval era.

Start: La Catedral
Distance: 1.5km
Duration: 1½ hours

Classic Photo: Stop 1 La Catedral

1 Before entering the cathedral, look at three Picasso friezes on the building facing the square. Next, wander through the magnificent **La Catedral** (p62).

ISMAIL ÇIYDEM/GETTY IMAGES ©

2 Pass through the city gates; turn right into **Plaça de Sant Felip Neri**. The shrapnel-scarred church was damaged by pro-Francist bombers in 1939.

3 Head west to the looming 14th-century **Església de Santa Maria del Pi** (p48), famed for its magnificent rose window.

IAKOV FILIMONOV/SHUTTERSTOCK ©

4 Follow the curving road to pretty **Plaça Reial** (p48). Flanking the fountain are Gaudí-designed lamp posts.

NIKADA/GETTY IMAGES ©

7 The final stop is picturesque **Plaça del Rei**. The former palace today houses a superb history museum, with significant Roman ruins.

PERESANZ/GETTY IMAGES ©

6 Cross Plaça de Sant Jaume and turn left after Carrer del Bisbe. You'll pass the entrance to a ruined **Roman Temple**, with four columns hidden in a small courtyard.

5 Nearby is El Call, the medieval Jewish quarter. Here you'll find **Sinagoga Major** (☎93 317 07 90; www.calldebarcelona.org; Carrer de Marlet 5; ⊙11am-5.30pm Mon-Fri, to 3pm Sat & Sun winter, 10.30am-6.30pm Mon-Fri, to 2.30pm Sat & Sun summer; MLiceu) FREE, one of Europe's oldest synagogues.

Take a Break...
In the heart of the Call, **Alcoba Azul** (⊙6pm-2.30am winter, noon-2am summer) is atmospheric.

Re-creation of a medieval ship at Museu Marítim

Museu Marítim

The mighty Reials Drassanes (Royal Shipyards) are an extraordinary piece of civilian architecture. From here, Don Juan of Austria's flagship galley was launched to lead a joint Spanish-Venetian fleet into the momentous Battle of Lepanto against the Turks in 1571. Today, the broad arches shelter the Museu Marítim, the city's seafaring-history museum and one of Barcelona's most intriguing institutions.

Great For...

ℹ Need to Know

☎93 342 99 20; www.mmb.cat; Avinguda de les Drassanes; adult/child €7/3.50, 3-8pm Sun free; ⊙10am-8pm; 🛜; MDrassanes

★ **Top Tip**

With your museum ticket, visit the **Pailebot de Santa Eulàlia** (www.mmb. cat; Moll de la Fusta; adult/child €3/free; ⊙10am-8.30pm Tue-Fri & Sun, 2-8.30pm Sat; Ⓜ Drassanes), **docked nearby**.

IAKOV FILIMONOV/SHUTTERSTOCK ©

Royal Shipyards

The shipyards were, in their heyday, among the greatest in Europe. Begun in the 13th century and completed by 1378, the long, arched bays (the highest arches reach 13m) once sloped off as slipways directly into the water, which lapped the seaward side of the Drassanes until at least the end of the 18th century. Shipbuilding was later moved to southern Spain, and the Drassanes became a barracks for artillery.

Replica of Don Juan of Austria's Flagship

The centre of the shipyards is dominated by a full-sized replica (made in the 1970s) of Don Juan of Austria's flagship. A clever audiovisual display aboard the vessel brings to life the ghastly existence of the slaves, prisoners and volunteers (!) who, at full steam, could haul this vessel along at 9 knots. They remained chained to their seats, four to an oar, at all times. Here they worked, drank (fresh water was stored below decks, where the infirmary was also located), ate, slept and went to the loo. You could smell a galley like this from miles away.

Exhibitions

Fishing vessels, old navigation charts, models and dioramas of the Barcelona waterfront make up the rest of this engaging museum. Temporary exhibitions are also held. The museum, which has seen major renovations in recent years, is scheduled to finally reopen in its entirety by early 2017. When it reopens, visitors will encounter a greatly expanded collection, with multi-media exhibits evoking more of Spain's epic history on the high seas.

Ictíneo

In the courtyard, you can have a look at a swollen replica of the *Ictíneo,* one of the

world's first submarines. It was invented and built in 1858 by Catalan polymath Narcis Monturiol, and was operated by hand-cranked propellers turned by friends of Monturiol who accompanied him on dozens of successful short dives (two hours maximum) in the harbour. He later developed an even larger submarine powered by a combustion engine that allowed it to dive to 30m and remain submerged for seven hours. Despite impressive demonstrations to awestruck crowds he never attracted the interest of the navy, and remains largely forgotten today.

What's Nearby?

L'Aquàrium   Aquarium
(☎93 221 74 74; www.aquariumbcn.com; Moll d'Espanya; adult/child €20/15, dive €300; ☺9.30am-11pm Jul & Aug, to 9pm Sep-Jun; Ⓜ Drassanes)

Museu Marítim

✕ **Take a Break**

The pleasant museum cafe offers courtyard seating, set lunches and a small assortment of bites.

It is hard not to shudder at the sight of a shark gliding above you, displaying its toothy, wide-mouthed grin. But this, the 80m shark tunnel, is the highlight of one of Europe's largest aquariums. It has the world's best Mediterranean collection and plenty of colourful fish from as far off as the Red Sea, the Caribbean and the Great Barrier Reef. All up, some 11,000 fish (including a dozen sharks) of 450 species reside here.

Museu d'Història de Catalunya   Museum

(Museum of Catalonian History; Map p250; ☑93 225 47 00; www.mhcat.net; Plaça de Pau Vila 3; adult/child €4.50/3.50, 1st Sun of month free; ☺10am-7pm Tue & Thu-Sat, to 8pm Wed, to 2.30pm Sun; Ⓜ Barceloneta) Inside the **Palau de Mar** (Map p250; Plaça de Pau Vila; Ⓜ Barceloneta), this worthwhile museum takes you from the Stone Age through to the early 1980s. It is a busy hotchpotch of dioramas, artefacts, videos, models, documents and interactive bits: all up, an entertaining exploration of 2000 years of Catalan history. Signage is in Catalan/Spanish.

Passeig Marítim de la Barceloneta   Promenade

(Ⓜ Barceloneta, Ciutadella Vila Olímpica) On La Barceloneta's seaward side are the first of Barcelona's beaches, which are popular on summer weekends. The pleasant Passeig Marítim de la Barceloneta, a 1.25km promenade from La Barceloneta to Port Olímpic, is a haunt for strollers and runners, with cyclists zipping by on a separate path nearby.

☑ **Don't Miss**
The replica of Don Juan of Austria's flagship.

GEWILDNATUURFOTOGRAFIE/GETTY IMAGES ©

FRANKIX/SHUTTERSTOCK ©

Palau Güell

This extraordinary neo-Gothic mansion, one of few major buildings of that era raised in the old city, is a magnificent example of the early days of Gaudí's fevered architectural imagination.

Great For...

☑ Don't Miss

The music room, the basement stables and the tiled chimney pots.

Gaudí & Güell

Gaudí built the palace just off La Rambla in the late 1880s for his wealthy and faithful patron, the industrialist Eusebi Güell, without whose support it is unlikely he'd have left a fraction of the creative legacy that is now so celebrated, but at the time was viewed with deep suspicion by much of Catalan society. Although it is a little sombre compared with some of his later whims, the Palau is still a characteristic riot of styles and materials. After the civil war the police occupied it and tortured political prisoners in the basement. The building was then abandoned, leading to its long-term disrepair. It finally reopened in 2012 after lengthy renovations.

ℹ **Need to Know**

Map p250; ☎93 472 57 75; www.palauguell. cat; Carrer Nou de la Rambla 3-5; adult/ concession/under 10 €12/9/free; ⊙10am-8pm Tue-Sun; Ⓜ Drassanes

✕ **Take a Break**

Bar Cañete (Map p250; ☎93 270 34 58; www.barcanete.com; Carrer de la Unió 17; tapas from €3.50; ⊙1pm-midnight Mon-Sat; Ⓜ Liceu), close by, is a great modern tapas stop.

★ **Top Tip**

Get here at 10am or in the afternoon to avoid the worst of the crowds.

The Building

The tour begins on the ground floor, once the coach house, and from there down to the basement, with squat mushroom-shaped brick pillars; this is where horses were stabled. Back upstairs admire the elaborate wrought iron of the main doors from the splendid vestibule, and the grand staircase lined with sandstone columns. Up another floor are the main hall and its annexes; check out the rosewood coffered ceilings and the gallery behind trelliswork, from where the family could spy on their guests as they arrived. Central to the structure is the magnificent music room with a rebuilt organ played during opening hours; the choir would sing from the mezzanine up on the other side. Alongside the alcove containing the organ is another that opened out to become the family chapel,

with booths to seat nobility and, above them, the servants. The hall is a parabolic pyramid – each wall an arch stretching up three floors and coming together to form a dome, giving a magnificent sense of space in what is a surprisingly narrow building, constructed on a site of just 500 square metres.

Above this, the main floor, are the family rooms, which are sometimes labyrinthine, and dotted with piercings of light or grand, stained-glass windows. The bright, diaphanous attic used to house the servants' quarters, but now houses a detailed exhibition on the history and renovation of the building. The roof is a tumult of tiled mosaics and fanciful chimney pots. The audio guide (included) is worth getting not only for the detailed description of the architecture, but also for the pieces of music and its photographic illustrations of the Güell family's life.

LUIS DAVILLA/GETTY IMAGES ©

Mercat de la Boqueria

One of the greatest sound, smell and colour sensations is Barcelona's central produce market, the Mercat de la Boqueria, slap bang on the Rambla, but still used by locals.

Great For...

☑ **Don't Miss**

Picking up fresh produce for a beach picnic.

The vibrant market spills over with all the rich and varied colour of fruit and vegetable stands, seemingly limitless varieties of sea critters, sausages, cheeses, meat (including the finest Jabugo ham) and sweets.

The Historic Market

Some chronicles place a market here as early as 1217. As much as it has become a modern-day attraction, this has always been the place where locals come to shop.

Between the 15th and 18th centuries a pig market known as Mercat de la Palla (Straw Market) stood here; it was considered part of a bigger market extending to Plaça del Pi. What we now know as La Boqueria didn't come to exist until the 19th century, when the local authorities decided to build a structure that would house fishmongers and butchers, as well as fruit and

ℹ **Need to Know**

Map p250; 📞93 412 13 15; www.boqueria.
info; La Rambla 91; ⊘8am-8.30pm Mon-Sat;
ⓜLiceu

✕ **Take a Break**

Take your pick from one of the many
eateries dotted through the market.

★ Top Tip

Stallholders aren't here for tourists:
give way to purchasers and ask per-
mission for photos.

vegetable sellers. The iron Modernista gate
was constructed in 1914.

Many of Barcelona's top restaurateurs
buy their produce here, although it's no
easy task getting past the crowds of tourists
to snare a slippery slab of sole or a tempting
piece of *queso de cabra* (goat's cheese).

What to Try?

La Boqueria is dotted with several unassuming places to eat, and eat well, with
stallholders opening up at lunchtime.
Whether you eat here or you're self-
catering, it's worth trying some of Catalonia's gastronomic specialities, such as
bacallà salat (dried salted cod), which usually comes in an *esqueixada,* a tomato, onion and black olive salad with frisée lettuce;
calçots (a cross between a leek and an onion), which are chargrilled and the insides
eaten as a messy whole; *cargols* (snails), a

Catalan staple best eaten baked as *cargols
a la llauna; peus de porc* (pig's trotters),
which are often stewed with snails; or
percebes (goose-necked barnacles). Much
loved across Spain, these crustaceans are
eaten with a garlic and parsley sauce.

What's Nearby?

Antic Hospital
de la Santa Creu   Historic Building

(Former Hospital of the Holy Cross; Map p249;
📞93 270 16 21; www.bcn.cat; Carrer de l'Hospital
56; ⊘9am-8pm Mon-Fri, to 2pm Sat; ⓜLiceu)
FREE Behind La Boqueria stands the Antic
Hospital de la Santa Creu, which was once
the city's main hospital. Begun in 1401,
it functioned until the 1930s, and was
considered one of the best in Europe in its
medieval heyday – it is the place where Antoni Gaudí died in 1926. Today it houses the
Biblioteca de Catalunya (National Library
of Catalonia), and the **Institut d'Estudis
Catalans** (Institute for Catalan Studies).
The hospital's Gothic chapel, **La Capella** (📞93 256 20 44; www.bcn.cat/lacapella;
⊘noon-8pm Tue-Sat, 11am-2pm Sun & holidays)
FREE, shows temporary exhibitions.

Els Quatre Gats (p95)

Modernista Wining & Dining

Barcelona's Modernista extravaganzas aren't just for daytime sightseeing. Several classic cafes and restaurants mean that you can enjoy their sinuous lines over a meal or cocktail in the evening, too. A couple of hotels add their weighty names to the mix; drop in for a drink if you're not staying.

Great For...

❶ Need to Know

Check the opening hours before making a route of these places.

★ **Top Tip**

The best people-watching time in cafes in Barcelona is early evening, around 7pm.

Casa Almirall
Bar

(Map p249; www.casaalmirall.com; Carrer de Joaquín Costa 33; ⏰6pm-2.30am Mon-Thu, 6.30pm-3am Fri, noon-3am Sat, noon-12.30am Sun; Ⓜ️Universitat) In business since the 1860s, this unchanged corner bar is dark and intriguing, with Modernista decor and a mixed clientele. There are some great original pieces in here, such as the marble counter, and the cast-iron statue of the muse of the Universal Exposition, held in Barcelona in 1888.

Hotel España
Hotel, Architecture

(📞93 550 00 00; www.hotelespanya.com; Carrer de Sant Pau 9-11; ❄️📶♨️; Ⓜ️Liceu) Best known for its wonderful Modernista interiors in the dining rooms and bar, in which architect Domènech i Montaner, sculptor Eusebi Arnau and painter Ramon Casas had a hand.

There's a small plunge pool and sun deck on the roof terrace, along with a bar.

London Bar
Bar

(Map p250; Carrer Nou de la Rambla 34-36; ⏰6pm-3am Mon-Thu & Sun, 6pm-3.30am Fri & Sat; Ⓜ️Liceu) Open since 1909, this Modernista bar started as a hang-out for circus hands and was later frequented by the likes of Picasso, Miró and Hemingway. Today it fills to the brim with punters at the long front bar and rickety old tables. On occasion you can attend concerts at the small stage right up the back.

Hotel Casa Fuster
Hotel, Architecture

(📞93 255 30 00; www.hotelcasafuster.com; Passeig de Gràcia 132; Ⓟ❄️@📶♨️; Ⓜ️Diagonal) This sumptuous Modernista mansion, built in 1908–11, is one of Barcelona's most luxurious hotels. Period features have

Escribà

been restored at considerable cost and the rooftop terrace (with pool) offers spectacular views.

The Café Vienés, once a meeting place for Barcelona's intellectuals, hosts excellent jazz nights (Thursdays from 9pm).

Els Quatre Gats
Catalan €€€

(Map p250; ☎93 302 41 40; www.4gats.com; Carrer de Montsió 3; mains €21-29; ⊗12.30-4.30pm & 6.30pm-1am; 🗟; ⓂUrquinaona) Once the lair of Barcelona's Modernista artists, Els Quatre Gats is a stunning example of the movement, inside and out, with its colourful tiles, geometric brickwork and wooden fittings. The restaurant is not quite as thrilling

☑ **Don't Miss**

Having a coffee in Els Quatre Gats, where the Modernista maestros used to hang out.

CARLOS SANCHEZ PEREYRA/GETTY IMAGES ©

as its setting, though you can just have a coffee and a croissant in the cafe (open from 9am to 1am) at the front.

El Paraigua
Live Music

(Map p250; ☎93 302 11 31; www.elparaigua.com; Carrer del Pas de l'Ensenyança 2; ⊗noon-midnight Sun-Wed, to 2am Thu, to 3am Fri & Sat; ⓂLiceu) A tiny chocolate box of dark tinted Modernisme, the 'Umbrella' has been serving up drinks since the 1960s. The turn-of-the-20th-century decor was transferred here from a shop knocked down elsewhere in the district and cobbled back together to create this cosy locale.

Cafè de l'Òpera
Cafe

(Map p250; ☎93 317 75 85; www.cafeopera bcn.com; La Rambla 74; ⊗8.30am-2.30am; 🗟; ⓂLiceu) Opposite the Gran Teatre del Liceu is La Rambla's most intriguing cafe. Operating since 1929, it is pleasant enough for an early evening libation or coffee and croissants. Head upstairs for an elevated seat above the busy boulevard. Can you be tempted by the *cafè de l'Òpera* (coffee with chocolate mousse)?

Escribà
Food & Drink

(Map p250; ☎93 301 60 27; www.escriba.es; La Rambla 83; ⊗9am-10pm; 🗟; ⓂLiceu) Chocolates, dainty pastries and mouth-watering cakes can be lapped up behind the Modernista mosaic facade here or taken away for private, guilt-ridden consumption. This Barcelona favourite is owned by the Escribà family, a name synonymous with sinfully good sweet things. More than that, it adds a touch of authenticity to La Rambla.

✕ **Take a Break**

Need a dose of non-Modernista reality? **El Colectivo** (Map p249; ☎93 318 63 80; Carrer del Pintor Fortuny 22; bocadillos from €4; ⊗9am-9pm Mon-Wed, 9am-midnight Thu, 9am-2am Fri & Sat) is a quiet, relaxing Raval cafe.

KARSOL/SHUTTERSTOCK ©

MACBA

Designed by Richard Meier and opened in 1995, MACBA (Museu d'Art Contemporani de Barcelona) has become the city's foremost contemporary art centre, with captivating exhibitions for the serious art lover.

Great For...

☑ Don't Miss

The permanent collection dedicated to 20th-century Spanish and Catalan art.

The ground and 1st floors of this great white bastion of contemporary art are generally given over to exhibitions from the gallery's own collections. There are some 3000 pieces centred on three periods: post-WWII; around 1968; and the years since the fall of the Berlin Wall in 1989, right up until the present day.

The Permanent Collection

The permanent collection is on the ground floor and dedicates itself to Spanish and Catalan art from the second half of the 20th century, with works by Antoni Tàpies, Joan Brossa and Miquel Barceló, among others, though international artists, such as Paul Klee, Bruce Nauman and John Cage, are also represented.

The gallery, across two floors, is dedicated to temporary visiting exhibitions that are

❶ Need to Know

Museu d'Art Contemporani de Barcelona; Map p249; ☑93 481 33 68; www.macba.cat; Plaça dels Àngels 1; adult/concession/under 12 €10/8/free; ◷11am-7.30pm Mon & Wed-Fri, 10am-9pm Sat, 10am-3pm Sun & holidays; ⓂUniversitat

✗ Take a Break

Stop in for tacos and homemade ginger beer at Caravelle (p135).

★ Top Tip

Before visiting, check the website for events that might coincide.

almost always challenging and intriguing. MACBA's 'philosophy' is to do away with the old model of a museum where an artwork is a spectacle and to create a space where art can be viewed critically, so the exhibitions are usually tied in with talks and events. This is food for the brain as well as the eyes.

Capella Macba

Across the square in front, where the city's skateboarders gather, the renovated 400-year-old Convent dels Àngels houses the Capella MACBA, where MACBA regularly rotates selections from its permanent collection. The Gothic framework of the one-time convent-church remains intact.

Fringe Attractions

The library and auditorium stage regular concerts, talks and events, all of which are either reasonably priced or free. The extensive art bookshop is fantastic for both stocking up on art and art theory books, as well as quirky gifts and small design objects.

What's Nearby?

Centre de Cultura Contemporània de Barcelona   Building

(CCCB; Map p249; ☑93 306 41 00; www.cccb. org; Carrer de Montalegre 5; adult/concession/ under 12 for 1 exhibition €6/4/free, 2 exhibitions €8/6/free, Sun 3-8pm free; ◷11am-8pm Tue-Sun; ⓂUniversitat) A complex of auditoriums, exhibition spaces and conference halls opened here in 1994 in what had been an 18th-century hospice, the Casa de la Caritat. The courtyard, with a vast glass wall on one side, is spectacular. With 4500 sq metres of exhibition space in four separate areas, the centre hosts a constantly changing program of exhibitions, film cycles and other events.

Palau de la Música Catalana's auditorium skylight

Palau de la Música Catalana

This concert hall is a high point of Barcelona's Modernista architecture, a symphony in tile, brick, sculpted stone and stained glass conceived as a temple for the Catalan Renaixença (Renaissance).

Great For...

☑ **Don't Miss**

The principal facade's mosaics and columns and the foyer and pillars in the restaurant.

Built by Domènech i Montaner between 1905 and 1908 for the Orfeo Català musical society, the *palau* (palace) was built with the help of some of the best Catalan artisans of the time, in the cloister of the former Convent de Sant Francesc. Since 1990 it has undergone several major changes.

The Facade

The *palau,* like a peacock, shows off much of its splendour on the outside. Take in the principal facade with its mosaics, floral capitals and the sculpture cluster representing Catalan popular music.

The Interior

Wander inside the foyer and restaurant areas to admire the spangled, tiled pillars. Best of all, however, is the richly colourful auditorium upstairs, with its ceiling of blue-and-gold stained glass and shimmering

❶ Need to Know

Map p254; ☎93 295 72 00; www.palau
musica.cat; Carrer de Palau de la Música
4-6; adult/concession/child €18/11/free;
⊙guided tours 10am-3.30pm, to 6pm Easter,
Jul & Aug; Ⓜ Urquinaona

✖ Take a Break

Le Cucine Mandarosso (☎93 269 07
80; www.lecucinemandarosso.com; Carrer de
Verdaguer i Callís 4; mains €12-14, menú del
día €11; ⊙1.30pm-1am Tue-Sat, 1.30-5pm &
8pm-midnight Sun; Ⓜ Urquinaona) is tops
for Italian comfort food.

★ Top Tip

Under 30? Take ID to the ticket office
to bag a discount.

---

skylight that looks like a giant, crystalline,
downward-thrusting nipple. Above a bust
of Beethoven on the stage towers a wind-
blown sculpture of Wagner's Valkyries
(Wagner was top of the Barcelona charts at
the time it was created). This can only be
savoured on a guided tour or by attending a
performance – either is highly recommended. Admission is by tour only, and tickets
can be bought up to a week in advance
by phone or online. Space is limited to a
maximum of 55 people.

Performances

This is the city's most traditional venue for
classical and choral music, although it has
a wide-ranging program, including flamenco, pop and – particularly – jazz. Just being
here for a performance is an experience.

A Controversial History

The original Modernista creation, now a
World Heritage site, did not meet with universal approval in its day. The doyen of Catalan literature, Josep Pla, did not hesitate
to condemn it as 'horrible' (although few
share his sentiments today). Domènech i
Montaner himself was also in a huff – he
failed to attend the opening ceremony in
response to unsettled bills.

The *palau* was at the centre of a
fraud scandal from 2009 to 2012, as its
president, Felix Millet, who subsequently
resigned, admitted to having siphoned off
millions of euros of its funds. He and his
partner were ordered to repay the embez-
zled money to the *palau* in March 2012.

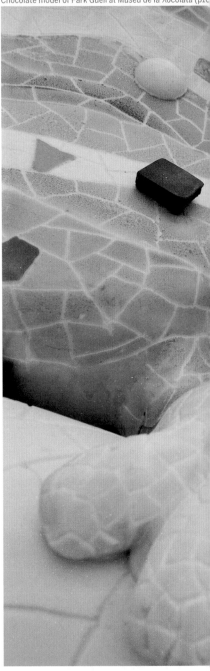

Chocolate model of Park Güell at Museu de la Xocolata (p1C

Foodie Trails in La Ribera

Gourmands and gastronomes will be thoroughly beguiled by the choice in La Ribera, home to a fabulous market and gourmet shops offering all sorts of delicacies. It's almost impossible to walk into its enticing pedestrian zone and come out without having tried, tasted or bought something.

Great For...

❶ Need to Know

Buying smallgoods? The Spanish phrase for 'vacuum pack' is '*envasar al vacío*'.

★ **Top Tip**
Get to La Ribera's market early; it's far more interesting in the morning.

Mercat de Santa Caterina · Market

(Map p250; ☎93 319 57 40; www.mercatsanta caterina.com; Avinguda de Francesc Cambó 16; ⏰7.30am-3.30pm Mon, Wed, Sat, to 8.30pm Tue, Thu, Fri, closed afternoons Jul & Aug; 🛜; Ⓜ Jaume I) This extraordinary-looking produce market was designed by Enric Miralles and Benedetta Tagliabue to replace its 19th-century predecessor. Finished in 2005, it is distinguished by its kaleido-scopic and undulating roof, held up above the bustling produce stands, restaurants, cafes and bars by twisting slender branch-es of what look like grey steel trees.

Museu de la Xocolata · Museum

(☎93 268 78 78; www.museuxocolata.cat; Carrer del Comerç 36; adult/under 7 €6/free; ⏰10am-7pm Mon-Sat, 10am-3pm Sun; 🛜; ⓂArc de Triomf) Chocoholics have a hard time containing themselves in this museum ded-icated to the fundamental foodstuff – par-ticularly when faced with the cocoa-based treats in the cafe at the exit. The displays trace the origins of chocolate, its arrival in Europe, and the many myths and images associated with it. Kids and grown-ups can join guided tours and occasionally take part in chocolate-making and tasting sessions.

Hofmann Pastisseria · Food

(Map p250; ☎93 268 82 21; www.hofmann-bcn. com; Carrer dels Flassaders 44; ⏰9am-2pm & 3.30-8pm Mon-Thu, to 8.30pm Fri & Sat, 9am-2.30pm Sun; ⓂBarceloneta) This bite-sized gourmet patisserie, linked to the prestig-ious Hofmann cooking school, tempts with jars of delicious chocolates, its renowned croissants, and an array of cakes and other sweet treats.

Casa Gispert

Casa Gispert   Food

(Map p250; ☑93 319 75 35; www.casagispert.com; Carrer dels Sombrerers 23; ☺10am-2pm & 4-8pm Mon-Sat; Ⓜ Jaume I) The wonderful, atmospheric and wood-fronted Casa Gispert has been toasting nuts and selling all manner of dried fruit since 1851. Pots and jars piled high on the shelves contain an unending variety of crunchy tidbits: some roasted, some honeyed, all of them moreish. Your order is shouted over to the till, along with the price, in a display of old-world accounting.

La Botifarreria   Food

(Map p250; ☑93 319 91 23; www.labotifarreria.com; Carrer de Santa Maria 4; ☺8.30am-2.30pm & 5-8.30pm Mon-Sat; Ⓜ Jaume I) Say it with a sausage! Although this delightful deli sells all sorts of goodies, the mainstay is an astounding variety of handcrafted sausages – the *botifarra*. Not just the regular pork kind either – these sausages are stuffed with anything from green pepper and whisky to apple curry.

El Magnífico   Coffee

(Map p250; ☑93 319 39 75; www.cafeselmagnifico.com; Carrer de l'Argenteria 64; ☺10am-8pm Mon-Sat; Ⓜ Jaume I) All sorts of coffee has been roasted here since the early 20th century. The variety of coffee (and tea) available is remarkable – and the aromas hit you as you walk in.

Vila Viniteca   Wine

(Map p250; ☑902 32 77 77; www.vilaviniteca.es; Carrer dels Agullers 7; ☺8.30am-8.30pm Mon-Sat; Ⓜ Jaume I) One of the best wine stores in Barcelona (and there are a few...), this place has been searching out the best local and imported wines since 1932. On a couple of November evenings it organises what has become an almost riotous wine-tasting event in Carrer dels Agullers and surrounding lanes, at which cellars from around Spain present their young new wines.

Olisoliva   Food

(Map p250; ☑93 268 14 72; www.olisoliva.com; Mercat de Santa Caterina; ☺9.30am-3.30pm Mon, Wed & Sat, to 8.30pm Tue & Thu; Ⓜ Jaume I) Inside the Mercat de Santa Caterina, this simple, glassed-in store is stacked with olive oils and vinegars from all over Spain. Taste some of the products before deciding.

Sans i Sans   Drink

(Map p250; ☑93 310 25 18; Carrer de l'Argenteria 59; ☺10am-8pm Mon-Sat; Ⓜ Jaume I) This exquisite tea shop is run by the same people who run El Magnífico across the road.

☑ **Don't Miss**

The Mercat de Santa Caterina: what a place.

MAREMAGNUM/GETTY IMAGES ©

★ **Top Tip**

In the Museu de la Xocolata, look for chocolate models of emblematic buildings such as La Sagrada Família.

Underground ruins at the museum

Museu d'Història de Barcelona

This fascinating museum in the Barri Gòtic takes you back through the centuries to the very foundations of Roman Barcino. It's an impressive display of archaeology and a most intriguing place to wander in the bowels of the old city, observing the layers of history spread out before you.

Great For...

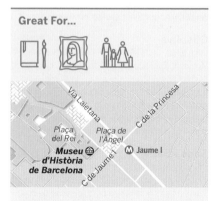

ⓘ Need to Know

MUHBA; Map p250; ☑93 256 21 00; www.museuhistoria.bcn.cat; Plaça del Rei; adult/concession/child €7/5/free, free 1st Sun of month & 3-8pm Sun; ⊙10am-7pm Tue-Sat, 10am-8pm Sun; 🛜; ⓂJaume I

★ **Top Tip**

Entry here includes admission to other MUHBA-run sites, such as the **Domus de Sant Honorat** (☎93 256 21 00; www.museuhistoria.bcn.cat; Carrer de la Fruita 2; ⊙10am-2pm Sun; Ⓜ Jaume I).

At the museum, you'll stroll amid extensive ruins of the town that flourished here following its founding by Emperor Augustus around 10 BC. Equally impressive is the setting inside the former Palau Reial Major (Grand Royal Palace), among the key locations of medieval princely power in Barcelona.

Casa Padellàs

Enter through Casa Padellàs, just south of Plaça del Rei. Casa Padellàs was built for a 16th-century noble family in Carrer dels Mercaders and moved here, stone by stone, in the 1930s. It has a courtyard typical of Barcelona's late-Gothic and baroque mansions, with a graceful external staircase up to the 1st floor. Today it leads to a restored Roman tower and a section of Roman wall (the exterior of which faces Plaça Ramon de Berenguer el Gran), as well as a section of the house set aside for temporary exhibitions.

Underground Ruins

Below ground is a remarkable walk through about 4 sq km of excavated Roman and Visigothic Barcelona. After the display on the typical Roman *domus* (villa), you reach a public laundry (outside in the street were containers for people to urinate into, as the urine was used as disinfectant). You pass more laundries and dyeing shops, a 6th-century public cold-water bath and more dye shops. As you hit the Cardo Minor (a main street), you turn right then left and reach various shops dedicated to the making of *garum*. This paste, a favourite food across the Roman Empire, was made of mashed-up fish intestines, eggs and blood. Occasionally prawns, cockles and herbs were added to create other flavours. Further on are fish-preserve stores. Fish were sliced

up (and all innards removed for making *garum*), laid in alternate layers using salt for preservation, and sat in troughs for about three weeks before being ready for sale and export.

Next come remnants of a 6th- to 7th-century church and episcopal buildings, followed by wine-making stores, with ducts for allowing the must to flow off, and ceramic, round-bottomed *dolia* for storing and ageing wine. Ramparts then wind around and upward, past remains of the gated patio of a Roman house, the medieval Palau Episcopal (Bishops' Palace) and into two broad vaulted halls with displays on medieval Barcelona.

Museu d'Història de Barcelona

☑ **Take a Break**

For a vegan burger and artisanal beer, hit **Cat Bar** (Carrer de la Bòria 17; mains €6.50-8.50; ⊘6-11.30pm Mon-Wed, 1-11pm Thu-Sat).

In Columbus' Footsteps

You eventually emerge at a hall and ticket office set up on the north side of Plaça del Rei. To your right is the Saló del Tinell, the banqueting hall of the royal palace and a fine example of Catalan Gothic (built 1359–70). Its broad arches and bare walls give a sense of solemnity that would have made an appropriate setting for Fernando and Isabel to hear Columbus' first reports of the New World. The hall is sometimes used for temporary exhibitions, which may cost extra and mean that your peaceful contemplation of its architectural majesty is somewhat obstructed.

A Chapel

As you leave the *saló* you come to the 14th-century Capella Reial de Santa Àgata, the palace chapel. Outside, a spindly bell tower rises from the northeast side of Plaça del Rei. Inside, all is bare except for the 15th-century altarpiece and the magnificent *techumbre* (decorated timber ceiling). The altarpiece is considered to be one of Jaume Huguet's finest surviving works.

Out to the Square

Head down the fan-shaped stairs into Plaça del Rei and look up to observe the Mirador del Rei Martí (lookout tower of King Martin), built in 1555, long after the king's death. It is part of the Arxiu de la Corona d'Aragón; the magnificent views over the old city are now enjoyed only by a privileged few.

> ☑ **Don't Miss**
> The public laundry and the wine-making stores.

AGF/GETTY IMAGES ©

DE AGOSTINI/C MAURY/GETTY IMAGES ©

Museu Frederic Marès

One of the wildest collections of historical curios lies inside this vast medieval complex, once part of the royal palace of the counts of Barcelona.

Great For...

☑ **Don't Miss**

Displays from the collector's cabinet.

The building holding the museum is an intriguing one. A rather worn coat of arms on the wall indicates that it was also, for a while, the seat of the Spanish Inquisition in Barcelona.

Sculpture

Frederic Marès i Deulovol (1893–1991) was a rich sculptor, traveller and obsessive collector. He specialised in medieval Spanish sculpture, huge quantities of which are displayed in the basement and on the ground and 1st floors – including some lovely polychrome wooden sculptures of the Crucifixion and the Virgin. Among the most eye-catching pieces is a reconstructed Romanesque doorway with four arches, taken from a 13th-century country church in the Aragonese province of Huesca.

Collector's Cabinet

The top two floors comprise 'the collector's
cabinet', a mind-boggling array of knick-
knacks, including medieval weaponry, finely
carved pipes, delicate ladies' fans, intricate
'floral' displays made of seashells, and
19th-century daguerreotypes and photographs. A room that once served as Marès'
study and library is now crammed with
sculptures. The shady courtyard houses a
pleasant summer cafe (Cafè de l'Estiu).

What's Nearby?

Plaça de Sant Jaume   Square

(Map p250, Ⓜ Liceu, Jaume I) In the 2000 or
so years since the Romans settled here, the
area around this square (often remodelled),
which started life as the forum, has been
the focus of Barcelona's civic life. This is
still the central staging area for Barcelona's
traditional festivals. Facing each other
across the square are the seat of Catalonia's regional government – the **Palau de
la Generalitat** (Map p250; www.president.
cat; Plaça de Sant Jaume; ⊘2nd & 4th weekend
of month; Ⓜ Jaume I), on the north side – and
the town hall, or **Ajuntament** (Casa de la Ciutat; Map p250; ☏93 402 70 00; www.barcelona
turisme.com; Plaça de Sant Jaume; ⊘10.30am-
1.30pm Sun; Ⓜ Jaume I) **FREE** to the south.

Museu d'Idees i
Invents de Barcelona   Museum

(Museum of Ideas & Inventions; Map p250; ☏93
332 79 30; www.mibamuseum.com; Carrer de la
Ciutat 7; adult/concession/under 4 €8/6/free;
⊘10am-2pm & 4-7pm Tue-Fri, 10am-8pm Sat, to
2pm Sun; Ⓜ Jaume I) Although the price is a
bit steep for such a small museum (though
they've now introduced a secondary
system of €0.20 per minute), the collection
makes for an amusing browse over an hour
or so. You'll find both brilliant and bizarre
inventions on display.

Walking Tour: Gràcia's Squares

One of Barcelona's most vibrant districts, Gràcia was an independent town until the 1890s. Explore the barrio's picturesque squares and experience its beauty, history and culture.

Start: Plaça de Joan Carles I
Distance: 1.9km
Duration: 50 minutes

7 Busy, elongated **Plaça de la Revolució de Setembre de 1868** commemorates the toppling of Queen Isabel II.

Take a Break...
La Nena (⊗9am-10pm) is a chaotic, exuberant, gem of a café.

Ⓜ

4 Plaça de la Llibertat (Liberty Sq) is home to a Modernista produce market (pictured), designed by Francesc Berenguer i Mestres, Gaudí's long-time assistant.

GLEB SOLOGUB/SHUTTERSTOCK ©

Gràcia Ⓡ

4

3

Travessera de Gràcia

C de Vic

C de Regàs

Via Augusta

3 Plaça de Galla Placidia recalls the brief sojourn of the Roman empress-to-be Galla Placidia in the 5th century AD.

2 Where Carrer Gran de Gràcia leads you into Gràcia proper, the grand **Modernista Casa Fuster** (p94) rises in all its glory.

JAN VAN DER HOEVEN/GETTY IMAGES ©

GRÀCIA

0 400 m
0 0.2 miles

FINISH

8

C d'Asturies
C de l'Or
C de Torrijos
C de la Perla
C de Terol
C de la Gràcia

7

C de Maspons
Travessera de Gràcia

6 C de Torrent de l'Olla

SANT GERVASI

5

C de Goya
C de Martínez de la Rosa
C de Francisco Giner
C de Mozart
C Gran de Gràcia

2

C de Bonavista
C de Sèneca
C de la Riera de Sant Miquel
C de Còrsega

START 1

Av Diagonal
Diagonal
Pg de Gràcia
Rambla de Catalunya

Diagonal Ⓜ

8 Pleasant terraces adorn pedestrianised **Plaça de la Virreina**, presided over by the 17th-century Església de Sant Joan.

SIQUI SANCHEZ/GETTY IMAGES ©

6 Possibly the rowdiest of Gràcia's squares, **Plaça del Sol** (Sun Sq) is lined with bars and eateries, which buzz on summer nights.

5 Popular **Plaça de la Vila de Gràcia** is home to the Torre del Rellotge (Clock Tower), long a symbol of Republican agitation.

BENC/GETTY IMAGES ©

1 The obelisk at **Plaça de Joan Carles I** honours Spain's present king for stifling an attempted coup d'état in 1981.

NITO/SHUTTERSTOCK ©

STEFANO POLITI MARKOVINA/GETTY IMAGES ©

Basílica de Santa Maria del Mar

At the southwest end of Passeig del Born stands the apse of Barcelona's finest Catalan Gothic church, Santa Maria del Mar (Our Lady of the Sea).

Great For...

☑ **Don't Miss**

The church's architects in memorial stone relief.

Built in the 14th century with record-breaking alacrity for the time (it took just 54 years), the church is remarkable for its architectural harmony and simplicity.

The People's Church

Its construction started in 1329, with Berenguer de Montagut and Ramon Despuig as the architects in charge. During construction the city's *bastaixos* (porters) spent a day each week carrying on their backs the stone required to build the church from royal quarries in Montjuïc. Their memory lives on in reliefs of them in the main doors and stone carvings elsewhere in the church. The walls, the side chapels and the facades were finished by 1350, and the entire structure was completed in 1383.

The Interior

The exterior gives an impression of stern-
ness, and the narrow streets surrounding
it are restrictive and claustrophobic. It may
come as a (pleasant) surprise then to find
a spacious and light interior – the central
nave and two flanking aisles separated by
slender octagonal pillars give an enormous
sense of lateral space.

The interior is almost devoid of imagery
of the sort to be found in Barcelona's other
large Gothic churches, but Santa Maria was
lacking in superfluous decoration even before anarchists gutted it in 1909 and 1936.
Keep an ear out for music recitals, often
baroque and classical.

Old Flame

Opposite Basílica de Santa Maria del Mar's
southern flank, an eternal flame burns over
an apparently anonymous sunken square.
This is El Fossar de les Moreres (The
Mulberry Cemetery), the site of a Roman
cemetery. It's also where Catalan resist-
ance fighters were buried after the siege of
Barcelona ended in defeat in September
1714, and for whom the flame burns.

What's Nearby?

Museu Europeu
d'Art Modern   Museum

(MEAM; Map p250; ☎93 319 56 93; www.meam.
es; Carrer Barra de Ferro 5; adult/concession/
under 10 €9/7/free; 🕘10am-8pm Tue-Sun;
Ⓜ Jaume I) The European Museum of Modern Art opened in the summer of 2011 in
the Palau Gomis, a handsome 18th-
century mansion around the corner from
the Museu Picasso. The art within is strictly
representational (the 'Modern' of the name
simply means 'contemporary') and is mostly from young Spanish artists, though there
are some works from elsewhere in Europe.

Jardí Botànic

IAKOV FILIMONOV/SHUTTERSTOCK ©

Exploring Montjuïc

The hill of Montjuïc overlooking the port has some top-notch art collections, but strolling through the succession of gardens admiring the vistas is another Barcelona must-do.

Great For...

☑ **Don't Miss**

The MNAC (p54) and Fundació Joan Miró (p58) are also top Montjuïc attractions.

Teleférico del Puerto   Cable Car

(Map p256; www.telefericodebarcelona.com; Av de Miramar, Jardins de Miramar; one way/return €11/16.50; ⊙11am-7pm; ⊡50, 153) The quickest way from the beach to the mountain is via the cable car that runs between Torre de Sant Sebastiá in La Barceloneta and the Miramar stop on Montjuïc (from mid-June to mid-September only). From Estació Parc Montjuïc, the separate **Telefèric de Montjuïc** (www.telefericdemontjuic.cat; Av de Miramar 30; adult/child one way €8/6.20; ⊙10am-9pm Jun-Sep, to 7pm Oct-May; ⊡55, 150) cable car carries you to the Castell de Montjuïc via the *mirador* (lookout point).

Funicular (Paral·lel)   Cable Car

(Map p256; ⊙7.30am-10pm Mon-Fri, 9am-10pm Apr-Oct, to 8pm Nov-Mar) The funicular runs every 10 minutes between Paral·lel metro station and Parc de Montjuïc. From there, catch the Telefèric up to the Castell de Montjuïc.

❶ Need to Know

Most of the gardens open at 10am.

✕ Take a Break

La Font del Gat (Map p256; ☎93 289 04 04; www.lafontdelgat.com; Passeig de Santa Madrona 28; mains €16-21; ⊗10am-6pm Tue-Fri, from noon Sat & Sun) has a lovely terrace, though you pay for the sublime view.

★ Top Tip

Get the funicular up if you don't fancy the climb.

Castell de Montjuïc — Fortress, Gardens

(Map p256; ☎93 256 44 45; www.bcn.cat/cas telldemontjuic; Carretera de Montjuïc 66; adult/child €5/free, Sun after 3pm free; ⊗10am-8pm Apr-Oct, to 6pm Nov-Mar; ⬛150, Telefèric de Montjuïc, Castell de Montjuïc) This forbidding *castell* (castle or fort) dominates the southeastern heights of Montjuïc and enjoys commanding views over the Mediterranean. It dates, in its present form, from the late 17th and 18th centuries. For most of its dark history, it has been used to watch over the city and as a political prison and killing ground.

Jardins de Mossèn Cinto de Verdaguer — Gardens

(Map p256; www.bcn.cat/parcsijardins; ⊗10am-sunset; ⬛55, 150) **FREE** Near the Estació Parc Montjuïc funicular/Telefèric station, these gardens are home to various kinds of bulbs and aquatic plants.

Jardí Botànic — Gardens

(Map p256; http://museuciencies.cat; Carrer del Doctor Font i Quer 2; adult/child €3.50/free, after 3pm Sun free; ⊗10am-7pm Apr-Sep, to 5pm Oct-Mar; ⬛55, 150) Jardí Botànic is dedicated to Mediterranean flora, with a collection of some 40,000 plants and 1500 species.

Jardins de Mossèn Costa i Llobera — Gardens

(Map p256; Carretera de Miramar 1; ⊗10am-sunset; ⬛Transbordador Aeri, Miramar) **FREE** Towards the foot of the part of Montjuïc below the castle, these gardens feature a good collection of tropical and desert plants – including a veritable forest of cacti.

Jardins de Joan Maragall — Gardens

(Map p256; Avinguda dels Montanyans 48; ⊗10am-3pm Sat & Sun; ⓂPlaça Espanya) **FREE** Near the Estadi Olímpic, these little-visited gardens include fountains, sculptures and a neo-classical palace (the Spanish royal family's residence in Barcelona).

Montjuïc

A ONE-DAY ITINERARY

Montjuïc, perhaps once the site of pre-Roman settlements, is today a hilltop green lung looking over city and sea. Interspersed across varied gardens are major art collections, a fortress, an Olympic stadium and more. A solid one-day itinerary can take in the key spots.

Alight at Espanya metro stop and make for **CaixaForum ❶**, always host to three or four free top-class exhibitions. The nearby **Pavelló Mies van der Rohe ❷** is an intriguing study in 1920s futurist housing by one of the 20th century's greatest architects. Uphill, the Romanesque art collection in the **Museu Nacional d'Art de Catalunya ❸** is a must, and its restaurant is a pleasant lunch stop. Escalators lead further up the hill towards the **Estadi Olímpic ❹**, scene of the 1992 Olympic Games. The road leads east to the **Fundació Joan Miró ❺**, a shrine to the master surrealist's creativity. Contemplate ancient relics in the **Museu d'Arqueologia de Catalunya ❻**, then have a break in the peaceful **Jardins de Mossèn Cinto Verdaguer ❼**, the prettiest on the hill, before taking the cable car to the **Castell de Montjuïc ❽**. If you pick the right day, you can round off with the gorgeously kitsch **La Font Màgica ❾** sound and light show, followed by drinks and dancing in an open-air nightspot in **Poble Espanyol ❿**.

TOP TIPS

» **Moving views** Ride the Transbordador Aeri from Barceloneta for a bird's eye approach to Montjuïc. Or take the Teleféric de Montjuïc cable car to the Castell for more aerial views.

» **Summer fun** The Castell de Montjuïc features outdoor summer cinema and concerts (see http://sala montjuic.org).

» **Beautiful bloomers** Bursting with colour and serenity, the Jardins de Mossèn Cinto Verdaguer are exquisitely laid out with bulbs, especially tulips, and aquatic flowers.

CaixaForum
This former factory and barracks designed by Josep Puig i Cadafalch is an outstanding work of Modernista architecture; like a Lego fantasy in brick.

Piscines Bernat Picornell

Olympic Needle

Poble Espanyol
Amid the rich variety of traditional Spanish architecture created in replica for the 1929 Barcelona World Exhibition, browse the art on show in the Fundació Fran Daurel.

Pavelló Mies van der Rohe
Admire the inventiveness of the great German architect Ludwig Mies van der Rohe in this recreation of his avant garde German pavillion for the 1929 World Exhibition.

La Font Màgica

Take a summer evening to behold the Magic Fountain come to life in a unique 15-minute sound and light performance, when the water glows like a cauldron of colour.

Museu Nacional d'Art de Catalunya

Make a beeline for the Romanesque art selection and the 12th-century polychrome image of Christ in majesty, which was recovered from the apse of a country chapel in northwest Catalonia.

Fundació Joan Miró

Take in some of Joan Miró's giant canvases, and discover little-known works from his early years in the Sala Joan Prats and Sala Pilar Juncosa.

Museu Etnològic

Teatre Grec

Museu Olímpic i de l'Esport

Estadi Olímpic

Jardí Botànic

Jardins de Mossèn Cinto Verdaguer

Castell de Montjuïc

Enjoy the sweeping views of the sea and city from atop this 17th-century fortress, once a political prison and long a symbol of oppression.

Museu d'Arqueologia de Catalunya

Seek out the Roman mosaic depicting the Three Graces, one of the most beautiful items in this museum, which was dedicated to the ancient past of Catalonia and neighbouring parts of Spain.

Walking Tour: Modernisme

Catalan modernism (Modernisme) abounds in the Barcelona's L'Eixample district. This walk introduces you to the movement's main form of expression, the architecture.

Start: Casa Calvet
Finish: Casa Macaya
Length: 4km; one hour

5 Completed in 1912, **Casa Thomas** was one of Domènech i Montaner's earlier efforts; the wrought-iron decoration is magnificent.

DAVID BORLAND/GETTY IMAGES ©

4 Casa Comalat, built in 1911 by Salvador Valeri, shows Gaudí's influence on the main facade, with its wavy roof and bulging balconies.

3 Puig i Cadafalch let his imagination loose on **Casa Serra** (1903–08), a neo-Gothic whimsy now home to government offices.

VITALYEDUSH/GETTY IMAGES ©

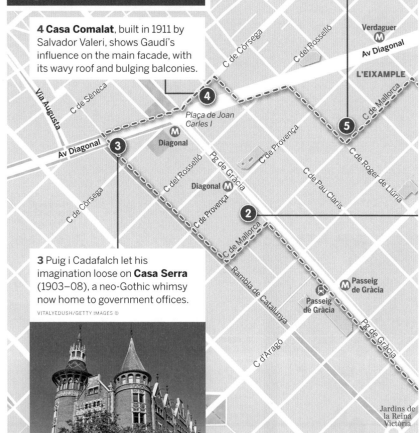

7 Puig i Cadafalch's **Casa Macaya** (1901) features the typical playful, pseudo-Gothic decoration that characterises many of the architect's projects.

Classic Photo: Stop 4 Casa Comalat

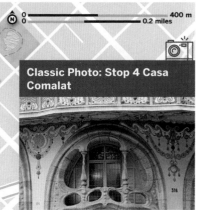

RICHARD CUMMINS/GETTY IMAGES ©

6 Casa Llopis i Bofill, designed by Antoni Gallissà in 1902, has a particularly striking graffiti-covered facade.

Take a Break...
Seek out **Casa Amalia** (☉1-3.30pm & 9-10.30pm Tue-Sat, 1-3.30pm Sun) for hearty Catalan cooking.

2 Casa Enric Batlló was completed in 1896 by Josep Vilaseca, part of the Comtes de Barcelona hotel.

1 Antoni Gaudí's most conventional contribution to L'Eixample is **Casa Calvet**, built in 1900. Inside, admire the staircase from the swanky restaurant.

ENGINEERVOSHKIN/SHUTTERSTOCK ©

400 m
0.2 miles

Pg. de Sant Joan

Ⓜ Verdaguer
7 (FINISH) Av Diagonal
Plaça de Mossèn Jacint Verdaguer

Pg. de Sant Joan

C d'Aragó

SANT GERVASI
C de València
6
C de Girona
C de Bailén

Gran Via de les Corts Catalanes

C de Casp
1 (START)
Via Laietana
Ronda de Sant Pere

Plaça de Joan Carles I
Urquinaona Ⓜ Plaça d'Urquinaona

Detail of Gaudí's church crypt

Colònia Güell

Apart from La Sagrada Família, Gaudí's last big project was the creation of a utopian textile workers' complex for magnate patron Eusebi Güell outside Barcelona at Santa Coloma de Cervelló.

Great For...

☑ **Don't Miss**

The church crypt built by Gaudí.

Gaudí's main role here was to erect the colony's church, Colònia Güell. Work began in 1908, but the idea fizzled eight years later when Eusebi Güell's business ventures took a downturn due to the First World War. In the end, Gaudí only finished the crypt, which still serves as a working church. It's 24km west of central Barcelona, but a quick journey on the train. The complex has been designated a Unesco World Heritage site and is well worth the trip out here for lovers of Gaudí's work.

The Structure

This structure is a key to understanding what the master had in mind for his magnum opus, La Sagrada Família. The mostly brick-clad columns that support the ribbed vaults in the ceiling are inclined at all angles in much the way you might expect trees in a forest to lean. That effect was deliberate, but

Ca L'Espinal building at Colònia Güell

SANNI PHOTOGRAPHY/GETTY IMAGES ©

★ **Top Tip**

FGC trains zip very regularly from Plaza Espanya station, taking 20 minutes.

ⓘ Need to Know

☑93 630 58 07; www.gaudicoloniaguell.org; Carrer de Claudi Güell; adult/student €7/5.50; ⊙10am-7pm Mon-Fri, to 3pm Sat & Sun, shorter hours outside of summer; 🚉FGC lines S4, S8, S33 to Colònia Güell

✕ **Take a Break**

There are some eating options in the former workers' cottages.

also grounded in physics. Gaudí worked out the angles so that their load would be transmitted from the ceiling to the earth without the help of extra buttressing. Similar thinking lay behind his plans for La Sagrada Família, the Gothic-inspired structure of which would tower above any medieval building, without requiring a single buttress. Gaudí's hand is visible even down to the wavy design of the pews. The primary colours in the curvaceous plant-shaped stained-glass windows are another reminder of the era in which the crypt was built. The broken mosaic tiling known as *trencadís* is typical of other Gaudí works. It was an elegant solution to the problem of using normal-sized tiles on his characteristically uneven, fluid surfaces.

Other Factory Buildings

Near the church spread the cute brick houses designed for the factory workers and still inhabited today. A short stroll away, the 23 factory buildings of a Modernista industrial complex, idle since the 1970s, were brought back to life in the early 2000s, with shops and businesses moving into the renovated complex.

In a five-room display with audiovisual and interactive material, the history and life of the industrial colony and the story of Gaudí's church are told in colourful fashion.

Platja de la Nova Icària

NITO/SHUTTERSTOCK ©

Beaches of Barcelona

A series of pleasant beaches stretches northeast from the Port Olímpic marina. They are largely artificial, but this doesn't stop an estimated seven million bathers from piling in every year.

Great For...

☑ **Don't Miss**

The vibrant bustle of Platja de la Nova Icària.

Platja de la Nova Icària

The southernmost of these beaches, Platja de la Nova Icària, is the busiest. Behind it, across the Avinguda del Litoral highway, is the Plaça dels Campions, site of the rusting three-tiered platform used to honour medallists in the sailing events of the 1992 games. Much of the athletes' housing-turned-apartments are in the blocks immediately behind Carrer de Salvador Espriu.

Platja de Bogatell

The next beach along is Platja de Bogatell. Just in from the beach is **Cementiri del Poblenou** (☎93 225 16 61; Av d'Icària, near Carrer del Taulat; ⊙8am-6pm), created in 1773. The cemetary was positioned outside the then city limits for health reasons. Its central monument commemorates the victims of a yellow-fever epidemic that swept

across Barcelona in 1821. The cemetery is full of bombastic family memorials, but an altogether disquieting touch is the sculpture *El Petó de la Mort* (the Kiss of Death), in which a winged skeleton kisses a young kneeling lifeless body.

There's a good skateboard area with half-pipes at the north end of the beach.

Other Beaches

Platja de la Mar Bella (which has a brief nudist strip and a sailing school) and Platja de la Nova Mar Bella follow, leading into the new residential and commercial waterfront strip, the Front Marítim, part of the Diagonal Mar project in the Fòrum district. It is fronted by the last of these artificial beaches to be created, Platja del Llevant.

❶ Need to Know

Line 4 (yellow) is the handiest Metro line, though it's a fair stroll to some beaches.

✗ Take a Break

The beaches are dotted with *chiringuitos*, snack bars that stay open until the wee hours.

★ Top Tip
The broad beachside boulevard is great for strolling, cycling or skating.

What's Nearby?
Museu Blau   Museum
(Blue Museum; ☏93 256 60 02; museucien cies.cat; Parc del Fòrum; adult/child €6/free; ☉10am-6pm Tue-Fri, to 7pm Sat, to 8pm Sun; ⓜEl Maresme Fòrum) Set inside the futuristic Edifici Fòrum, the Museu Blau takes visitors on a journey across the natural world. Multimedia and interactive exhibits explore topics like the history of evolution, earth's formation and the scientists who have helped shaped human knowledge. There are also specimens from the animal, plant and mineral kingdoms – plus dinosaur skeletons – all rather dramatically set amid the sprawling 9000 sq metres of exhibition space.

El Fòrum   Area
(ⓜEl Maresme Fòrum) Once an urban wasteland, this area has seen dramatic changes in the last 20 years, with sparkling new buildings, open plazas and waterfront recreation areas. The most striking element is the eerily blue, triangular *2001: A Space Odyssey*–style **Edifici Fòrum** building by Swiss architects Herzog & de Meuron.

Giant tree display within an ascending helix

JUAN AUNION/SHUTTERSTOCK ©

CosmoCaixa

Kids (and kids at heart) are fascinated by displays here, and this entertaining, interactive museum has become one of the city's most popular attractions.

Great For...

☑ **Don't Miss**

A tropical storm in the Amazon.

The Amazon

The single greatest highlight of Cosmo-Caixa is the recreation of over 1 sq km of flooded Amazon rainforest (Bosc Inundat). More than 100 species of Amazon flora and fauna (including anacondas, colourful poisonous frogs and caimans) prosper in this unique, living diorama in which you can even watch a tropical downpour.

Geology

In another original section, the Mur Geològic, seven great chunks of rock (90 metric tons in all) have been assembled to create a Geological Wall.

Planetarium & More

Also worthwhile are the 3D shows in the Planetari (Planetarium), which are

Seed collection

DIEGO MORENO DELGADO/GETTY IMAGES ©

❶ Need to Know

Museu de la Ciència; 📞93 212 60 50; www.
fundacio.lacaixa.es; Carrer de Isaac Newton
26; adult/child €4/free; ⊙10am-8pm Tue-
Sun; 🚌60, 🚊FGC Avinguda Tibidabo

✕ Take a Break

El Asador de Aranda (p147) offers
wood-oven delicacies in an art-nouveau
building.

★ Top Tip

Outside, stroll extensive Plaça de la
Ciència, the modest garden of which
flourishes with Mediterranean flora.

screened several times a day. Shows
typically run for 35 minutes and cost €4;
headsets provide commentary in English
and other languages.

These and other displays on the lower
5th floor (the bulk of the museum is underground) cover many fascinating areas of
science, from fossils to physics, and from
the alphabet to outer space.

What's Nearby?

Tibidabo   Mountain
Framing the north end of the city, the
forest-covered mountain of Tibidabo, which
tops out at 512m, is the highest peak in
Serra de Collserola. Aside from the superb
views from the top, Tibidabo's highlights
include the 8000-hectare **Parc de Collserola** (📞93 280 35 52; www.parcnaturalcoll
serola.cat; Carretera de l'Església 92; ⊙Centre

d'Informació 9.30am-3pm, Can Coll 9.30am-3pm
Sun & holidays, closed Jul & Aug; 🚊FGC Baixador
de Vallvidrera, 🚊de Vallvidrera), an old-
fashioned **amusement park** (📞93 211 79 42;
www.tibidabo.cat; Plaça de Tibidabo 3-4; adult/
child €30/11; ⊙closed Jan & Feb; 🚌T2A from
Plaça de Catalunya), a **telecommunications
tower** (📞93 406 93 54; www.torredecollserola.
com; Carretera de Vallvidrera al Tibidabo; adult/
child €6/4; ⊙noon-2pm & 3.30-8pm Wed-Sun Jul
& Aug, noon-2pm & 3.30-6pm Sat & Sun Sep-Dec
& Mar-Jun, closed Jan & Feb; 🚌111, 🚊Funicular
de Vallvidrera) with viewing platform, and a
looming **church** (Church of the Sacred Heart;
📞93 417 56 86; Plaça de Tibidabo; lift €2.50;
⊙8am-8pm, lift 10am-2pm & 3-7pm; 🚌T2A from
Plaça de Catalunya) **FREE** that's visible from
many parts of the city.

Tibidabo gets its name from the devil,
who, trying to tempt Christ, took him to a
high place and said, in Latin: *'Haec omnia tibi
dabo si cadens adoraberis me'* ('All this I will
give you if you fall down and worship me').

DINING OUT

From tapas to world-renowned restaurants

Dining Out

Barcelona has a celebrated food scene fuelled by a combination of world-class chefs, imaginative recipes and magnificent ingredients fresh from farms and the sea. Catalan culinary masterminds such as Ferran Adrià and Carles Abellan have become international icons, famous for their crazy riffs on the themes of traditional local cooking. Meanwhile, traditional Catalan recipes, with their roots in the local market hall, continue to earn accolades in dining rooms and tapas bars across the city.

In This Section

Price Ranges

The following price symbols represent the cost of a main course:

€	less than €10
€€	€10 to €20
€€€	over €20

Tipping

Service is rarely included in the bill. Locals aren't big tippers, but if you're particularly happy, 5% is generally fine.

Gràcia & Park Güell
Hip and characterful
tapas bars and taverns
(p145)

**Camp Nou, Pedrables
& La Zona Alta**
Culinary gems well worth the trip
(p147)

**La Sagrada Família
& L'Eixample**
Some of Barcelona's
best restaurants
(p140)

La Ribera
Atmospheric and
avant-garde restaurants
(p136)

*Port
Olímpic*

El Raval
Classic, budget and
artful newcomers
(p134)

**La Rambla &
Barri Gòtic**
Both touristy and
well-respected eateries
(p132)

**Barceloneta &
the Waterfront**
Top choice for
seafood and paella
(p138)

**Montjuïc, Poble Sec
& Sant Antoni**
Historic taverns, famed tapas bars,
new trendsetters
(p144)

*Port
Vell*

*Mediterranean
Sea*

Useful Phrases

The bill, please.	*La cuenta, por favor.*	la *kwen*·ta por fa·*vor.*
I'd/We'd like...	Quería/ queríamos...	ke·*ria*/ ke·*ria*·mos
A dish of... chicken	Una de... pollo	*oo*·na de... *pol*·yo
I'm allergic to...	Tengo alergía a...	*ten*·go al·er·hi·ya a
I don't eat... meat	No como... carne	No *ko*·mo... *kar*·ne
Very good, thank you!	Muy rico, gracias!	Mwee *ri*·ko *gra*·thyas!

Classic Dishes

Calçots Barbecued leek/spring onion cross.

Escalivada Grilled and cooled sliced vegetables with oil.

Esqueixada Salad of salt cod with vegetables and beans.

Botifarra amb mongetes Pork sausage with white beans.

Cargols/Caracoles Snails, often stewed with rabbit.

Fideuà Like seafood paella, but with vermicelli noodles.

The Best...

Experience Barcelona's top restaurants and cafes

By Budget

€

La Cova Fumada (p138) Barceloneta hole-in-the-wall with excellent small plates.

Bormuth (p136) Tasty tapas in an old-city setting.

€€

Suculent (p135) Carles Abellan's bistro serves excellent Catalan cooking.

Casa Delfín (p137) Delicious Mediterranean fare in an atmospheric setting.

€€€

Disfrutar (p143) Expect the unexpected – this is Catalan cooking at its most experimental.

Koy Shunka (p134) Avant-garde Japanese fare; probably Barcelona's best.

For Vegetarians

Aguaribay (p139) First-rate prix fixe lunches and a small but well-executed evening à la carte menu.

Cererìa (p133) Pizzas and galettes in an old-fashioned setting.

Flax & Kale (p135) Vast, colourful salads and a truly creative approach.

Rasoterra (p133) Airy vegetarian charmer in the Barri Gòtic.

Cafes

Copasetic (p140) Vintage-filled cafe.

Federal (p144) Unnervingly hip, but the food is excellent and the service friendly.

Čaj Chai (p132) Teas and lively chatter in the Barri Gòtic.

La Nena (p145) Kid-friendly cafe in Gràcia.

For Seafood

Barraca (p139) Sparkling waterfront restaurant with unique and flavour-rich seafood.

Can Ros (p139) Traditional, family-owned seafood restaurant.

Kaiku (p139) Creative takes on top-quality seafood.

Can Maño (p139) Unfussy place with great dishes at low prices.

For Carnivores

Patagonia Beef & Wine (p141) Feast on Argentine steaks.
Bilbao (p146) A classic spot for steaks and Spanish reds.
El Asador de Aranda (p147) Roast lamb in a Modernista setting.

For Brunch

Federal (p144) Excellent brunches and a small roof terrace.
Milk (p133) Serves brunch daily (till 4.30pm).
Dos Trece (p135) Fabulous Sunday brunches in El Raval.
En Aparté (p136) French eatery serving tasty brunch fare on weekends.
Copasetic (p140) Vintage filled cafe with weekend brunch.

For Catalan Cuisine

Vivanda (p147) Magnificent Catalan cooking with year-round garden dining.
Roig Robí (p147) A pillar of traditional Catalan cooking.
Cafè de l'Acadèmia (p133) High-quality dishes that never disappoint.
Can Culleretes (p133) The city's oldest restaurant, with great-value traditional dishes.

★ For Gastronomes

Disfrutar (p143) Set up by three alumni of El Bulli, this is one to watch.
Cinc Sentits (p143) Serves a magnificent tasting menu of the freshest, highest-quality ingredients.
Tickets (p145) Celebrated restaurant of Albert Adrià, showcasing Barcelona's best nueva cocina española.

✕ La Rambla & Barri Gòtic

Caelum   Cafe €
(Map p250; 📞 93 302 69 93; www.caelumbarce
lona.com; Carrer de la Palla 8; ⏰10.30am-8.30pm
Mon-Thu, 10.30am-11pm Fri & Sat, 10.30am-
9pm Sun; Ⓜ Liceu) Centuries of heavenly
gastronomic tradition from across Spain
are concentrated in this exquisite medieval
space in the heart of the city. The upstairs
cafe is a dainty setting for decadent cakes
and pastries, while descending into the
underground chamber with its stone walls
and flickering candles is like stepping into
the Middle Ages.

La Granja   Cafe €
(Map p250; 📞 93 302 69 75; Carrer dels Banys
Nous 4; ⏰9am-9pm; Ⓜ Jaume I) This long-
running cafe serves up thick, rich cups of
chocolate, in varying formats, but it doesn't
make its own churros. Buy them a few
doors down at **Xurreria** (Map p250; 📞 93
318 76 91; Carrer dels Banys Nous 8; cone €1.20;
⏰7.30am-1.30pm & 3.30-8.15pm; Ⓜ Jaume I)
and bring them here for the perfect combo

of churros dipped in chocolate. Also worth
a look is the section of Roman wall visible
at the back.

Salterio   Cafe €
(Map p250; Carrer de Sant Domènec del Call 4;
⏰11am-midnight, to 1am Fri & Sat; 📶; Ⓜ Jaume
I) A wonderfully photogenic candlelit spot
tucked down a tiny lane in El Call, Salterio
serves refreshing teas, Turkish coffee,
authentic mint teas and snacks amid
stone walls, incense and ambient Middle
Eastern music. If hunger strikes, try the
sardo (grilled flatbread covered with pesto,
cheese or other toppings).

Čaj Chai   Cafe €
(Map p250; 📞 93 301 95 92; www.cajchai.com;
Carrer de Sant Domènec del Call 12; ⏰10.30am-
10pm; Ⓜ Jaume I) Inspired by Prague's bohemian tearooms, this bright and buzzing
cafe in the heart of the old Jewish quarter
is a tea connoisseur's paradise. Čaj Chai
stocks over 100 teas from China, India,
Korea, Japan, Nepal, Morocco and beyond.
It's a much-loved local haunt.

Chocolate con churros

BADMANPRODUCTION/GETTY IMAGES ©

La Vinateria del Call Spanish €€

(Map p250; 93 302 60 92; www.lavinateria
delcall.com; Carrer de Sant Domènec del Call 9;
small plates €7-12; 7.30pm-1am; Jaume I)
In a magical setting in the former Jewish
quarter, this tiny jewel box of a restaurant
(recently extended to add another dining
room) serves up tasty Iberian dishes
including Galician octopus, cider-cooked
chorizo and the Catalan *escalivada* (roasted peppers, aubergine and onions) with
anchovies. Portions are small and made for
sharing, and there's a good and affordable
selection of wines.

Belmonte Tapas €€

(Map p250; 93 310 76 84; Carrer de la Mercè
29; tapas €4-10, mains €12; 8pm-midnight Tue-
Sat, plus 1-3.30pm Sat; ; Jaume I) This tiny
tapas joint in the southern reaches of the
Barri Gòtic whips up beautifully prepared
small plates – including an excellent *truita*
(tortilla), rich *patatons a la sal* (salted new
potatoes with romesco sauce) and tender
carpaccio de pop (octopus carpaccio).
Wash it down with the housemade *vermut*
(vermouth).

Can Culleretes Catalan €€

(Map p250; 93 317 30 22; www.culleretes.com;
Carrer Quintana 5; mains €10-17; 1.30-4pm &
9-11pm Tue-Sat, 1.30-4pm Sun; Liceu) Founded in 1786, Barcelona's oldest restaurant is
still going strong, with tourists and locals
flocking here to enjoy its rambling interior,
old-fashioned tile-filled decor, and enormous helpings of traditional Catalan food,
including fresh seafood and sticky stews.

Cafè de l'Acadèmia Catalan €€

(Map p250; 93 319 82 53; Carrer dels Lledó
1; mains €14-18; 1-3.30pm & 8-11pm Mon-Fri;
; Jaume I) Expect a mix of traditional
Catalan dishes with the occasional creative
twist. At lunchtime, local *ajuntament* (town
hall) office workers pounce on the *menú
del día* (€14.30). In the evening it is rather
more romantic, as low lighting emphasises
the intimacy of the beamed ceiling and
stone walls. On warm days you can also
dine on the pretty square at the front.

Chocolate con Churros

Barcelona has some irresistible temptations for those with a sweet tooth.
Chocolate lovers won't want to miss
Carrer del Petritxol, which is home to
several famous *granjas* (milk bars) that
dole out thick cups of hot chocolate,
best accompanied by churros.

Rasoterra Vegetarian €€

(Map p250; 93 318 69 26; www.rasoterra.
cat; Carrer del Palau 5; mains €13; 7-11pm
Tue, 1-4pm & 7-11pm Wed-Sun; ; Jaume
I) A delightful addition to the Barri Gòtic,
Rasoterra cooks up first-rate vegetarian
dishes in a Zen-like setting with tall ceilings,
low-playing jazz and fresh flowers on the
tables. The creative, globally influenced
menu changes regularly and might feature
Vietnamese-style coconut pancakes with
tofu and vegetables, or pear and goat
cheese quesadillas. Has good vegan and
gluten-free options.

Cerería Vegetarian €€

(Map p250; 93 301 85 10; Baixada de Sant
Miquel 3; mains €7-11; 1pm-midnight Tue-Sat,
1pm-5pm Sun; ; Jaume I) Black-and-
white marble floors, a smattering of old
wooden tables and ramshackle displays
of musical instruments lend a certain
bohemian charm to this small vegetarian
restaurant. The pizzas are delicious, and
feature organic ingredients – as do the
flavourful galettes, dessert crêpes and
bountiful salads. Vegan options too.

Milk Brunch €€

(Map p250; 93 268 09 22; www.milkbarcelona.
com; Carrer d'en Gignàs 21; mains €8-12; 9am-
2am Sun-Thu, to 3am Fri & Sat; ; Jaume I)
It's known as an enticing cocktail spot, but
Milk's key role for local night owls is pro-
viding morning-after brunches (served till
4.30pm). Avoid direct sunlight and tuck into
pancakes, eggs Benedict and other hang-
over dishes in a cosy lounge-like setting.

🍽️ Market Dining

Barcelona has some fantastic food markets. Foodies will enjoy the sounds, smells and, most importantly, tastes of all of them. While the Mercat de la Boqueria (p90) and Mercat de Santa Caterina (p102) are the most famous, you can find temptations of all sorts – plump fruit and veg, fresh-squeezed juices, artisanal cheeses, smoked meats, seafood and pastries – in several others, including the Mercat de Sant Antoni (p164), **Mercat del Ninot** (☑93 323 49 09; www.mercatdelninot.com; Carrer de Mallorca 157; ⊙9am-8pm Mon-Fri, 9am-2pm Sat; 🛜; ⓂHospital Clínic), **Mercat de la Llibertat** (☑93 217 09 95; www.mercatlliibertat.com; Plaça de la Llibertat 27; ⊙8am-8pm Mon-Fri, 8am-3pm Sat; 🚉FGC Gràcia) and Mercat de l'Abaceria Central (p167).

Mercat de la Boqueria (p90)
MICHAEL HEFFERNAN/LONELY PLANET ©

Onofre   Spanish €€
(Map p250; ☑93 317 69 37; www.onofre.net; Carrer de les Magdalenes 19; mains €9-14; ⊙10am-4pm & 7.30pm-midnight Mon-Sat; 🛜; ⓂJaume I) Famed for its (good, affordable) wine selections, Onofre is a small, modern eatery (and wine shop and delicatessen) that has a strong local following for its delicious tapas (think duck confit and codfish carpaccio) and great-value lunch specials (three-course prix fixe for €10.75, or €14.75 on Saturdays).

Koy Shunka   Japanese €€€
(Map p250; ☑93 412 79 39; www.koyshunka.com; Carrer de Copons 7; multicourse menu €82-128; ⊙1.30-3pm & 8.30-11pm Tue-Sat, 1.30-3pm Sun; ⓂUrquinaona) Down a narrow lane north of the cathedral, Koy Shunka opens a portal to exquisite dishes from the East – mouthwatering sushi, sashimi, seared Wagyu beef and flavour-rich seaweed salads are served alongside inventive cooked fushion dishes like steamed clams with sake. Don't miss the house specialty of tender *toro* (tuna belly).

Pla   Fusion €€€
(Map p250; ☑93 412 65 52; www.restaurantpla.cat; Carrer de la Bellafila 5; mains €17-23; ⊙7pm-11.30pm Sun-Thu, to midnight Fri & Sat; ⓂJaume I) One of Gòtic's long-standing favourites, Pla is a stylish, romantically lit medieval dining room where the cooks churn out such temptations as oxtail braised in red wine, seared tuna with oven-roasted peppers, and polenta with seasonal mushrooms. It has a tasting menu for €52 Sunday to Thursday.

✗ El Raval

Bar Pinotxo   Tapas €€
(Map p250; www.pinotxobar.com; Mercat de la Boqueria; mains €8-17; ⊙6am-4pm Mon-Sat; ⓂLiceu) This is arguably La Boqueria's, and even Barcelona's, best tapas bar. It sits among the half-dozen or so informal eateries within the market, and the popular owner, Juanito, might serve up chickpeas with pine nuts and raisins, a soft mix of potato and spinach sprinkled with salt, soft baby squid with cannellini beans, or a quivering cube of caramel-sweet pork belly.

Mam i Teca   Catalan €€
(Map p249; ☑93 441 33 35; Carrer de la Lluna 4; mains €9-12; ⊙1-4pm & 8pm-midnight Mon, Wed-Fri & Sun, 8pm-midnight Sat; ⓂSant Antoni) A tiny place with half a dozen tables, Mam i Teca is as much a lifestyle choice as a restaurant. Locals hang at the bar, and diners are treated to Catalan dishes that are made with locally sourced products and adhere

to Slow Food principles (such as cod fried in olive oil with garlic and red pepper, or pork ribs with chickpeas).

Suculent
Catalan €€

(Map p250; 📞93 443 65 79; www.suculent.com; Rambla del Raval 43; mains €13-21; 🕐1-4pm & 8.30-11.30pm Wed-Sun; Ⓜ Liceu) Michelin-starred chef Carles Abellan adds to his stable with this old-style bistro, which showcases the best of Catalan cuisine. From the cod brandade to the oxtail stew with truffled sweet potato, only the best ingredients are used. Be warned that the prices can mount up a bit, but this is a great place to sample regional highlights.

Caravelle
International €€

(Map p249; 📞93 317 98 92; Carrer del Pintor Fortuny 31; mains €10-13; 🕐9.30am-5.30pm Mon-Wed, 8.30am-midnight Thu, 10am-1am Sat, 10am-5.30pm Sun; Ⓜ Liceu) A bright little joint, beloved of the hipster element of the Raval and anyone with a discerning palate. Tacos as you've never tasted them (cod, lime *alioli* and radish, and pulled pork with roast corn and avocado); a superior steak sandwich

on homemade brioche with pickled celeri-ac; and all manner of soul food.

Dos Trece
International €€

(Map p249; 📞93 301 73 06; www.dostrece.es; Carrer del Carme 40; mains €10-15; 🕐10am-midnight; 📶✏; Ⓜ Liceu) Lively, sunny and fun, Dos Trece is great for brunches (including vegie and vegan options) that are available all day, as well as late-night bites. The menu ranges from juicy burgers to a more sophisticated rack of lamb, and the bar serves a good array of cocktails. There are a few tables outside, next to the kids' playground.

Flax & Kale
Vegetarian €€

(Map p249; 📞93 317 56 64; teresacarles.com/fk; Carrer dels Tallers 74; mains €12.50-16.50; 🕐10am-11.30pm; 📶✏; Ⓜ Universitat) A far cry from the vegie restaurants of old, Flax & Kale marks a new approach (for Barcelona, at least), that declares that going meat-free does not mean giving up on choice or

> *a great place to sample regional highlights*

Alfresco dining, Plaça Reial

From left: Mercat de la Boqueria (p90); Paella; A Barri Gòtic cake shop

creativity, and is entirely possible in stylish surroundings. There are gluten-free and vegan options, and dishes include tacos with guacamole, aubergine, shiitake mushrooms and sour cashew cream, or Penang red curry.

✖ La Ribera

Bormuth   Tapas €
(Map p250; ☑93 310 21 86; Carrer del Rec 31; tapas from €4; ⊙1pm-midnight; 🛜; Ⓜ Jaume I) Opened on the pedestrian Carrer del Rec in 2013, Bormuth has tapped into the vogue for old-school tapas with modern-times service and decor, and serves all the old favourites – *patatas bravas* (potato chunks in a slightly spicy tomato sauce), *ensaladilla* (Russian salad), tortilla – along with some less predictable and superbly prepared numbers (try the chargrilled red pepper with black pudding).

A lunchtime deal offers three tapas and a drink for €8.90, or two tapas and a drink for €5.90.

En Aparté   French €
(☑93 269 13 35; www.enaparte.es; Carrer Lluís el Piados 2; mains €7-10; ⊙10am-1.30am Mon-Thu, to 2am Fri & Sat, to 12.30am Sun; 🛜; Ⓜ Arc de Triomf, Urquinaona) A great low-key place to eat good-quality French food, just off the quiet Plaça de Sant Pere. The restaurant is small but spacious, with sewing-machine tables and vintage details. Floor-to-ceiling windows bring in some wonderful early-afternoon sunlight.

The lunch menu (€12.50) is excellent, offering a salad (such as beetroot, apple and walnut), and a quiche or another dish, such as stuffed peppers with a potato gratin. Brunch is served on weekends.

Euskal Etxea   Tapas €
(Map p250; ☑93 310 21 85; Placeta de Montcada 1; tapas €1.95; ⊙10am-12.30am Sun-Thu, to 1am Fri & Sat; Ⓜ Jaume I) Barcelona has plenty of Basque and pseudo-Basque eateries, but this is the real deal. It captures the feel of San Sebastián better than many of its newer competitors. Choose your *pintxos* (tapas mounted on slices of bread), sip *txacolí* wine, and keep the toothpicks so

the staff can count them up and work out your bill.

Paradiso
Smokery €

(Map p250; ☑639 310671; www.rooftopsmoke house.com; Carrer de Rera Palau 4; mains €8; ⊙cocktail bar 7pm-2am Sun-Thu, to 3am Fri & Sat, pastrami bar noon-2am Sun-Thu, to 3am Fri & Sat; MBarceloneta) A kind of Narnia in reverse, Paradiso is fronted with a snowy-white space, not much bigger than a wardrobe, and in itself reason enough to linger, with pastrami sandwiches, smoked duck and other home-cured delights.

Casa Delfín
Catalan €€

(Map p250; ☑93 319 50 88; www.tallerdeta pas.com; Passeig del Born 36; mains €10-15; ⊙8am-midnight Sun-Thu, to 1am Fri & Sat; ☎; MBarceloneta) One of Barcelona's culinary delights, Casa Delfín is everything you dream of when you think of Catalan (and Mediterranean) cooking. Start with the tangy and sweet *calçots* (a cross between a leek and an onion; February and March only) or salt-strewn *padron* peppers, moving on to grilled sardines speckled with

parsley, then tackle the meaty monkfish roasted in white wine and garlic.

El Atril
International €€

(☑93 310 12 20; www.atrilbarcelona.com; Carrer dels Carders 23; mains €11-15; ⊙noon-midnight Mon-Thu, to 1am Fri & Sat, 11.30am-11.30pm Sun; ☎; MJaume I) Aussie owner Brenden is influenced by culinary flavours from all over the globe, so while you'll see plenty of tapas (the *patatas bravas* are recommended for their homemade sauce), you'll also find kangaroo fillet, salmon and date rolls with mascarpone, chargrilled turkey with fried yucca, and plenty more.

Cal Pep
Tapas €€

(Map p250; ☑93 310 79 61; www.calpep.com; Plaça de les Olles 8; mains €13-20; ⊙7.30-11.30pm Mon, 1-3.45pm & 7.30-11.30pm Tue-Sat, closed last 3 weeks Aug; MBarceloneta) Getting a foot in the door of this legendary fish restaurant can be a problem – there can be queues out into the square. And if you want one of the five tables out the back, you'll need to call ahead. Most people are happy elbowing their way to the bar for some of the tastiest seafood tapas in town.

A haute cuisine seafood dish

Pep recommends *cloïsses amb pernil* (clams and ham) or the *trifàsic* (combo of calamari, whitebait and prawns). The restaurant's other pièce de résistance is a super-smooth *tortilla de patatas* (Spanish omelette) and tuna tartare.

✗ Barceloneta & the Waterfront

La Cova Fumada   Tapas €
(☑93 221 40 61; Carrer del Baluard 56; tapas €4-8; ⊗9am-3.20pm Mon-Wed, 9am-3.20pm & 6-8.15pm Thu & Fri, 9am-1pm Sat; Ⓜ Barceloneta) There's no sign and the setting is decidedly downmarket, but this tiny, buzzing family-run tapas spot always packs in a crowd. The secret? Mouthwatering *pulpo* (octopus), *calamar, sardinias* and 15 or so other small plates cooked to perfection in the small open kitchen. The *bombas* (potato croquettes served with *alioli*) and grilled *carxofes* (artichokes) are good, but everything is amazingly fresh.

Can Dendê   American €
(☑646 325551; Carrer de la Ciutat de Granada 44; mains €6-11; ⊗8.30am-5pm Mon-Fri, from 10.30am Sat & Sun; Ⓜ Llacuna) An eclectic crowd gathers at this bright, bohemian Brazilian-run eatery in Poblenou. Anytime brunch is the culinary star here; tuck into eggs Benedict with smoked salmon, fluffy pancakes or pulled pork sandwiches while watching the cooks in action.

Can Recasens   Catalan €€
(☑93 300 81 23; Rambla del Poblenou 102; mains €7-15; ⊗9pm-1am Mon-Sat & 1-4pm Sat; Ⓜ Poblenou) One of Poblenou's most romantic settings, Can Recasens hides a warren of warmly lit rooms full of oil paintings, flickering candles, fairy lights and baskets of fruit. The food is outstanding, with a mix of salads, fondues, smoked meats, cheeses, and open-faced sandwiches piled high with delicacies like wild mushrooms and Brie or *escalivada* (grilled vegetables) and Gruyère.

El 58   Tapas €€
(Le cinquante huit; Rambla del Poblenou 58; sharing plates €4-11; ⊗1.30pm-midnight

Tue-Sat; MLlacuna) This French-Catalan eatery serves imaginative, beautifully prepared tapas dishes that earn rave reviews from both locals and expats. Solo diners can grab a seat at the marble-topped front bar and get dining tips from the friendly multilingual baristas. The back dining room with its exposed brick walls, industrial light fixtures and curious artworks is a lively place to linger over a long meal.

Codfish balls with romesco sauce, scallop ceviche, *tartiflette* (a cheese, ham and potato casserole), salmon sashimi: it's all good here.

Aguaribay — Vegetarian €€
(📞93 300 37 90; Carrer de Ramon Turró 181; mains €9-14; ⏰1-4pm Mon-Wed, 1-4pm & 8.30-11pm Thu-Sun ; 🍴; MLlacuna) This polished eatery in Poblenou serves a small, well-executed à la carte menu by night: miso and smoked tofu meatballs, soba noodles with shiitake mushrooms, and seasonal vegetables and a rich black rice. At lunchtime, stop in for the prix fixe lunch specials, which change daily. Craft beers and biodynamic wines round out the menu.

Kaiku — Seafood €€
(📞93 221 90 82; http://restaurantkaiku.cat; Plaça del Mar 1; mains for 2 €28-36; ⏰1-3.30pm Tue-Sun; MBarceloneta) Overlooking the waterfront at the south end of Barceloneta, Kaiku has a solid reputation for its creative seafood plates. Mouth-watering ingredients are sourced from the nearby fish market, and artfully prepared in dishes like crayfish with mint, swordfish carpaccio with avocado and sundried tomatoes, chilli-smeared tuna with green apples and mushrooms, and the outstanding rice dishes for two.

Can Maño — Spanish €€
(Carrer del Baluard 12; mains €8-14; ⏰9am-4pm Tue-Sat & 8-11pm Mon-Fri; MBarceloneta) It may look like a dive, but you'll need to be prepared to wait before being squeezed in at a packed table for a raucous night of *raciones* (full-plate tapas serving; posted on a board at the back) over a bottle of *turbio* – a cloudy white plonk. The seafood is

Seafood Spots

There are a wealth of restaurants specialising in seafood. Not surprisingly, Barceloneta, which lies near the sea, is packed with eateries of all shapes and sizes doling out decadent paellas, cauldrons of bubbling molluscs, grilled catches of the day and other delights. Nearest the sea, you'll find pricier open-air places with Mediterranean views; plunge into the narrow lanes to find the real gems, including bustling family-run places that serve first-rate plates at great prices.

abundant with first-rate squid, shrimp and fish served at rock-bottom prices.

Barraca — Seafood €€€
(📞93 224 12 53; www.barraca-barcelona.com; Passeig Marítim de la Barceloneta 1; mains €19-24; ⏰12.30pm-midnight; MBarceloneta) This buzzing space has a great location fronting the Mediterranean – a key reference point in the excellent seafood dishes served here. Start off with a cauldron of chilli-infused clams, cockles and mussels before moving on to the lavish paellas and other rice dishes, which steal the show.

Els Pescadors — Seafood €€€
(📞93 225 20 18; www.elspescadors.com; Plaça de Prim 1; mains €19-40; ⏰1-3.45pm & 8-11.30pm; MPoblenou) Set on a picturesque square lined with low houses and *bella ombre* trees long ago imported from South America, this quaint family restaurant continues to serve some of the city's best grilled fish and seafood-and-rice dishes. There are three dining areas inside, but on warm nights, try for a table outside.

Can Ros — Seafood €€€
(📞93 221 45 79; Carrer del Almirall Aixada 7; mains €16-30; ⏰1-4pm & 7-11pm Tue-Sun; 🚌45, 57, 59, 64, 157, MBarceloneta) The fifth generation is now at the controls of this

Set Meals

The *menú del día,* a full set meal with water and wine (and usually with several meal options), is a great way to cap prices at lunchtime. They start from around €10 and can move as high as €25 for more elaborate offerings.

Many high-end restaurants offer a *menú de degustación,* a multicourse tasting menu involving samples of different dishes. This can be a great way to get a broader view of what the restaurant does and has the advantage of coming at a fixed price. At gastronomic restaurants, this is always the best, and often the only, option.

immutable seafood favourite, which first opened in 1911. In a restaurant where the decor is a reminder of simpler times, there's a straightforward guiding principle: serve juicy fresh fish cooked with a light touch.

Can Ros also does a rich *arròs a la marinera* (seafood rice), *fideuá* (similar to paella, but using vermicelli noodles as the base) with squid and mussels, and a grilled fish and seafood platter.

✗ La Sagrada Família & L'Eixample

Cafè del Centre   Cafe €
(Map p254; ☑93 488 11 01; Carrer de Girona 69; ⊙10am-midnight Mon-Fri, noon-midnight Sat; 🛜; MGirona) Step back a century in this cafe, in business since 1873. The wooden bar extends down the right side as you enter, fronted by a slew of marble-topped tables and wooden chairs. It exudes an almost melancholy air by day but gets busy at night. It stocks 50 beers, and there is a lunchtime *menú* for €11.

Copasetic   Cafe €
(Map p249; ☑93 532 76 66; www.copasetic barcelona.com; Carrer de la Diputació 55;

mains €8-12; ⊙10.30am-midnight Tue & Wed, 10.30am-1am Thu, 10.30am-2am Fri & Sat, 10.30am-5.30pm Sun; 🛜🖉; MRocafort) A fun and friendly cafe, decked out with retro furniture. The menu holds plenty for everyone, whether your thing is eggs Benedict, wild-berry tartlets or a juicy fat burger. There are lots of vegetarian, gluten-free and organic options, and superb (and reasonably priced) brunches on weekends. Wednesday night is ladies' night, with cheap cocktails. Lunch *menús* (Tuesday to Friday) cost between €9.50 and €11.

Cremeria Toscana   Gelateria €
(☑93 539 38 25; www.cremeriatoscana.es; Carrer de Muntaner 161; ice cream from €2.80; ⊙1pm-midnight daily Easter-Oct, 1-10pm Sun-Thu, 1pm-midnight Fri & Sat Nov-Easter; MHospital Clínic) Yes, you can stumble across quite reasonable ice cream in Barcelona, but close your eyes and imagine yourself across the Mediterranean with the real ice-cream wizards. Creamy *stracciatella* and wavy *nocciola* and myriad other flavours await at the most authentic gelato outlet in town.

Tapas 24   Tapas €€
(Map p254; ☑93 488 09 77; www.carlesabellan. com; Carrer de la Diputació 269; tapas €4-9; ⊙9am-midnight; 🛜; MPasseig de Gràcia) Carles Abellan, master of the now-defunct Comerç 24 in La Ribera, runs this basement tapas haven known for its gourmet versions of old faves. Specials include the *bikini* (toasted ham and cheese sandwich – here the ham is cured and the truffle makes all the difference) and a thick black *arròs negre de sípia* (squid-ink black rice).

The inventive McFoie-Burger is fantastic and, for dessert, choose *xocolata amb pa, sal i oli* (delicious balls of chocolate in olive oil with a touch of salt and wafer). You can't book but it's worth the wait.

Cata 1.81   Tapas €€
(Map p254; ☑93 323 68 18; www.cata181. com; Carrer de València 181; tapas €5.50-8; ⊙6pm-midnight Mon-Sat; MPasseig de Gràcia) A beautifully designed venue (with lots of

Pintxos (Basque tapas)

small lights, some trapped in birdcages), this is the place to come for fine wines and dainty gourmet dishes like *raviolis amb bacallà* (salt-cod dumplings) or *truita de patates i tòfona negre* (thick potato tortilla with a delicate trace of black truffle). The best idea is to choose from one of several tasting-menu options.

Can Kenji   Japanese €€

(Map p254; ☑93 476 18 23; www.cankenji.com; Carrer del Rosselló 325; mains €10-14; ⊗1-3.30pm & 8.30-11.30pm; Ⓜ Verdaguer) If you want to go Japanese in Barcelona, this is the place. The chef of this understated little *izakaya* (the Japanese version of a tavern) gets his ingredients fresh from the city's markets, with traditional Japanese recipes receiving a Mediterranean touch. This is fusion at its very best.

Choices include sardine tempura with an aubergine, miso and anchovy purée, or *tataki* (lightly grilled meat) of *bonito* (tuna) with *salmorejo* (a Cordoban cold tomato and bread soup).

Tapas 24 is known for its gourmet versions of old faves

Chicha Limoná   Mediterranean, Pizzeria €€

(Map p254; ☑93 277 64 03; www.chichalimona. com; Passeig de Sant Joan 80; mains €10-16; ⊗8.30am-1am Tue-Thu, 8.30am-2am Fri, 9.30am-2am Sat, 9.30am-5pm Sun; 🛜; Ⓜ Tetuan) Passeig de Sant Joan has become the newest haunt for the hussar-moustached, turned-up-cigarette-pants brigade, and bright, bustling Chicha Limoná has provided them with somewhere great to eat. Grilled octopus with quince jelly, pork with apple compote, and pear tatin with crème anglaise are among the oft-changing dishes (set menu €12.90), along with pizzas.

Patagonia Beef & Wine   South American €€

(Map p254; ☑93 304 37 35; www.patagoniabw. com; Gran Via de les Corts Catalanes 660; mains €18-30; ⊗1.30-3.30pm & 7-11pm Mon-Thu, to 11.30pm Fri, to 10.30pm Sat; Ⓜ Passeig de Gràcia)

Barcelona on a Plate

Semi-dried tomatoes

Marinated guindilla peppers

Fried chicken drumsticks

Keep the toothpicks for totting up the bill

Marinated olives with feta

MICHAEL HEFFERNAN/GETTY IMAGES ©

Try Some Tasty Tapas

How to Eat Tapas Like a Local

Though you can certainly take a table, basically the idea of tapas is that you choose and eat them at the bar, often elbow-to-elbow with your fellow munchers. Whether it's a traditional tavern with dusty brandy bottles or a sleek modern spot reinventing classic dishes with a touch of molecular wizardry, it's an involved, social experience.

Tapas at El Xampanyet (p178)
FLOORTJE/GETTY IMAGES ©

★ Top Five Tapas Spots

Bormuth (p136) Serves both the classic and the new wave, plus tasty vermouths.

Quimet i Quimet (p144) Mouth-watering morsels served to a standing crowd.

Palo Cortao (p144) A new star in Poble Sec with outstanding sharing plates.

Bar Pinotxo (p134) Pull up a bar stool at this legendary Boqueria joint.

Tapas 24 (p140) Everyone's favourite gourmet tapas bar.

This stylish restaurant does exactly what it says on the tin – which is offer an Argentine meat-fest. Start with *empanadas* (small pies filled with various meats), then head for a hearty meat main, such as a juicy beef *medallón con salsa de colmenillas* (a medallion in a morel sauce) or such classics as the *bife de chorizo* (sirloin strip) or Brazilian *picanha* (rump).

Entrepanes Díaz   Sandwiches €€

(Map p254; ☑93 415 75 82; Carrer de Pau Claris 189; sandwiches €6-8, salads €12; ⏰11am-midnight Tue-Sat, 11am-6pm Sun; Ⓜ Diagonal) A new concept in upmarket gourmet sandwiches, from roast beef to suckling pig, along with sharing plates of Spanish specialties such as sea urchins and shrimp fritters, in a sparkling old-style bar. The policy of only hiring experienced waiters over 50 lends a certain gravitas to the operation and some especially charming service.

Disfrutar   Modern European €€€

(☑93 348 68 96; www.en.disfrutarbarcelona. com; Carrer de Vilarroel 163; tasting menus €75, €105 & €135; ⏰1-4pm & 8-11pm Tue-Sat; Ⓜ Hospital Clínic) In its first few months of life, Disfrutar rose stratospherically to become the city's finest restaurant – book now while it's still possible to get a table. Run by alumni of Ferran Adrià's game-changing El Bulli restaurant, it operates along similar lines.

Nothing is as it seems, from red and green peppers that are actually chocolate ganache coated in, respectively, chilli and mint-flavoured gelatine, to an iced hare consommé in a brandy snifter.

Cinc Sentits   International €€€

(Map p254; ☑93 323 94 90; www.cincsentits.com; Carrer d'Aribau 58; tasting menus €100 & €120; ⏰1.30-3pm & 8.30-10pm Tue-Sat; Ⓜ Passeig de Gràcia) Enter the realm of the 'Five Senses' to indulge in a jaw-dropping tasting menu consisting of a series of small, experimental dishes (there is no à la carte, although dishes can be tweaked to suit diners' requests). There is a lunch *menú* for €55.

The use of fresh local produce, such as fish landed on the Costa Brava and suckling

¡◯¡ Common Tapas

If you opt for *tapes/*tapas, it is handy to recognise some of the common items:

Bombes/bombas Meat and potato croquettes

Boquerons/boquerones White anchovies in vinegar – delicious and tangy

Carxofes/alcachofas Artichokes

Gambes/gambas Prawns, either done *al all/al ajillo* (with garlic), or *a la plantxa/plancha* (grilled)

Navalles/navajas Razor clams

Patates braves/patatas bravas Potato chunks in a slightly spicy tomato sauce, sometimes mixed with mayonnaise

Pop a feira/pulpo a la gallega Tender boiled octopus with paprika

Truita de patates/tortilla de patatas Potato-filled omelette; one with vegetables is a *tortilla de verduras*

Xampinyons/champiñones Mushrooms

pig from Extremadura, is key, along with the kind of creative genius that has earned chef Jordi Artal a Michelin star.

Casa Calvet   Catalan €€€

(Map p254; ☑93 412 40 12; www.casacalvet.es; Carrer de Casp 48; mains €28-31; ⏰1-3.30pm & 8.30-11pm Mon-Sat; Ⓜ Urquinaona) An early Gaudí masterpiece loaded with his trademark curvy features houses a swish restaurant (just to the right of the building's main entrance). Dress up and ask for an intimate *taula cabina* (wooden booth). You could opt for scallops and razor clams with pesto and buckwheat, or venison with juniper and porcini sauce.

It has various tasting menus for up to €70, and a lunch menu for €36.

Monvínic   Spanish €€€

(Map p254; ☑93 272 61 87; www.monvinic.com; Carrer de la Diputació 249; mains €24-32; ⏰1.30-3.30pm & 8-10.30pm Tue-Fri, 8-10.30pm Mon & Sat; Ⓜ Passeig de Gràcia) ✒ Formerly known

🍴 Vegetarian Food

Vegetarians and vegans can have a hard time in Spain, but in Barcelona a growing battery of vegetarian restaurants offers welcome relief. Be careful when ordering salads (such as the *amanida catalana*), which may contain popular 'vegetables' such as ham or tuna.

as Fastvínic, this is the *'espacio culinario'* of world-famous wine emporium Monvínic. The menu has advanced from sandwiches and snacks to elaborate confections such as wild mushroom polenta with pigeon, and beetroot tatin. It's a project in sustainability; ingredients, wine and building materials all sourced from Catalonia, and there are air-purifying plants and a water- and food-recycling system.

✖ Montjuïc, Poble Sec & Sant Antoni

Spice   Cafe €
(Map p256; http://spicecafe.es; Carrer de Margarit 13; desserts around €4; ⊘4-9pm Tue-Thu, 11am-9pm Fri-Sun; 🛜; Ⓜ Poble Sec) Spice is a delightful cafe that's earned quite a following (among expats and locals) for its delicious homemade desserts – especially its moist, creamy carrot cake (the best in town). Good coffees, loose-leaf teas, friendly English-speaking staff and heavenly temptations in the glass front counter may inspire multiple visits.

Quimet i Quimet   Tapas €€
(Map p256; ☑ 93 442 31 42; Carrer del Poeta Cabanyes 25; tapas €4-10, montaditos around €3; ⊘noon-4pm & 7-10.30pm Mon-Fri, noon-4pm Sat; Ⓜ Paral·lel) There's barely space to swing a *calamar* in this bottle-lined, standing-room-only place, a family-run business that has been passed down from generation to generation. It is a treat for the palate, with *montaditos* (tapas on a slice of bread) made to order. Try delectable combinations like artichoke, cheese and caviar, or tuna belly with sea urchin, and order a drop of fine wine to accompany your meal.

Palo Cortao   Tapas €€
(Map p256; ☑ 93 188 90 67; www.palocortao. es; Carrer de Nou de la Rambla 14; mains €10-15; ⊘8pm-1am Tue-Sun & 1-5pm Sat & Sun; Ⓜ Paral·lel) Palo Cortao has a solid reputation for its beautifully executed seafood and meat dishes, served at fair prices. Highlights include octopus with white bean hummus, skirt steak with foie armagnac, and tuna tataki tempura. You can order half sizes of all plates – which will allow you to try more dishes. Friendly English-speaking staff can help guide you through the food and wine list.

Bodega 1900   Tapas €€
(Map p256; ☑ 93 325 26 59; www.bodega1900. com; Carrer de Tamarit 91; tapas €5-14; ⊘noon-4pm & 7-11.30pm; Ⓜ Sant Antoni) The latest venture from the world-famous Adrià brothers, Bodega 1900 mimics an old-school tapas and vermouth bar, but this is no ordinary spit-and-sawdust joint serving *patatas bravas* and tortilla. Witness, for example, the *mollete de calamars,* probably the best squid sandwich in the world, hot from the pan and served with chipotle mayonnaise, kimchi and lemon zest; or the 'spherified' false olives.

Federal   Cafe €€
(Map p256; ☑ 93 187 36 07; www.federalcafe.es; Carrer del Parlament 39; mains €9-12; ⊘8am-11pm Mon-Thu, 8am-1am Fri, 9am-1am Sat, 9am-5.30pm Sun; 🛜📶; Ⓜ Sant Antoni) On a stretch that now teems with cafes, Australian-run Federal was the trailbazer, with its breezy chic and superb brunches. Later in the day there is healthy, tasty cooking from vegie burgers to grilled salmon with soba noodles, not to mention snacks (like prawn toast or polenta chips with Gorgonzola) and good coffee.

Head to the roof for a small, leafy terrace on which to browse the day's papers.

Casa Xica   Fusion €€

(Map p256; ☑93 600 58 58; Carrer de la França Xica 20; sharing plates €9-15; ☉1.30-3pm & 8.30-11.30pm Mon-Sat; Ⓜ Poble Sec) On the parlour floor of an old house, Casa Xica is a casual, but artfully designed space that fuses elements of the Far East with fresh Catalan ingredients. The creative menu, which changes regularly, features sharing plates like prawn and cod liver *gyoza* (Japanese dumplings), oxtail with sweet potato and ginger, and Iberian pork cured with kimchi and soy. It's a bit of an uphill slog from the metro station.

Tickets   Modern Spanish €€€

(Map p256; ☑606 225545; www.ticketsbar.es; Avinguda del Paral·lel 164; tapas €5-27; ☉6.30-10.30pm Tue-Fri, 1-3pm & 7-10.30pm Sat, closed Aug; Ⓜ Paral·lel) This is, literally, one of the sizzling tickets in the restaurant world, a tapas bar opened by Ferran Adrià, of the legendary El Bulli, and his brother Albert. Unlike El Bulli, it's an affordable venture – if you can book a table, that is. You can only book online, and two months in advance (or call for last-minute cancellations).

The food veers towards the deliciously surreal in concoctions like spherical olives, 'airbaguette' with dry aged Rubia Gallega beef, or the wild carrot cone with cardamom yoghurt, sugared sesame and carrot ice cream.

✗ Gràcia & Park Güell

La Nena   Cafe €

(Map p254; ☑93 285 14 76; www.chocolateria lanena.com; Carrer de Ramon i Cajal 36; desserts from €4.50; ☉9am-10pm; 📶; Ⓜ Fontana) A French team has created this delightfully chaotic space for indulging in cups of *suïssos* (rich hot chocolate) served with a plate of heavy whipped cream and *melindros* (spongy sweet biscuits), fine desserts and a few savoury dishes (including crêpes). The place is strewn with books, and you can help yourself to the board games on the shelves. It's an ideal family rest stop.

> *the food veers towards the deliciously surreal*

A dish at Tickets

DAVID RAMOS / STRINGER/GETTY IMAGES ©

Chivuo's Sandwiches €

(📞93 218 51 34; www.chivuos.com; Carrer del Torrent de l'Olla 175; sandwiches €7-9; ⏰1-5pm & 7pm-midnight Mon-Fri, 6pm-midnight Sat; Ⓜ️Lesseps, Fontana) Satisfying grilled sandwiches and delicious craft brews make a fine pair at this buzzing little snack den in Gràcia. A mostly local crowd comes for the slow-roasted pork, tuna melts, bacon-covered burgers and 'philli cheese steaks'. The rotating selection of eight craft brews includes mostly Catalan and Spanish brews, including excellent ales from Barcelona-based Edge Brewing (p181).

La Panxa del Bisbe Tapas €€

(Map p254; 📞93 213 70 49; Carrer del Torrent de les Flors 156; tapas €8-14, tasting menus from €30; ⏰1.30-3.30pm & 8.30pm-midnight Tue-Sat; Ⓜ️Joanic) With low lighting and an artfully minimalist interior, the 'Bishop's Belly' serves up creative tapas that earn high praise from the mostly local crowd. Feast on grilled razor clams, tender morsels of tuna tataki or *picanya* (grilled rump steak) served with chips and Béarnaise sauce.

Bilbao Spanish €€

(Map p254; 📞93 458 96 24; Carrer del Perill 33; mains €16-28; ⏰1-4pm & 9-11pm Mon-Sat, closed Aug; Ⓜ️Diagonal) It doesn't look much from the outside, but Bilbao is a timeless classic, where reservations for dinner are imperative. The back dining room, with bottle-lined walls, stout timber tables and a yellow light evocative of a country tavern, sets the stage for feasting on hearty meat and rich seafood dishes, matched by good Spanish wine selections.

Standouts include roast suckling pig, oxtail in red wine sauce, codfish with garlic mousse and fresh market fish.

Con Gracia Fusion €€€

(Map p254; 📞93 238 02 01; www.congracia.es; Carrer de Martínez de la Rosa 8; set menu €65, with wine pairing €95; ⏰7-11pm Tue-Sat; Ⓜ️Diagonal) This teeny hideaway (seating about 20 in total) is a hive of originality, producing delicately balanced Mediterranean cuisine with Asian touches. On offer is a regularly changing surprise tasting menu or the set 'traditional' one, with dishes like squid

Barbecued vegetables and romesco sauce

NITO/SHUTTERSTOCK ©

stuffed with *jamón ibérico* and black truffle, and juicy black Angus steak. Book ahead.

Roig Robí
Catalan €€€

(Map p254; ☎93 218 92 22; www.roigrobi.com; Carrer de Sèneca 20; mains €24-40; ☺1.30-4pm & 8.30-11.30pm Mon-Fri, 8.30-11.30pm Sat; ⓂDiagonal) This is an altar to refined traditional cooking. The menu changes seasonally, and serves as a showcase for beautifully presented creations with local and organic ingredients. Start off with sautéed baby squids with chickpeas before moving on to outstanding seafood rice dishes, grilled fresh fish baked with salt or slow-roasted young lamb. Call ahead to score a table on the vine-draped back patio.

Botafumeiro
Seafood €€€

(☎93 218 42 30; www.botafumeiro.es; Carrer Gran de Gràcia 81; mains €20-48; ☺noon-1am; ⓂFontana) It is hard not to mention this classic temple of Galician shellfish and other briny delights, long a magnet for VIPs visiting Barcelona. You can bring the price down by sharing a few *medias raciones* (half-rations; large tapas plates) to taste a range of marine offerings. It's a good place to try *percebes*, the strangely twisted goose barnacles harvested along Galicia's north Atlantic coast, which many Spaniards consider the ultimate seafood delicacy.

✕ Camp Nou, Pedrables & La Zona Alta

Vivanda
Catalan €€

(☎93 203 19 18; www.vivanda.cat; Carrer Major de Sarrià 134; sharing plates €8-18; ☺1.30-3.30pm Tue-Sun & 9-11pm Tue-Sat; ⓇFGC Reina Elisenda) With a menu designed by celebrated Catalan chef Jordi Vilà, diners are in for a treat at this Sarrià classic. The changing dishes showcase seasonal fare (like eggs with truffles, rice with cuttlefish, and artichokes with romesco sauce).

One of Vivanda's best features is the garden-like terrace behind the restaurant. It has heat lamps and is open year-round.

Ajoblanco
Tapas €€

(☎93 667 87 66; www.ajoblancorestaurant.com; Carrer de Tuset 20; sharing plates €8-21; ☺noon-1am Sun-Wed, to 3am Thu-Sat; ✐; ⓇFGC Gràcia) This beautifully designed space serves up a mix of classic and creative tapas plates that go nicely with the imaginative cocktail menu. Sip the house vermouth while munching on crispy aubergine with goat's cheese, slow-roasted lamb shoulder, or wild sea bass ceviche with mango and chilli.

ABaC
Catalan €€€

(☎93 319 66 00; www.abacbarcelona.com; Avinguda del Tibidabo 1; mains €45-75, tasting menus €135-165; ☺1.30-4pm & 8.30-11pm Tue-Sat; ⓇFGC Tibidabo) Led by celebrated chef Jordi Cruz, ABaC offers one of Barcelona's most memorable dining experiences (and also one of its priciest). Expect creative, mouthwatering perfection in dishes like sea urchin curry with lime, and roasted sea bass with artichokes and oysters.

La Balsa
Mediterranean €€€

(☎93 211 50 48; www.labalsarestaurant.com; Carrer de la Infanta Isabel 4; mains €20-28; ☺1.30-3.30pm Tue-Sun & 8.30-11pm Tue-Sat; ⓇFGC Avinguda Tibidabo) With its grand ceiling and the scented gardens that surround the main terrace dining area, La Balsa is one of the city's top dining experiences. The menu changes frequently and is a mix of traditional Catalan and off-centre inventiveness. Lounge over a cocktail at the bar before being ushered to your table.

El Asador de Aranda
Spanish €€€

(☎93 417 01 15; www.asadordearanda.com; Avinguda del Tibidabo 31; mains €17-24; ☺1-4.30pm daily & 7.45-11.30pm Mon-Sat; ⓇFGC Avinguda Tibidabo) A great place for a meal after visiting Tibidabo, El Asador de Aranda is set in a striking art-nouveau building, complete with stained-glass windows, Moorish-style brick arches and elaborate ceilings. You'll find a fine assortment of tapas plates for sharing, though the speciality is the meat (roast lamb, spare ribs, beef), beautifully prepared in a wood oven.

TREASURE HUNT

Begin your shopping adventure

Treasure Hunt

If your doctor has prescribed an intense round of retail therapy to deal with the blues, then Barcelona is the place. Barcelona's food markets are among Europe's best and the streets of La Ribera are a gourmet paradise. And across Ciutat Vella (Barri Gòtic, El Raval and La Ribera), L'Eixample and Gràcia is spread a thick mantle of boutiques, historic shops, original one-off stores, gourmet corners, wine dens and more designer labels than you can shake your gold card at. You name it, you'll find it here.

In This Section

Useful Phrases

I'd like to buy...	Quería comprar...	ke·*ria* kom·prar...
I'm just looking	Sólo estoy mirando	*so*·lo es·*toy* mee·*ran*·do
Can I look at it?	¿Puedo verlo?	*pwe*·do *ver*·lo
Do you have other sizes?	¿Tienes más tallas?	*tyen*·es mas·*tie*·yas
How much is it?	¿Cuanto cuesta?	*kwan*·to *kwes*·ta

Gràcia & Park Güell
A bit of everything in this intriguing, locally focused district
(p164)

Camp Nou, Pedrables & La Zona Alta
Large-scale shops and the FC Barcelona stadium store
(p167)

La Sagrada Família & L'Eixample
Big-name designers and upmarket boutiques
(p161)

La Ribera
Great market and numerous gourmet food outlets
(p158)

El Raval
Alternative, bohemian design, clothing and vintage stores
(p156)

La Rambla & Barri Gòtic
Intriguing quirky shops on narrow lanes among tourist traps
(p154)

Barceloneta & the Waterfront
Great flea market and craft market choices
(p160)

Port Olímpic

Mediterranean Sea

Port Vell

Montjuïc, Poble Sec & Sant Antoni
Small, quirky boutiques, pop-ups and cutting-edge streetwear
(p164)

Opening Hours

In general, most businesses open from 10am to 1.30pm or 2pm and 4.30pm or 5pm to 8pm or 8.30pm Monday to Friday. Many open on Saturdays, too, sometimes only in the morning. Large supermarkets, malls and department stores open from 10am to 10pm Monday to Saturday, while many fashion boutiques open from 10am to 8pm Monday to Saturday.

Sales

The winter sales start after Reis (6 January) and, depending on the shop, can go on well into February. Summer sales start in July, with shops trying to entice locals in before they flood out of the city on holiday in August. Some shops prolong sales to August's end.

The Best...

Experience Barcelona's best shopping

For Design & Craft

Drap Art (p155) Weird and wonderful recycled art and accessories.

Arlequí Màscares (p158) Handmade masks to rival any in Venice; the perfect souvenir.

Fantastik (p156) A temple to kitsch, with kooky wonders from all around the world.

Teranyina (p157) The 'Spider's Web', so-called for its intricate designs in intricate textiles.

For Fashion

Coquette (pictured above; p158) Offbeat women's clothes with an ethereal elegance.

Holala! Plaza (p157) Today vintage is the new designer, and nowhere has a better selection than Holala!

Bagués-Masriera (p161) Exquisite jewellery from a company with a long tradition.

Custo Barcelona (p158) Quirky, colourful clothes that are not for the shy.

Loisaida (p158) Cute, smart and somewhat retro clothing for men and women.

Markets

Mercat de Santa Caterina (p102) A colourful alternative to La Boqueria, with fewer crowds and lower prices.

Els Encants Vells (p160) A sprawling flea market in a spanking new building.

El Bulevard dels Antiquaris (p161) A labyrinth of tiny antique shops that merits a morning's browsing.

For Food & Wine

Casa Gispert (p103) The speciality is roast nuts, but you'll also find chocolate, conserves and olive oils, attractively labelled.

Vila Viniteca (p103) A jaw-dropping cathedral of wines from Catalonia and elsewhere in Spain, tucked away in a Born side street.

Barcelona Reykjavik (p156) The place to come for that organic spelt loaf or buttery croissant.

Caelum (p132) Deliciously wicked sweet treats made by nuns, with a little tea room downstairs.

For Vintage

L'Arca (p154) Ethereal gowns, often used for film sets, in the heart of the Barri Gòtic.

El Bulevard dels Antiquaris (p161) A quirky hotchpotch of antique shops.

Els Encants Vells (p160) Stunningly re-modelled flea market where you can unearth retro homeware and kitschy bric-a-brac.

Port Antic (p160) A quirky street market with finds from vintage toys to tiny oil paintings.

★ Lonely Planet's Top Choices

Mercat de la Boqueria (pictured above; p90) Stock up on budget delicacies amid one of Europe's most vibrant food markets.

Vila Viniteca (p103) Oenophiles unite at this wonderful wine shop.

Coquette (p158) Simple and beautiful designer clothes for women.

Loisalda (p158) Men's and women's fashion, antiques and retro vinyl.

⌂La Rambla & Barri Gòtic

L'Arca   Vintage, Clothing

(Map p250; ☑93 302 15 98; www.larca.es; Carrer dels Banys Nous 20; ☉11am-2pm & 4.30-8.30pm Mon-Sat; Ⓜ Liceu) Step inside this enchanting shop for a glimpse of beautifully crafted apparel from the past, including 18th-century embroidered silk vests, elaborate silk kimonos, and wedding dresses and shawls from the 1920s. Thanks to its incredible collection, it has provided clothing for films including *Titanic, Talk to Her* and *Perfume: The Story of a Murderer*.

Sabater Hermanos   Beauty

(Map p250; ☑93 301 98 32; www.shnos.com. ar; Plaça de Sant Felip Neri 1; ☉10.30am-9pm; Ⓜ Jaume I) This fragrant little shop sells handcrafted soaps of all sizes. Varieties like fig, cinnamon, grapefruit and chocolate smell good enough to eat, while sandalwood, magnolia, mint, cedar and jasmine add spice to any sink or bathtub.

Herboristeria del Rei   Beauty

(Map p250; ☑93 318 05 12; www.herboristeria delrei.blogspot.com; Carrer del Vidre 1; ☉2-8.30pm Mon, 10am-8.30pm Tue-Sat; Ⓜ Liceu) Once patronised by Queen Isabel II, this timeless corner store flogs all sorts of weird and wonderful herbs, spices and medicinal plants. It's been doing so since 1823 and the decor has barely changed since the 1860s. However, some of the products have, and you'll find anything from fragrant soaps to massage oil nowadays. Film director Tom Tykwer shot scenes from *Perfume: The Story of a Murderer* here.

Formatgeria La Seu   Food

(Map p250; ☑93 412 65 48; www.formatgeria laseu.com; Carrer de la Dagueria 16; ☉10am-2pm & 5-8pm Tue-Sat, closed Aug; Ⓜ Jaume I) Dedicated to artisan cheeses from across Spain, this small shop is run by the oh-so-knowledgable Katherine McLaughlin and is the antithesis of mass production – it sells only the best from small-scale farmers and the stock changes regularly. Wine and cheese tastings in the cosy room at the back are fun.

Loisaida (p158)

Torrons Vicens · Food

(Map p250; ☑93 304 37 36; www.vicens.com; Carrer del Petritxol 15; ☺10am-8.30pm Mon-Sat, 11am-8pm Sun; ⓂLiceu) You can find the *turrón* (nougat) treat year-round at Torrons Vicens, which has been selling its signature sweets since 1775.

Drap Art · Arts & Crafts

(Map p250; ☑93 268 48 89; www.drapart.org; Carrer Groc 1; ☺11am-2pm & 5-8pm Tue-Fri, 6-9pm Sat; ⓂJaume I) A nonprofit arts organisation runs this small store and gallery space, which exhibits wild designs from artists near and far. Works change regularly, but you might find sculptures, jewellery, handbags and other accessories made from recycled products, as well as mixed-media installations.

FC Botiga · Souvenirs

(Map p250; ☑93 269 15 32; Carrer de Jaume I 18; ☺10am-9pm Mon-Sat; ⓂJaume I) Need a Lionel Messi football jersey, a blue-and-burgundy ball, or any other football paraphernalia pertaining to what many locals consider the greatest team in the world? This is a convenient spot to load up without traipsing to the stadium.

Cereria Subirà · Homewares

(Map p250; ☑93 315 26 06; Baixada de la Llibreteria 7; ☺9.30am-1.30pm & 4-8pm Mon-Thu, 9.30am-8pm Fri, 10am-8pm Sat; ⓂJaume I) Even if you're not interested in myriad mounds of colourful wax, pop in just so you've been to the oldest shop in Barcelona. Cereria Subirà has been churning out candles since 1761 and at this address since the 19th century; the interior has a beautifully baroque quality, with a picturesque *Gone With the Wind* staircase.

Art & Crafts Market · Market

(Mostra d'Art; Map p250; Plaça de Sant Josep Oriol; ☺11am-8.30pm Sat, 10am-3pm Sun; ⓂLiceu) The Barri Gòtic is enlivened by an art and crafts market on Saturday and Sunday.

Artesania Catalunya · Handicrafts

(Map p250; ☑93 342 75 20; www.bcncrafts. com; Carrer dels Banys Nous 11; ☺10am-8pm

🛍 Barri Gòtic Shopping

A handful of interesting shops dots La Rambla, but the real fun starts inside the labyrinth. Young fashion on Carrer d'Avinyó, a mixed bag on Avinguda del Portal de l'Àngel, some cute old shops on Carrer de la Dagueria and lots of exploring in tight old lanes awaits.

Mon-Sat, to 2pm Sun; ⓂLiceu) A celebration of Catalan products, this nicely designed store is a great place to browse for unique gifts. You'll find jewellery with designs inspired by Roman iconography (as well as works that reference Gaudí and Barcelona's Gothic era), plus pottery, wooden toys, silk scarves, notebooks, housewares and more.

Cómplices · Books

(Map p250; www.libreriacomplices.com; Carrer de Cervantes 4; ☺10.30am-8pm Mon-Fri, noon-8pm Sat; ⓂJaume I) One of the most extensive gay and lesbian bookshops in the city has a mix of erotica in the form of DVDs and comics as well as books. It's a welcoming place for all ages and orientations.

El Corte Inglés · Department Store

(Map p250; Portal de l'Àngel 19-21; ☺9.30am-9.30pm Mon-Sat; ⓂCatalunya) A secondary branch of Spain's only remaining department store, selling electronics, fashion, stationery and sports gear.

La Basilica Galeria · Jewellery

(Map p250; ☑93 304 20 47; www.labasilica galeria.com; Carrer Sant Sever 7; ☺11am-8.30pm; 🗑; ⓂJaume I) A pure wonderland for the senses, La Basilica Galeria is a whimsical jewellery store with artful displays set among crystal- and flower-covered mannequins. In addition to eye-catching necklaces, delicate rings and fairy-tale pendants, there are a few original paintings for sale, though there's more artwork a few doors down in Basilica's gallery and perfume shop.

from corner-store days as kids. Watch the sticky sweets being made before your eyes.

Xocoa   Food

(Map p250; ☑93 301 82 91; www.xocoa-bcn.com; Carrer del Petritxol 11-13; ⊙9.30am-9pm; Ⓜ Liceu) Tucked along 'chocolate street' Carrer del Petritxol, this den of dental devilry displays ranks and ranks of original bars in stunning designs, chocolates stuffed with sweet stuff, gooey pastries and more. It has various other branches scattered about town.

🔒 El Raval

Les Topettes   Beauty

(Map p249; ☑93 500 55 64; www.lestopettes. com; Carrer de Joaquín Costa 33; ⊙11am-2pm & 4-9pm Tue-Sat; Ⓜ Universitat) It's a sign of the times that such a chic little temple to soap and perfume can exist in the Raval. The items in Les Topettes' collection have been picked for their designs as much as the products themselves, and you'll find gorgeously packaged scents, candles and unguents from Diptyque, Cowshed and L'Artisan Parfumeur, among others.

Fantastik   Arts & Crafts

(Map p249; ☑93 301 30 68; www.fantastik. es; Carrer de Joaquín Costa 62; ⊙11am-2pm & 4-8.30pm Mon-Fri, noon-9pm Sat; Ⓜ Universitat) Over 400 products, including a Mexican skull rattle, robot moon explorer from China and recycled plastic zebras from South Africa, are in this colourful shop, which sources its items from Mexico, India, Bulgaria, Russia, Senegal and 20 other countries. It's a perfect place to buy all the things you don't need but can't live without.

Barcelona Reykjavik   Food

(Map p249; ☑93 302 09 21; www.barcelonareyk javik.com; Carrer del Doctor Dou 12; ⊙10am-9pm Mon-Sat, 9.30am-8pm Sun; Ⓜ Catalunya) Bread lovers, rejoice! Good bread can be hard to find in Barcelona, but Reykjavik saves the day. All loaves are made using organic flour – spelt, wholemeal, mixed cereals and

🛍 Vintage Shopping

El Raval is best for vintage fashion. You'll discover old-time stores that are irresistible to browsers, and a colourful array of affordable, mostly secondhand clothes boutiques. The central axis here is Carrer de la Riera Baixa, which plays host to '70s threads and military cast-offs. Carrer dels Tallers is also attracting a growing number of clothing and shoe shops (although CDs remain its core business). Small galleries, designer shops and arty bookshops huddle together along the streets running east of MACBA (Museu d'Art Contemporani de Barcelona) towards La Rambla.

Old books for sale
J2R/SHUTTERSTOCK ©

La Manual Alpargatera   Shoes

(Map p250; ☑93 301 01 72; lamanualalparga tera.es; Carrer d'Avinyó 7; ⊙9.30am-1.30pm & 4.30-8pm Mon-Fri, from 10am Sat; Ⓜ Liceu) Clients from Salvador Dalí to Jean Paul Gaultier have ordered a pair of espadrilles (rope-soled canvas shoes) from this famous store. The shop was founded just after the Spanish Civil War, though the roots of the simple shoe design date back hundreds of years and originated in the Catalan Pyrenees.

Papabubble   Food

(Map p250; ☑93 268 86 25; www.papabubble. com; Carrer Ample 28; ⊙10am-2pm & 3.30-8pm Mon-Fri, 10am-8pm Sat; Ⓜ Jaume I) It feels like a step into another era in this candy store, which makes up pots of rainbow-coloured boiled lollies, just like some of us remember

Pottery display, Barri Gòtic

so on – and sourdough yeast, though this does make for fairly high prices. The bakery also produces excellent cakes. Three more shops can be found in El Born, Gràcia and L'Eixample.

Holala! Plaza   Fashion

(Map p249; www.holala-ibiza.com; Plaça de Castella 2; ⊗11am-9pm Mon-Sat; MUniversitat) Backing on to Carrer de Valldonzella, where it boasts an exhibition space (Gallery) for temporary art displays, this Ibiza import is inspired by that island's long established (and somewhat commercialised) hippie tradition. Vintage clothes are the name of the game, along with an eclectic program of exhibitions and activities.

Teranyina   Arts & Crafts

(Map p249; www.textilteranyina.com; Carrer del Notariat 10; ⊗11am-3pm & 5-8pm Mon-Fri; MCatalunya) Artist Teresa Rosa Aguayo runs this textile workshop in the heart of the artsy bit of El Raval. You can join courses at the loom, admire some of the rugs and other works that Teresa has created, and, of course, buy them.

> *Fantastik is a perfect place to buy all the things you don't need but can't live without*

Discos Castelló   Music

(Map p249; Carrer dels Tallers 7; ⊗10am-8.30pm Mon-Sat; MCatalunya) Castelló used to dominate this street, which contained instrument and CD shops. But the recession took its toll and now only this store remains, selling new and secondhand CDs of all types of music, from metal to classical, along with a selection of related books and paraphernalia.

La Portorriqueña   Coffee

(Map p249; Carrer d'en Xuclà 25; ⊗9am-2pm & 5-8pm Mon-Fri, 9am-2pm Sat; MCatalunya) Coffee beans from around the world, freshly ground before your eyes, have been the winning formula in this store since 1902. It also offers all sorts of chocolate goodies. The street it's on is good for little old-fashioned food boutiques.

Waterfront Markets

On weekends Port Vell springs to life with a handful of markets at key points along the waterfront selling a mix of antiques and contemporary art and crafts.

Near the Palau de Mar, you'll find **Feria de Artesanía del Palau de Mar** (Moll del Dipòsit; ⊙11am-8.30pm Sat & Sun; MBarceloneta), with artisans selling a range of crafty items, including jewellery, graphic T-shirts, handwoven hats, fragrant candles and soaps, scarves and decorative items. In July and August the market runs daily.

Take a stroll along the pedestrian-only Rambla de Mar to reach the weekend art fair **Mercado de Pintores** (Passeig d'Ítaca; ⊙10am-8pm Sat & Sun; MDrassanes), with a broad selection of paintings both collectable and forgettable.

And at the base of La Rambla is the small Port Antic market (p160).

La Ribera

Loisaida
Clothing, Antiques
(Map p250; ☑93 295 54 92; www.loisaidabcn.com; Carrer dels Flassaders 42; ⊙11am-9pm Mon-Sat, 11am-2pm & 4-8pm Sun; MJaume I) A sight in its own right, housed in what was once the coach house and stables for the Royal Mint, Loisaida (from the Spanglish for 'Lower East Side') is a deceptively large emporium of colourful, retro and somewhat preppy clothing for men and women, costume jewellery, music from the 1940s and '50s and some covetable antiques.

Coquette
Fashion
(Map p250; ☑93 319 29 76; www.coquettebcn.com; Carrer del Rec 65; ⊙11am-3pm & 5-9pm Mon-Fri, 11.30am-9pm Sat; MBarceloneta) With its spare, cut-back and designer look, this friendly fashion store is attractive in its own right. Women can browse through casual, feminine wear by such designers as Humanoid, Vanessa Bruno, UKE, Hoss

Intropia and others, with a further collection nearby at Carrer de Bonaire 5. (Map p250; ☑93 310 35 35; Carrer de Bonaire 5; ⊙11am-3pm & 5-9pm Mon-Fri, 11.30am-9pm Sat; MBarceloneta)

El Rei de la Màgia
Magic
(Map p250; ☑93 319 39 20; www.elreydela magia.com; Carrer de la Princesa 11; ⊙10.30am-2pm & 4-7.30pm Mon-Sat; MJaume I) For more than 100 years, the people behind this box of tricks have been keeping locals both astounded and amused. Should you decide to stay in Barcelona and make a living as a magician, this is the place to buy levitation brooms, glasses of disappearing milk and decks of magic cards.

Arlequí Màscares
Arts & Crafts
(Map p250; ☑93 268 27 52; www.arlequimask.com; Carrer de la Princesa 7; ⊙10.30am-8.30pm Mon-Sat, 10.30am-3pm & 4-7.30pm Sun; MJaume I) A wonderful little oasis of originality, this shop specialises in masks for costume and decoration. There's also a beautiful range of decorative boxes in Catalan themes, and some old-style marionettes.

Custo Barcelona
Fashion
(Map p250; ☑93 268 78 93; www.custo.com; Plaça de les Olles 7; ⊙10am-9pm Mon-Sat, noon-8pm Sun; MBarceloneta) The psychedelic decor and casual atmosphere lend this avant-garde Barcelona fashion store a youthful edge. Custo presents daring new women's and men's collections each year on the New York catwalks. The dazzling colours and cut of everything from dinner jackets to hot pants are for the uninhibited. It has three other stores around town.

Nu Sabates
Shoes, Accessories
(Map p250; ☑93 268 03 83; www.nusabates.com; Carrer dels Cotoners 14; ⊙11am-9pm Mon-Sat; MJaume I) A couple of modern-day Catalan cobblers have put together some original handmade leather shoes for men and women (and a handful of bags and other leather items) in their friendly and stylish locale, which is enlivened by some inspired music selections.

IAKOV FILIMONOV/SHUTTERSTOCK ©

★ Where to Shop

For high fashion, design, jewellery and department stores, the principal shopping axis starts on Plaça de Catalunya, proceeds up Passeig de Gràcia and turns left into Avinguda Diagonal, along which it extends as far as Plaça de la Reina Maria Cristina. The densely packed section between Plaça de Francesc Macià and Plaça de la Reina Maria Cristina is an especially good hunting ground.

LEFT: KRIS UBACH AND QUIM ROSER/GETTY IMAGES © RIGHT: DIEGO LEZAMA/GETTY IMAGES ©

Top: Els Encants Vells (p160); Left: Clothes shopping; Above: Shoe shopping in El Born

🛍Barceloneta & the Waterfront

Els Encants Vells — Market
(Fira de Bellcaire; ☎93 246 30 30; www.
encantsbcn.com; Plaça de les Glòries Catalanes;
⊙9am-8pm Mon, Wed, Fri & Sat; Ⓜ Glòries)
In a gleaming open-sided complex, the
'Old Charms' flea market is the biggest of
its kind in Barcelona. Over 500 vendors
ply their wares, from antique furniture to
secondhand clothes. A lot of it is junk, but
occasionally you'll find a *ganga* (bargain).

The most interesting time to be here
is from 7.30am to 8.30am on Monday,
Wednesday and Friday, when the *subastas*
(public auctions) take place.

Port Antic — Market
(Plaça del Portal de la Pau; ⊙10am-8pm Sat &
Sun; Ⓜ Drassanes) At the base of La Rambla,
this small market is a requisite stop for
shopping-minded strollers and antique
hunters. Here you'll find old photographs,
frames, oil paintings, records, shawls, cameras, vintage toys and other odds and ends.
Go early to beat the crowds.

Ultra-Local Records — Music
(☎661 017638; www.ultralocalrecords.com;
Carrer de Pujades 113; ⊙3-8.30pm Mon-Fri,
from 11am Sat; Ⓜ Llacuna) Tucked along a
fairly empty stretch of Poblenou, this
small, well-curated shop sells mostly used
records (plus some re-releases and albums
by current indie rock darlings) from Catalan, Spanish, French, American and British
artists. Vinyl aside, you'll find a smaller CD
selection, plus zines and a few other curiosities. There's a €1 bargain bin, too.

Bestiari — Books, Handicrafts
(Map p250; Plaça de Pau Vila 3; ⊙10am-7pm
Tue-Sat, to 2.30pm Sun; Ⓜ Barceloneta) On the
ground floor of the Museu d'Història de
Catalunya, this nicely stocked shop sells
books in English, Spanish and Catalan for
all ages, plus lots of Catalan-themed gift
ideas: CDs, T-shirts, umbrellas, bags, chess
sets, mugs and toys (along the lines of the
build-your-own Gothic or Gaudí structures).

Bazart — Accessories
(☎633 45 53 78; Carrer de la Ciutat de Granada
44; ⊙10.30am-6pm Mon-Fri, to 2.30pm Sat;
Ⓜ Llacuna) If you can't make it to South

Window shopping in L'Eixample

America's handicrafts markets, Bazart may be your next-best option. This colourfully decorated shop stocks handcrafted goods from across the Andes. There are lots of great gift ideas, including silver jewellery from Ecuador, woven pillowcases from Bolivia, and alpaca gloves, scarves and blankets from Chile.

System Action — Clothing

(☎93 225 79 90; systemaction.es; Carrer de Pere IV 122; ⏰10am-7pm Mon-Sat; Ⓜ Llacuna) If you like discovering local producers, then look no further than this outlet store on Pere IV. Though System Action has stores all across Catalonia (and in Madrid), its design headquarters are a few blocks south in a former Poblenou ice factory. Fashions are feminine but rugged, with good basics, very wearable scarves, sweaters, skirts and even shoes available. Prices are reasonable – especially when sales are underway.

🛍 La Sagrada Família & L'Eixample

Bagués-Masriera — Jewellery

(Map p254; ☎93 216 01 74; www.bagues-masri era.com; Passeig de Gràcia 41; ⏰10am-8.30pm Mon-Fri, 11am-8pm Sat; Ⓜ Passeig de Gràcia) This jewellery store, in business since the 19th century, is in thematic harmony with its location in the Modernista Casa Amatller. Some of the classic pieces to come out of the Bagués clan's workshops have an equally playful, Modernista bent.

El Bulevard dels Antiquaris — Antiques

(Map p254; ☎93 215 44 99; www.bulevarddels antiquaris.com; Passeig de Gràcia 55; ⏰10.30am-8.30pm Mon-Sat; Ⓜ Passeig de Gràcia) More than 70 stores (be warned: most close for lunch) are gathered under one roof (on the floor above the more general Bulevard Rosa arcade) to offer the most varied selection of collector's pieces. These range from old porcelain dolls to fine crystal, from Asian antique furniture to old French goods, and from ethnic art to jewellery.

🛍 Shopping Strips in Barcelona

Avinguda del Portal de l'Àngel This broad pedestrian avenue is lined with high-street chains, shoe shops, book-shops and more. It feeds into Carrer dels Boters and Carrer de la Portaferrissa, characterised by shops offering light-hearted costume jewellery and youth-oriented streetwear.

Avinguda Diagonal This boulevard is loaded with international fashion names and design boutiques, suitably interspersed with cafes to allow weary shoppers to take a load off.

Carrer d'Avinyó Once a fairly squalid old street, Carrer d'Avinyó has morphed into a dynamic young fashion street.

Carrer de la Riera Baixa The place to look for a gaggle of shops flogging preloved threads.

Carrer del Consell de Cent The heart of the private art-gallery scene in Barcelona, between Passeig de Gràcia and Carrer de Muntaner.

Carrer del Petritxol Best for chocolate shops and art.

Carrer del Rec Another threads street, this one-time stream is lined with bright and cool boutiques. Check out Carrer del Bonaire and Carrer de l'Esparteria, too. You'll find discount outlets and original local designers.

Carrer dels Banys Nous Along with nearby Carrer de la Palla, this is the place to look for antiques.

Passeig de Gràcia This is the premier shopping boulevard, chic with a capital 'C', and mostly given over to big-name international brands.

Flores Navarro — Flowers

(Map p254; ☎93 457 40 99; www.floristerias navarro.com; Carrer de València 320; ⏰24hr; Ⓜ Diagonal) You never know when you might need flowers, and this florist never closes.

DOMINGO LEIVA/GETTY IMAGES ©

A shopfront in El Born

> *The medieval streets of El Born hide an abundance of shopping intrigue*

It's a vast space (or couple of spaces, in fact), and worth a visit just for the bank of colour and wonderful fragrance.

Altaïr
Books

(Map p254; ☎93 342 71 71; www.altair.es; Gran Via de les Corts Catalanes 616; ⊙10am-8.30pm Mon-Sat; ☎; MCatalunya) Enter a wonderland of travel in this extensive bookshop, which is a mecca for guidebooks, maps, travel literature and all sorts of other books likely to induce a severe case of itchy feet. It has a travellers' noticeboard and, downstairs, a travel agent.

Norma Comics
Books

(☎93 244 81 25; www.normacomics.com; Passeig de Sant Joan 7-9; ⊙10.30am-8.30pm Mon-Sat; MArc de Triomf) With a huge range of comics, both Spanish and international, this is Spain's biggest dealer – everything from Tintin to some of the weirdest sci-fi

and sex comics can be found here. Also on show are armies of model superheroes and other characters. Kids from nine to 99 can be seen snapping up items to add to their collections.

Camper
Shoes

(Map p254; ☎93 215 63 90; www.camper.com; Carrer de València 249; ⊙10am-9pm Mon-Sat; MPasseig de Gràcia) What started as a modest Mallorcan family business (the island has a long shoemaking tradition) has, over the decades, and particularly with the success of the 'bowling shoe' in the '90s, become the Clarks of Spain. The shoes, from the eminently sensible to the stylishly fashionable, are known for solid reliability and are sold all over the world. Camper now has shops all over Barcelona.

Cacao Sampaka
Food

(Map p254; ☎93 272 08 33; www.cacaosam paka.com; Carrer del Consell de Cent 292; ⊙9am-9pm Mon-Sat; MPasseig de Gràcia) Chocoholics will be convinced they have died and passed on to a better place. Load up in the shop or head for the bar out the back where you can have a classic *xocolata* (hot chocolate) and munch on exquisite chocolate cakes, tarts, ice cream, sweets and sandwiches. The bonbons make particularly good presents.

Antinous   Books

(Map p249; ✆93 301 90 70; www.antinous libros.com; Carrer de Casanova 72; ☯11am-2pm & 5-8pm Mon-Sat; Ⓜ Universitat) Gay and lesbian travellers may want to browse in this spacious and relaxed gay bookshop, which recently moved to the Gaixample from its long-held home in the Barri Gòtic. There are also regular titles, kids' book and comic books.

Joan Múrria   Food

(Map p254; ✆93 215 57 89; www.murria.cat; Carrer de Roger de Llúria 85; ☯9am-2pm & 5-8pm Mon-Fri; Ⓜ Passeig de Gràcia) Ramon Casas designed the century-old Modernista shop-front advertisements featured at this culinary temple. For a century the gluttonous have trembled at this altar of speciality food goods from around Catalonia and beyond.

Adolfo Domínguez   Fashion

(Map p254; ✆93 487 41 70; www.adolfo dominguez.com; Passeig de Gràcia 32; ☯10am-9pm Mon-Sat; Ⓜ Passeig de Gràcia) One of the stars of Spanish prét-à-porter, this label produces classic men's and women's garments from quality materials. Encompassing anything from regal party gowns to kids' outfits (that might have you thinking of British aristocracy), the broad range generally oozes a conservative air, with elegant cuts that make no concessions to rebellious urban ideals.

Cubiña   Homewares

(Map p254; ✆93 476 57 21; www.cubinya.es; Carrer de Mallorca 291; ☯10am-2pm & 4.30-8.30pm Mon-Sat; Ⓜ Verdaguer) Even if interior design doesn't ring your bell, it's worth a visit to this extensive temple to furniture, lamps and just about any home accessory your heart might desire, just to see this Domènech i Montaner building. Admire

🛍 Shopping Malls

Barcelona has no shortage of shopping malls. One of the first to arrive was **L'Illa Diagonal** (✆93 444 00 00; www.lilla.com; Avinguda Diagonal 549; ☯10am-9.30pm Mon-Sat; Ⓜ Maria Cristina), designed by star Spanish architect Rafael Moneo. The **Centre Comercial Diagonal Mar** (✆93 567 76 37; www.diagonalmar.com; Avinguda Diagonal 3; ☯10am-10pm Mon-Sat; Ⓜ El Maresme Fòrum), by the sea, is one of the latest additions.

The city's other emporia include **Centre Comercial de les Glòries** (✆93 486 04 04; www.lesglories.com; Gran Via de les Corts Catalanes 208; ☯10am-1am; Ⓜ Glòries), in the former Olivetti factory; **Heron City** (✆93 276 50 70; www.heron citybarcelona.com; Avinguda de Rio de Janeiro 42; ☯stores 10am-10pm Mon-Sat, cinema & restaurants 7am-1am daily; Ⓜ Fabra i Puig), just off Avinguda Meridiana, about 4km north of Plaça de les Glòries Catalanes; and the **Centre Comercial Gran Via 2** (✆902 301444; www.granvia2.com; Gran Via de les Corts Catalanes 75; ☯shops 10am-8pm Mon-Sat, restaurants & cinema 10am-1am daily; Ⓡ FGC Ildefons Cerdà) in L'Hospitalet de Llobregat.

the enormous and whimsical wrought-iron decoration at street level before heading inside to marvel at the ceiling, timberwork, brick columns and windows.

Loewe   Fashion

(Map p254; ✆93 216 04 00; www.loewe.com; Passeig de Gràcia 35; ☯10am-8.30pm Mon-Sat; Ⓜ Passeig de Gràcia) Loewe is one of Spain's leading and oldest fashion stores, founded in 1846. It specialises in luxury leather (shoes, accessories and travel bags), and also has lines in perfume, sunglasses, cuff links, silk scarves and jewellery. This branch opened in 1943 in the Modernista Casa Lleó Morera.

🔒 Montjuïc, Poble Sec & Sant Antoni

Galeri   Arts & Crafts
(Map p256; ☎93 124 13 30; Carrer de Viladomat 27; ⊙11am-2pm & 5-9pm Tue-Sat; Ⓜ️Poble Sec) This brightly lit gallery sells prints by Catalan artists as well as unusual graphic T-shirts, canvas bags and small ceramics – delicate conversation pieces, just small enough to fit in a carry-on bag. There are also a few original paintings and sculptures, from an ever-changing collection.

Mercat de Sant Antoni   Market
(Map p249; ☎93 426 35 21; www.mercatdesant antoni.com; Carrer de Comte d'Urgell 1; ⊙7am-2.30pm & 5-8.30pm Mon-Thu, 7am-8.30pm Fri & Sat; Ⓜ️Sant Antoni) Just beyond the western edge of El Raval is Mercat de Sant Antoni, a glorious old iron and brick building that has been undergoing renovation since 2009. In the meantime, a huge marquee has been erected alongside to house a food market. The secondhand book market still takes place alongside on Sunday mornings.

The latest estimates for the market's reopening was slated for the end of 2017.

GI Joe   Fashion
(Map p249; ☎93 329 96 52; www.gijoebcn. com; Ronda de Sant Antoni 49; ⊙10am-2pm & 4.30-8.30pm Mon-Sat; Ⓜ️Universitat) This is the best central army-surplus warehouse. Get your khakis here, along with urban army fashion T-shirts, and throw in a holster, gas mask or sky-blue UN helmet for a kinkier effect. You can also find vintage WWII items.

🔒 Gràcia & Park Güell

Amapola Vegan Shop   Clothing
(Map p254; ☎93 010 62 73; http://amapola veganshop.com; Travessera de Gràcia 129; ⊙11am-2.30pm & 5-8.30pm Mon-Sat; Ⓜ️Fontana, Diagonal) A shop with a heart of gold, Amapola proves that you need not toss your ethics aside in the quest for stylish clothing and accessories. You'll find sleek leather alternatives for wallets, handbags and messenger bags by Matt & Nat, dainty ballerina-style flats by Victoria and elegant scarves by Barts.

Other finds: socks made from bamboo, soft but wool-free gloves and cheeky T-shirts – with slogans like 'Another Fucking Vegan' and 'No como mis amigos' (I don't eat my friends).

Be   Gifts
(Map p254; ☎93 218 89 49; www.bethestore. com; Carrer de Bonavista 7; ⊙10.30am-9pm Mon-Sat; Ⓜ️Diagonal) Be is a fun place to browse for accessories and gift ideas. Among the eye candy you'll find rugged vintage-looking satchels, leather handbags, stylish (and reflective) Happy Socks, portable record players, sneakers (Vans, Pumas, old-school Nikes) and gadgets (including richly hued Pantone micro speakers and Polaroid digital cameras).

La Festival   Wine
(Map p254; ☎93 023 22 81; Carrer de Verdi 67; ⊙5.30-9.30pm Mon, 10.30am-9.30pm Tue-Sat, 11am-2pm Sun; Ⓜ️Fontana) This handsomely designed shop earns high marks for its knowledgable (and English-speaking) staff, who can give you a wealth of information about the many excellent wines for sale here. Most bottles are from Spanish producers, though there are a few French options, and some organic as well as biodynamic wines.

You can also refill your bottle with wine or vermouth from one of the casks at the front, starting at €3 a bottle.

Lady Loquita   Clothing
(Map p254; ☎93 217 82 92; www.ladyloquita. com; Travessera de Gràcia 126; ⊙11am-2pm & 5-8.30pm Mon-Sat; Ⓜ️Fontana) Lady Loquita is a hip little shop, where you can browse through light summer dresses by Tiralahilacha, evening wear by Japamala and handmade jewellery by local design label Klimbim. There are also whimsical odds and ends: dinner plates with dog-people portraits and digital prints on wood by About Paola.

A shopfront on Passeig de Gràcia (p161)

Magnesia Accessories

(📞93 119 01 87; www.magnesiabcn.com; Carrer del Torrent de l'Olla 192; ⏱10.30am-2pm & 4.30-8pm Mon-Fri, 10.30am-2pm Sat; Ⓜ Lesseps, Fontana) Tucked away on a quiet corner of Gràcia, Magnesia is a petite store so packed with intrigue that you might want to just gift-wrap the whole thing and slip it into your handbag. There's bespoke stationery, fairy-tale-esque greeting cards, one-of-a-kind framed illustrations, statement-piece jewellery and ceramics (tiny bowls, tea cups), herb-infused candles and chunky puzzles (and other gift ideas) for kids.

Tintin Shop Children

(Map p254; 📞932 89 25 24; www.tintinshopbcn.com; Travessera de Gràcia 176; ⏱10.30am-2.30pm & 5-8.30pm Mon-Fri, 11am-2.30pm Sat) Fans of the French-speaking boy wonder should make a beeline to this Gràcia store, where you'll find Tintin T-shirts, posters, action figures, book bags, wristwatches, pencil cases, and even a soft, irresistible Snowy (Tintin's wire fox terrier) – plus, of course, the books that made him famous (with titles in Spanish, Catalan and French).

Nostàlgic Photography

(Map p254; 📞93 368 57 57; www.nostalgic.es; Carrer de Goya 18; ⏱11am-2.30pm & 5-8.30pm Tue-Sat; Ⓜ Fontana) A beautiful space with exposed-brick walls and wooden furniture specialising in all kinds of modern and vintage photography equipment – you'll find camera bags and tripods for the digital snappers, and the inevitable collection of Lomo cameras, with their quirky variations. There is also a decent collection of photography books to buy or browse.

Doctor Paper Barcelona Accessories, Toys

(Map p254; 📞93 237 58 57; http://doctorpaper bcn.com; Travessera de Gràcia 130; ⏱10.30am-2pm & 5-8.30pm Mon-Sat; ®FGC Gràcia) Doctor Paper is a fun little shop to explore, with shelves crammed full of whimsical objects and retro crafts. Wind-up robots, make-your-own-aeroplane kits, vintage postcards with irreverent sayings (in Spanish), action figures, painted enamel cups and teapots, glowing mushroom lamps and travel journals with Barcelona street scenes are just a small part of the treasure trove.

5 Must-Buy Mementos

❶ Cured Meat

Instead of *jamón* (cured ham), go for some local sausage such as *fuet* or *botifarra*. It's best bought in one of the market halls. They'll vacuum-pack it for you.

❷ FC Barcelona Gear

Yes, everyone seems to have a Messi shirt these days, but you can find harder-to-come-by Barça mementoes in their official shops.

❸ Wine

Look for something you can't get back home – some small-producer Catalan red, or a hard-to-get *cava (sparkling wine)*. Wine shops in La Ribera have an ample supply.

❺ Build a Gaudí

We might not have the maestro's imagination, but by damn we can reconstruct his buildings in miniature. Available in most museum and Gaudí-building shops.

❹ Fashion

Seek out a small local design boutique to ensure you head home wearing something unique.

Bodega Bonavista   Wine

(Map p254; ☑93 218 81 99; Carrer de Bonavista 10; ☺10am-2.30pm & 5-9pm Mon-Fri, noon-3pm & 6-9pm Sat, noon-3pm Sun; Ⓜ️Fontana) An excellent little neighbourhood wine shop that endeavours to seek out great wines at reasonable prices. The stock is mostly from Catalonia and elsewhere in Spain, but there's also a good selection from France. The Bonavista also acts as a deli, and there are some especially good cheeses.

Mushi Mushi   Fashion

(Map p254; ☑93 292 29 74; www.mushimushi collection.com; Carrer de Bonavista 12; ☺11am-3pm & 4.30-8.30pm Mon-Sat; Ⓜ️Fontana) A gorgeous little fashion boutique in an area that's not short of them, Mushi Mushi specialises in quirky but elegant women's fashion and accessories. It stocks labels that include Des Petits Hauts, Sessùn, Orion London and small French labels like Five. The collection changes frequently, with only a few of each item being stocked, so a return visit can pay off.

Surco   Music

(Map p254; ☑93 218 34 39; Travessera de Gràcia 144; ☺10.30am-2pm & 5.30-9pm Mon-Sat; Ⓜ️Fontana, FGC Gràcia) Surco is an obligatory stop for music lovers – especially for fans of vinyl. You'll find loads of new and used records and CDs here, with a mix of Tom Waits, Mishima (a Catalan band), Calexico and more.

Cabinet BCN   Homewares

(Map p254; ☑93 368 43 82; www.cabinetbcn. com; Carrer de Sant Domènec 5; ☺11am-2.30pm & 5-8.30pm Tue-Sun; Ⓜ️Fontana) A charming addition to the Gràcia neighbourhood is Cabinet BCN, an interiors shop with a tasteful selection of things for the home – including throws, cushions, bowls, candles and lamps, as well as quirky ornaments – that would make excellent presents.

**Mercat de
l'Abaceria Central**   Market

(Map p254; Travessera de Gràcia 186; ☺7am-2.30pm & 5.30-8pm Mon-Sat; Ⓜ️Fontana) This sprawling iron and brick market, which dates back to the 1890s, is a fine place to browse for fresh produce, delicious cheeses, bakery items and snack foods. There's also a sushi stand and several inexpensive food stalls where you can grab a quick bite on the cheap.

🛍Camp Nou, Pedralbes & La Zona Alta

FC Botiga Megastore   Souvenirs

(☑93 409 02 71; www.fcbmegastore.com; Gate 9, off Avinguda Joan de XXIII; ☺10am-7pm Mon-Sat, to 3pm Sun; Ⓜ️Palau Reial, Collblanc) This sprawling three-storey shop in Camp Nou has footballs, shirts, scarves, socks, wallets, bags, sneakers, smartphone covers – pretty much anything you can think of – featuring Barça's famous red-and-blue insignia.

Labperfum   Beauty

(Carrer de Santaló 45; ☺11am-2pm & 5-8pm Mon-Sat; ⓇFGC Muntaner) This tiny shop looks like an old apothecary, with its shelves lined with pretty glass bottles. What's for sale are extraordinary fragrances (for men and women) that are made in-house. Scents diverge from run-of-the-mill Obsession, with varieties like tobacco, black orchid and leather. You can also buy scented candles, soaps and creams. It offers beautiful packaging and fair prices (starting at €14 for 50ml).

Tomates Fritos   Fashion

(☑93 209 26 17; tomatesfritos.es; Carrer del Tenor Viñas 7; ☺10.30am-8.30pm Mon-Fri, 10.30am-3pm & 5-8.30pm Sat; ⓇFGC Muntaner) One of a growing number of boutiques along this street, Tomates Fritos is an obligatory stop for design-minded shoppers, and carries a trove of unique wares. The cache of global designers includes denim by IRO, handbags by Liebeskind, blouses and jackets by The Kooples and beautifully tailored tops by Scotch & Soda.

BAR OPEN

Cocktails, *cava* and clubs galore

Bar Open

Barcelona is a nightlife-lovers' town, with an enticing spread of candlelit wine bars, old-school taverns, stylish lounges and kaleidoscopic nightclubs where the party continues until daybreak. For something a little more sedate, the city's atmospheric cafes and teahouses make a fine retreat when the skies turn grey. Wherever you end up, keep in mind that eating and drinking go hand in hand in Barcelona, and some of the liveliest bars serve up as many tapas as they do alcoholic tipples.

In This Section

Opening Hours

Bars Typically open around 6pm and close at 2am (3am on weekends). Get lively around 11pm or midnight.

Clubs Open from midnight until 6am, Thursday to Saturday. Clubs don't start filling up until around 2am.

Beach bars 10am to around midnight (later on weekends) from April through October.

Gràcia & Park Güell
Young hipster crowd
(p187)

Camp Nou, Pedrables & La Zona Alta
High-end clubs
(p189)

La Sagrada Família & L'Eixample
Student bars, tiny lounges, LGBT venues
(p182)

La Ribera
Cava and wine bars, lounges
(p178)

El Raval
Bohemian bars, small clubs
(p176)

La Rambla & Barri Gòtic
Atmospheric bars, cafes, outdoor spots, clubs
(p174)

Barceloneta & the Waterfront
Neighbourhood taverns, seaside bars, touristy clubs
(p180)

Montjuïc, Poble Sec & Sant Antoni
Art-minded bars, trendy cafes, open-air spots
(p186)

Port Olímpic

Port Vell

Mediterranean Sea

Costs/Tipping

A coffee costs €1.20 to €1.70, a glass of wine will run €2 to €3.50 in most places, and mixed drinks and cocktails will set you back €6 to €10.

Nightclubs charge anywhere from nothing to €20 for admission.

Tipping is not customary nor necessary.

Useful Words

Coffee

con leche – half coffee, half milk

solo – an espresso

cortado – an espresso with a dash of milk

Beer

cerveza – beer (bottle)

caña – small draught beer

tubo – large draught beer

quinto – a 200ml bottle

tercio – a 330ml bottle

clara – a shandy; a beer with a hefty dash of lemonade

The Best...

Experience Barcelona's best drinking & nightlife spots

For Dancing

Marula Cafè (p174) Barri Gòtic favourite for its lively dance floor.

Moog (p177) A small Raval club that draws a fun, dance-loving crowd.

Antilla BCN (p183) The top name in town for salsa lovers.

City Hall (p185) A legendary Eixample dance club.

For Cocktails

Balius (p181) Beautifully mixed elixirs in Poblenou.

Elephanta (p187) The place to linger over a creative concoction.

Dry Martini (p182) Expertly made cocktails in a classy setting.

Juanra Falces (p178) White-jacketed waiters serve up artful elixirs.

Boadas (p176) An iconic drinking den that's been going strong since the 1930s.

The Mint (p181) Atmospheric drinkery with outstanding mojitos and infused gins.

For Craft Beer

Edge Brewing (p181) Take a tour and taste some of Barcelona's best brews.

BlackLab (p180) Innovative IPAs and APAs on the waterfront.

La Cervecita Nuestra de Cada Día (p181) Outstanding selection of rare brews.

La Cerveteca (p175) A Barri Gòtic gem that was one of the city's first beer-focused drinking spots.

The Beer Shop (p189) Order a tasting flight, then take a few bottles home.

For Wine Lovers

Viblioteca (p187) A small, modern space famed for its wine (and cheese) selections.

Monvínic (p183) With a staggering 3000 varieties of wines, you won't lack for options.

La Vinya del Senyor (p179) Outdoor wine-sipping facing Basílica de Santa Maria del Mar.

Beachfront Spots

Santa Marta (p182) Sit at outdoor tables and watch the passing people parade.

CDLC (p182) Come early for a beach-facing outdoor table, stay for dancing.

Guingueta del Bogatell (p182) Sit on the seafront far from the mayhem.

Bohemian Hang-Outs

Gran Bodega Saltó (p200) Poble Sec icon with psychedelic decor and an eclectic crowd.

Madame George (p182) Tiny, dramatically designed space with soulful DJs.

El Rouge (p186) Bordello-esque lounge with great people-watching.

Gipsy Lou (p196) For a night of surprises in El Raval.

For Rock Lovers

Alfa (p189) A rock-loving Gràcia staple.

Magic (p179) Basement club with rock and pop in heavy rotation.

Musical Maria (p188) Classic rock lives on in this neighbourhood favorite.

★ Lonely Planet's Top Choices

Ocaña (p175) Stylish spot on pretty Plaça Reial with a beautifully designed interior.

Ginger (p174) An art-deco gem in the Barri Gòtic.

La Caseta del Migdia (p186) An open-air charmer, hidden in the thickets of Montjuïc.

Sor Rita (p174) Join festive crowds in a whimsical Almodóvar-esque world.

El Xampanyet (p178) Sip cava (sparkling wine) and munch on tapas in this garrulous icon in El Born.

Dry Martini (p182) This elegant drinking den serves perfect martinis and goldfish-bowl-sized gin and tonics.

🍷 La Rambla & Barri Gòtic

Ginger   Cocktail Bar

(Map p250; 📞93 310 53 09; www.ginger.cat; Carrer de Palma de Sant Just 1; ⏰7.30pm-2.30am Tue-Thu, to 3am Fri & Sat; Ⓜ Jaume I) Tucked away just off peaceful Plaça de Sant Just, Ginger is an art deco–style multilevel drinking den with low lighting, finely crafted cocktails and good ambient sounds (provided by vinyl-spinning DJs some nights). It's a mellow spot that's great for sipping wine and sampling from the gourmet tapas menu.

Marula Cafè   Bar

(Map p250; 📞93 318 76 90; www.marulacafe. com; Carrer dels Escudellers 49; ⏰11pm-6am Wed-Sun; Ⓜ Liceu) A fantastic find in the heart of the Barri Gòtic, Marula will transport you to the 1970s and the best in funk and soul. James Brown fans will think they've died and gone to heaven. It's not, however, a monothematic place and DJs slip in other tunes, from breakbeat to house. Samba and other Brazilian dance sounds also penetrate here.

Sor Rita   Bar

(Map p250; 📞93 176 62 66; www.sorritabar.es; Carrer de la Mercè 27; ⏰7pm-3am Sun-Thu, to 3.30am Fri & Sat; 📶; Ⓜ Jaume I) A lover of all things kitsch, Sor Rita is pure eye candy, from its leopard-print wallpaper to its high-heel-festooned ceiling and deliciously irreverent decorations inspired by the films of Almodóvar. It's a fun and festive scene, with special-event nights including tarot readings on Mondays, €5 all-you-can-eat snack buffets on Tuesdays, karaoke or cabaret on Wednesdays and gin specials on Thursdays.

L'Ascensor   Bar

(Map p250; 📞93 318 53 47; Carrer de la Bellafila 3; ⏰6pm-2.30am Sun-Thu, to 3am Fri & Sat; 📶; Ⓜ Jaume I) Named after the lift (elevator) doors that serve as the front door, this elegant drinking den with its vaulted brick ceilings, vintage mirrors and marble-topped bar gathers a faithful crowd that comes for old-fashioned cocktails and lively conversation against a soundtrack of up-tempo jazz and funk.

A bar in El Born

STEFANO POLITI MARKOVINA/GETTY IMAGES ©

Karma
Club

(Map p250; ☑93 302 56 80; www.karmadisco.
com; Plaça Reial 10; ⊘6pm-5.30am; ⓂLiceu)
During the week Karma plays good, mainstream indie music, while on weekends
the DJs spin anything from rock to disco. A
golden oldie in Barcelona, tunnel-shaped
Karma is small and becomes quite tightly
packed (claustrophobic for some) with a
good-natured crowd of locals and out-of-
towners. The bar and terrace on the Plaça
Reial open at 6pm, and the club opens at
midnight.

Ocaña
Bar

(Map p250; ☑93 676 48 14; www.ocana.cat;
Plaça Reial 13; ⊘noon-2.30am Mon-Fri, 11am-
2.30am Sat & Sun; 🛜; ⓂLiceu) Named after a
flamboyant artist who once lived on Plaça
Reial, Ocaña is a beautifully designed space
with chandeliers and plush furnishings.
Have a seat on the terrace and watch the
passing people parade, or head downstairs
to the Moorish-inspired Apotheke bar or
the chic lounge a few steps away, where
DJs spin for a mix of beauties and bohemi-
ans on weekend nights.

La Macarena
Club

(Map p250; ☑637 416647; www.macarenaclub.
com; Carrer Nou de Sant Francesc 5; €5-10;
⊘midnight-5am Sun-Thu, to 6am Fri & Sat;
ⓂDrassanes) You won't believe this was
once a tile-lined Andalucian flamenco
musos' bar. Now it is a dark dance space, of
the kind where it is possible to sit at the bar,
meet people around you and then stand
up for a bit of a shake to the DJ's electro
and house offerings, all within a couple of
square metres.

La Cerveteca
Bar

(Map p250; www.lacerveteca.com; Carrer d'en
Gignàs 25; ⊘6pm-midnight Tue-Fri, noon-3.30pm
& 6pm-midnight Sat, noon-3.30pm Sun; ⓂJaume
I) An unmissable stop for beer lovers, La
Cerveteca serves an impressive variety of
global craft brews. In addition to scores of
bottled beers, there's a frequent rotation of
draught beers. Cheeses, *jamón ibérico* and

🔭 Drinks with a View

Barcelona has a handful of rooftop bars
and hillside drinking spaces that provide
an enchanting view over the city. Depending on the neighbourhood, the vis-
ta may take in the rooftops of the Ciutat
Vella (Old City), the curving beachfront,
or the entire expanse of the city centre
with the Collserola Hills and Tibidabo
in the distance. Most of these drinking
spots are perched atop high-end hotels,
but are not solely the domain of visiting
foreigners. An increasing number of
style-minded *barcelonins* (people of
Barcelona) are drawn to these spaces.
Late in the evening you'll find a mostly
local crowd.

A few top picks:
Barceló Raval (☑93 320 14 90; www.
barceloraval.com; Rambla del Raval 17-21; r
from €128; ❄🛜; ⓂLiceu) Boasts dramatic
360-degree views from its rooftop
terrace; its location in Raval makes it
a good place to start off the evening
before heading to nearby nightspots.

La Isabala (☑93 552 95 52; www.hotel
1898.com; La Rambla 109; d €235; ❄🛜❄;
ⓂLiceu) On the 7th-floor terrace of Hotel
1898, this handsomely designed summertime spot is a peaceful oasis from
La Rambla down below.

Mirablau (p189) At the foot of Tibidabo,
this open-air spot is a city icon, famous
for its unrivalled views over the city.

La Caseta del Migdia (p186) Open-air
space on Montjuïc.

★ **Tapas & Tipples**

Planning a big night out ? Wherever you end up, keep in mind that eating and drinking go hand in hand in Barcelona, and some of the liveliest bars serve up as many tapas as they do alcoholic tipples.

From left: Tapas and beer; Waiter pouring sparkling wine; La Confitería

other charcuterie selections are on hand, including *cecina* (cured horse meat).

The standing cask tables (with a few seats at the back) are a fine setting to an early evening pick-me-up.

Manchester   Bar

(Map p250; www.manchesterbar.com; Carrer de Milans 5; ⏱6.30pm-2.30am Sun-Thu, to 3am Fri & Sat; 🛜; Ⓜ Liceu) A drinking den that has undergone several transformations over the years now treats you to the sounds of great Manchester bands, from Joy Division to Oasis, but probably not the Hollies. It has a pleasing rough-and-tumble feel, with tables jammed in every which way. There are DJs on Thursdays.

Polaroid   Bar

(Map p250; ☑93 186 66 69; www.polaroidbar.es; Carrer dels Còdols 29; ⏱7pm-2.30am Sun-Thu, to 3am Fri & Sat; Ⓜ Drassanes) For a dash of 1980s nostalgia, Polaroid is a blast from the past, with its wall-mounted VHS tapes, old film posters, comic-book-covered tables, action-figure displays and other kitschy decor. Not surprisingly, it draws a fun, unpretentious crowd who comes for cheap

cañas (draught beer), mojitos and free popcorn.

🍷 El Raval

La Confitería   Bar

(Map p256; Carrer de Sant Pau 128; ⏱7.30pm-2.30am Mon-Thu, 6pm-3.30am Fri, 5pm-3.30am Sat, 12.45pm-2.45am Sun; Ⓜ Paral·lel) This is a trip into the 19th century. Until the 1980s it was a confectioner's shop, and although the original cabinets are now lined with booze, the look of the place barely changed with its conversion into a laid-back bar. A quiet enough spot for a house *vermut* (vermouth; €3; add your own soda) in the early evening.

Boadas   Cocktail Bar

(Map p250; www.boadascocktails.com; Carrer dels Tallers 1; ⏱noon-2am Mon-Thu, to 3am Fri & Sat; Ⓜ Catalunya) One of the city's oldest cocktail bars, Boadas is famed for its daiquiris. Bow-tied waiters have been serving up unique, drinkable creations since Miguel Boadas opened it in 1933 – in fact Miró

and Hemingway both drank here. Miguel was born in Havana, where he was the first barman at the immortal La Floridita.

Moog   Club

(Map p250; www.masimas.com/moog; Carrer de l'Arc del Teatre 3; ⏱midnight-5am Mon-Thu & Sun, to 6am Fri & Sat; MDrassanes) This fun and minuscule club is a standing favourite with the downtown crowd. In the main dance area, DJs dish out house, techno and electro, while upstairs you can groove to a nice blend of indie and occasional classic-pop throwbacks. Admission is €5.

Negroni   Cocktail Bar

(Map p249; www.negronicocktailbar.com; Carrer de Joaquín Costa 46; ⏱7pm-2.30am Mon-Thu, to 3am Fri & Sat; MUniversitat) Good things come in small packages and this dark, teeny cocktail bar confirms the rule. The mostly black decor lures in a largely student set to try out the cocktails, among them, of course, the celebrated negroni, a Florentine invention with one part Campari, one part gin and one part sweet vermouth.

Bar La Concha   Bar, Gay

(Map p250; http://laconchadelraval.com; Carrer de la Guàrdia 14; ⏱5pm-2am; MDrassanes) This place is dedicated to the worshipping of the actress Sara Montiel: the walls groan with more than 250 photos of the sultry star. La Concha used to be a largely gay and trans-vestite haunt, but anyone is welcome and bound to have fun – especially when the drag queens come out to play. Moroccan ownership means you're also likely to see belly dancing.

33|45   Bar

(Map p249; Carrer de Joaquín Costa 4; ⏱4pm-2am Mon-Thu, to 3am Fri & Sat, to 1.30am Sun; 🛜; MUniversitat) A super-trendy bar on a street that's not short of them, this place has excellent mojitos – even pink and strawberry ones – and a fashionable crowd. The main area has DJ music and lots of excited noise-making, while the back room is scattered with sofas and armchairs for a post-dancing slump. On occasional Sundays the venue has lunchtime live gigs.

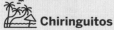 **Chiringuitos**

During summer small wooden beach bars, affectionately known as *chiringuitos*, open up along the strand, from Barceloneta all the way up to Platja de la Nova Mar Bella. Here you can dip your toes in the sand and nurse a cocktail while watching the city at play against the backdrop of the deep-blue Mediterranean. Ambient grooves add to the laid-back environment. *Chiringuitos* are also great spots for a snack – particularly the **Guingueta de la Barceloneta** (Platja de Sant Sebastià; sandwiches €6-12; ⊙9am-midnight Mar-Nov; ⓂBarceloneta) and Guingueta del Bogatell (p182) run by Michelin-starred chef Carles Abellan. The drink of choice at either is a refreshing *cava* (sparkling wine) sangría.
One of the liveliest beachside bars lies northeast of the city on Cavaió beach in Arenys de Mar (accessible from Barcelona by train). **Lasal** (www.lasal.com) hosts top-notch DJs and has a tropical-themed party atmosphere. It opens daily from mid-May to September.

Bar Marsella Bar

(Map p250; ☎93 442 72 63; Carrer de Sant Pau 65; ⊙10pm-2.30am Mon-Thu, to 3am Fri & Sat; ⓂLiceu) This bar has been in business since 1820, and has served the likes of Hemingway, who was known to slump here over an *absenta* (absinthe). The bar still specialises in absinthe, a drink to be treated with respect.

Betty Ford's Bar

(Map p249; www.bettyfords.es; Carrer de Joaquín Costa 56; ⊙5pm-3am Sat-Tue, 1pm-3am Wed-Fri; ⓂUniversitat) This enticing corner bar is one of several good stops along the student-jammed run of Carrer de Joaquín Costa. It puts together some nice cocktails and the place fills with an even mix of locals and foreigners, generally aged not much over 30. There's a decent line in burgers and soups, too.

Bar Pastís Bar

(Map p250; www.barpastis.com; Carrer de Santa Mònica 4; ⊙7.30pm-2am; ⓂDrassanes) A French cabaret theme (with lots of Piaf in the background) dominates this tiny, cluttered classic. It's been going, on and off, since the end of WWII. You'll need to be in here before 9pm to have any hope of sitting, getting near the bar or anything much else. On some nights it features live acts, usually performing French chansons.

🍷 La Ribera

El Xampanyet Wine Bar

(Map p250; ☎93 319 70 03; Carrer de Montcada 22; ⊙noon-4pm & 7-11pm Tue-Sat, noon-4pm Sun; ⓂJaume I) Nothing has changed for decades in this, one of the city's best-known *cava* bars. Plant yourself at the bar or seek out a table against the decoratively tiled walls for a glass or three of the cheap house *cava* and an assortment of tapas, such as the tangy *boquerones en vinagre* (fresh anchovies in vinegar).

Juanra Falces Cocktail Bar

(Map p250; ☎93 310 10 27; Carrer del Rec 24; ⊙8pm-3am Tue-Sat, 10pm-3am Sun & Mon; ⓂJaume I) Transport yourself to a Humphrey Bogart movie in this narrow little bar, formerly (and still, at least among the locals) known as Gimlet. White-jacketed bar staff with all the appropriate aplomb will whip you up a gimlet or any other classic cocktail (around €10) that your heart desires.

La Vinya del Senyor · Wine Bar

(Map p250; ☎93 310 33 79; Plaça de Santa Maria del Mar 5; ☺noon-1am Mon-Thu, to 2am Fri & Sat, to midnight Sun; 🛜; ⓂJaume I) Relax on the terrace, which lies in the shadow of the Basílica de Santa Maria del Mar, or crowd inside at the tiny bar. The wine list is as long as *War and Peace* and there's a table upstairs for those who opt to sample by the bottle rather than the glass.

Guzzo · Cocktail Bar

(Map p250; ☎93 667 00 36; www.guzzo.es; Plaça Comercial 10; ☺6pm-3am Tue-Thu, to 3.30am Fri & Sat, noon-3am Sun; 🛜; ⓂBarceloneta) A swish but relaxed cocktail bar, run by much-loved Barcelona DJ Fred Guzzo, who is often to be found at the decks, spinning his delicious selection of funk, soul and rare groove. You'll also find frequent live-music acts of consistently decent quality, and a funky atmosphere at almost any time of day.

Magic · Club

(Map p250; ☎93 310 72 67; www.magic-club.net; Passeig de Picasso 40; ☺11pm-6am Thu-Sun; ⓂBarceloneta) Although it sometimes hosts live acts in its sweaty, smoky basement, Magic is basically a straightforward, subterranean nightclub offering rock, mainstream dance faves and Spanish pop.

Rubí · Bar

(Map p250; ☎647 773707; Carrer dels Banys Vells 6; ☺7.30pm-2.30am Sun-Thu, to 3am Fri & Sat; ⓂJaume I) With its boudoir lighting and cheap mojitos, Rubí is where the Born's cognoscenti head for a nightcap – or several. It's a narrow, cosy space – push through to the back where you might just get one of the coveted tables, with superior bar food, from Vietnamese rolls to more traditional selections of cheese and ham.

Miramelindo · Bar

(Map p250; ☎93 310 37 27; www.barmiramelindo bcn.com; Passeig del Born 15; ☺8pm-2am; 🛜; ⓂJaume I) A spacious tavern in a Gothic building, this remains a classic on Passeig

> *a French cabaret theme dominates this tiny, cluttered classic*

Bar Pastís

del Born for mixed drinks, while soft jazz and soul sounds float overhead. Try for a comfy seat at a table towards the back before it fills to bursting. A couple of similarly barn-sized places sit on this side of the *passeig*.

🍷 Barceloneta & the Waterfront

Absenta   Bar
(www.absentabar.es; Carrer de Sant Carles 36; ⊙7pm-1am Tue & Wed, from 11am Thu-Mon; MBarceloneta) Decorated with old paintings, vintage lamps and curious sculpture (including a dangling butterfly woman and face-painted TVs), this whimsical and creative drinking den takes its liquor seriously. Stop in for the house-made vermouth or for more bite try one of the many absinthes on hand. Just go easy: with an alcohol content of 50% to 90%, these spirits have kick!

Can Paixano   Wine Bar
(Map p250; ☎93 310 08 39; Carrer de la Reina Cristina 7; ⊙9am-10.30pm Mon-Sat; MBarceloneta) This lofty old champagne bar (also called La Xampanyeria) has long been run on a winning formula. The standard poison is bubbly rosé in elegant little glasses, combined with bite-sized *bocadillos* (filled rolls) and tapas (€3 to €7). Note that this place is usually jammed to the rafters, and elbowing your way to the bar can be a titanic struggle.

BlackLab   Microbrewery
(Map p250; ☎93 221 83 60; www.blacklab.es; Plaça Pau Vila 1; ⊙noon-1.30am; MBarceloneta) Inside the historic Palau de Mar, BlackLab was Barcelona's first brewhouse to open way back in 2014. With 20 taps (including 18 housemade brews, including *saisons*, double IPAs and dry stouts), it's an impressive operation, and the brewmasters are constantly experimenting with new flavours.

There's plenty to eat: burgers and barbecue pulled pork as well as Asian dishes:

A Barceloneta beach bar

bahn mì (Vietnamese sandwiches), vegie dumplings and braised oxtail ramen.

BlackLab also runs tasting tours (currently on Sundays at 5pm), where you'll get a behind-the-scenes look at the brewers in action.

Edge Brewing — Brewery

(edgebrewing.com; Carrer de Llull 62; tours including beer tastings €20; ⊘tours by appointment; Ⓜ Bogatell) Founded by two Americans back in 2013, Edge Brewing has already racked up some impressive awards for its craft beers (among other things it was named top new brewer in the world in 2014 by RateBeer.com). On a brewery tour, you'll get a behind-the-scenes look at Edge's operations, and get to taste some of its classic (like the Hoptimista, an award-winning 6.6% IPA) and seasonal brews (the summertime Apassionada is a passionfruit sour ale).

Check the website for upcoming tours and other events, including 'members' nights in the tasting room (though you can become a member just by signing up online).

Balius — Cocktail Bar

(☑93 315 86 50; www.facebook.com/BaliusBar; Carrer de Pujades 196; ⊘5pm-1am Tue-Fri, from 1pm Sat & Sun; Ⓜ Poblenou) There's an old-fashioned jauntiness to this vintage cocktail den in Poblenou. Friendly barkeeps pour a fair mix of classic libations as well as vermouths, and there's a small tapas menu. Stop by on Sundays to catch live jazz, starting around 7.30pm.

The Mint — Cocktail Bar

(Map p250; ☑647 737707; Passeig d'Isabel II, 4; ⊘7.30pm-2.30am; Ⓜ Barceloneta) Named after the prized cocktail ingredients, this mojito-loving drinkery has a little something for everyone. Linger upstairs with the grown-ups to peruse the first-rate house-infused gins (over 20 on hand, including creative blends like lemongrass and Jamaican pepper), or head downstairs with

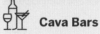

Cava Bars

Cava bars tend to be more about the festive ambience than the actual drinking of *cava*, a sparkling white or rosé, most of which is produced in Catalonia's Penedès region. At the more famous *cava* bars you'll have to nudge your way through the garrulous crowds and enjoy your bubbly standing up. Two of the most famous cava bars are El Xampanyet (p178) in La Ribera and Can Paixano (p180) in Barceloneta.

the kids to the brick-vaulted cellars, where red lights and driving beats create a more celebratory vibe.

It's a fun setting for a night out, and well-located for a bar-hop through El Born before or after.

La Cervecita Nuestra de Cada Día — Bar

(Carrer de Llull 184; ⊘5.30-9.30pm Sun & Mon, 11.30am-2pm & 5.30-9.30pm Tue-Sat; Ⓜ Llacuna) Equal parts beer shop and craft brew bar, La Cervicita has a changing selection of unique beers from around Europe and the USA. You might stumble across a Catalan sour fruit beer, a rare English stout, a potent Belgian triple ale or half a dozen other drafts on hand – plus many more varieties by the bottle.

Low-playing music and minimal decorations keep the focus on beer chatter.

Madame George
Lounge

(www.madamegeorgebar.com; Carrer de Pujades 179; ⏰7pm-1am Sun-Thu, to 3am Fri & Sat; Ⓜ️Poblenou) A theatrical (veering towards campy) elegance marks the interior of this small, chandelier-lit lounge just off the Rambla del Poblenou. Deft bartenders stir up nicely balanced cocktails to a friendly, eclectic crowd, while off in the corner a DJ spins vintage soul and funk (bonus points for using vinyl).

Santa Marta
Bar

(Carrer de Guitert 60; ⏰11am-11pm; 🚌45, 57, 59, 157, Ⓜ️Barceloneta) This chilled bar set just back from the beach attracts a garrulous mix of locals and expats, who come for light meals, beers and prime people-watching at one of the outdoor tables near the boardwalk. It has some tempting food too: a mix of local and Italian items, with a range of satisfying sandwiches.

Guingueta del Bogatell
Bar

(Platja del Bogatell; ⏰9am-10.30pm May-Sep) At this summertime spot, you can dig your feet in the sand and enjoy a cold brew while watching the lapping waves.

CDLC
Lounge

(📞93 224 04 70; www.cdlcbarcelona.com; Passeig Marítim de la Barceloneta 32; ⏰noon-4am; Ⓜ️Ciutadella Vila Olímpica) Seize the night by the scruff at the Carpe Diem Lounge Club, where you can lounge in Asian-inspired surrounds. Ideal for a slow warm-up before heading to the nearby clubs. You can come for the food (quite good, but pricey) or wait until about midnight, when the tables are rolled away and the DJs and dancers take full control.

🍷 La Sagrada Família & L'Eixample

Dry Martini
Bar

(📞93 217 50 80; www.drymartiniorg.com; Carrer d'Aribau 162-166; ⏰1pm-2.30am Mon-Thu, 6pm-3am Fri & Sat, 7pm-2.30am Sun; Ⓜ️Diagonal) Waiters with a discreetly knowing smile will attend to your cocktail needs and make uncannily good suggestions, but the house drink, taken at the bar or in one of the plush green leather banquettes, is a safe bet. The gin and tonic comes in an enormous

From left: Mercat de la Boqueria (p90); El Xampanyet (p178); Bar Marsella (p178)

mug-sized glass – one will take you most of the night.

Out the back is a superb if pricey restaurant, **Speakeasy** (93 217 50 80; www.speakeasy-bcn.com; mains €22-28; 1-4pm & 8pm-midnight Mon-Sat; Diagonal).

Monvínic — Wine Bar

(Map p254; 93 272 61 87; www.monvinic.com; Carrer de la Diputació 249; 1-11pm Tue-Fri, 7-11pm Mon & Sat; Passeig de Gràcia) Apparently considered unmissable by El Bulli's sommelier, Monvínic is an ode, a rhapsody even, to wine loving. The interactive wine list sits on the bar for you to browse, on a digital tablet similar to an iPad, and boasts more than 3000 varieties.

But that's not to say that it's for connoisseurs only; enthusiasts can also come here to taste wine by the glass – there are 60 selections. You can search by origin, year or grape, from a vast international range. Prices start at €3.50 for a glass of Albariño, and go up – and you can, of course, order by the bottle too. There is an emphasis on affordability, but if you want to splash out, there are fantastic vintage wines. Feel free to talk to one of the six sommeliers who work on the list. At the back is the restaurant, which specialises in Mediterranean cuisine, with ingredients that are sourced locally from Catalan farmers.

Quilombo — Bar

(93 439 54 06; Carrer d'Aribau 149; 9.30pm-2.30am Wed-Sun; FGC Provença) Some formulas just work, and this place has been working since the 1970s. Set up a few guitars in the back room, which you pack with tables and chairs, add some cheapish pre-prepared mojitos and plastic tubs of nuts, and let the punters do the rest. They pour in, creating plenty of *quilombo* (fuss).

Antilla BCN — Club

(Map p249; 93 451 45 64; www.antillasalsa.com; Carrer d'Aragó 141; Wed-Thu free, Fri & Sat €10; 10pm-5am Wed, 11pm-5am Thu, 11pm-6am Fri & Sat, 7pm-5am Sun; Urgell) Known as *the salsateca* in town, this is the place to come for Cuban *son*, merengue, salsa and a whole lot more. There are dance classes from around 8pm or 9pm from Tuesday to Friday. Check www.antillaescueladesalsa.com for details.

MATT MUNRO/LONELY PLANET ©

Barcelona in a Glass

400 ml fresh
orange juice

100ml fresh
lemon juice

Add sugar (optional) to
taste, plus ice

Add a good splash
of orange liqueur

Some sliced
fresh fruit

Top up with a
bottle of *cava*

BONCHAN/GETTY IMAGES ©

Salut! Sangría de Cava

A Golden Drop

The refreshing summery blend of wine, fruit, sugar and a dash of something harder is given a twist in Catalonia by using local sparkling wine, *cava*, instead of cheap red. Sangría originated as a colonial drink in Latin America, adding an appealing freshness to wine in the steamy climate. Though its name refers to the colour of blood *(sangre)*, the *cava* version is a light golden hue. *¡Salud!*

★ Where to drink Sangría de Cava

Tapas 24 (p140)

Xiringuito D'Escribà (☎93 221 07 29; www.xiringuitoescriba.com; Ronda del Litoral 42; mains €18-32; ⊙1-4.30pm year-round, 8pm-midnight Thu-Sat Apr-Sep; ⓂLlacuna) One of Barcelona's most popular waterfront seafood eateries, this is a fine spot for a drink, too.

Cerveseria Catalana (Map p254; ☎93 216 03 68; Carrer de Mallorca 236; tapas €4-11; ⊙8am-1.30am Mon-Fri, 9am-1.30am Sat & Sun; ⓂPasseig de Gràcia) At the 'Catalan Brewery', you can sit at the bar, on the pavement terrace or in the restaurant at the back. The variety of hot tapas, salads and other snacks draws a well-dressed crowd of locals and outsiders, making it a good spot for people-watching as you sip a sangría de *cava*.

FUNKYFROGSTOCK/GETTY IMAGES ©

Les Gens Que J'Aime
Bar

(Map p254; ☑93 215 68 79; www.lesgensque jaime.com; Carrer de València 286; ⊙6pm-2.30am Sun-Thu, 7pm-3am Fri & Sat; Ⓜ️Passeig de Gràcia) This intimate basement relic of the 1960s follows a deceptively simple formula: chilled jazz music in the background, minimal lighting from an assortment of flea-market lamps and a cosy, cramped scattering of red-velvet-backed lounges around tiny dark tables.

Milano
Cocktail Bar

(Map p254; ☑93 112 71 50; www.camparimilano. com; Ronda de la Universitat 35; ⊙noon-2.30am Mon-Sat, 6pm-2.30am Sun; Ⓜ️Catalunya) An absolute gem of hidden Barcelona nightlife, Milano is a subterranean old-school cocktail bar with velvet banquettes and glass-fronted cabinets, presided over by white-jacketed waiters, and completely invisible from street level. Check the website for details on occasional live music.

Napar BCN
Brewery

(Map p254; ☑606 546467; www.naparbcn.com; Carrer de la Diputació 223; ⊙noon-midnight Tue-Thu, to 2am Fri & Sat, noon-5pm Sun; 🛜; Ⓜ️Universitat) The latest bar to open as part of Barcelona's burgeoning craft-beer scene, Napar has 12 beers on tap, six of which are brewed on-site, including a mix of IPAs, pale ale and stout. There's also an accomplished list of bottled beers. It's a stunning space, with a gleaming steampunk aesthetic, and serves some excellent food should hunger strike.

Michael Collins Pub
Pub

(Map p254; ☑93 459 19 64; www.michaelcollins pubs.com; Plaça de la Sagrada Família 4; ⊙1pm-2.30am Sun-Thu, to 3am Fri & Sat; 🛜; Ⓜ️Sagrada Família) Locals and expats alike patronise this place, one of the city's best-loved Irish pubs. To be sure of a little Catalan-Irish *craic*, this barn-sized pub is just the ticket. It's ideal for football fans wanting big-screen action over their pints, too.

⚣ The Gaixample

Barcelona has a vibrant LGBT scene, with a fine array of restaurants, bars and clubs in the the 'Gaixample' (a conjoining of Gay and L'Eixample), an area southwest of Passeig de Gràcia around Carrer del Consell de Cent.

City Hall
Club

(Map p254; ☑93 238 07 22; www.cityhallbarce lona.com; Rambla de Catalunya 2-4; €10-15, incl 1 drink; ⊙midnight-5am Wed & Thu, midnight-6am Fri & Sat, 11pm-5am Sun; Ⓜ️Catalunya) A long corridor leads to the dance floor of this venerable and popular club, located in a former theatre. House and other electric sounds dominate, with occasional funk nights, and – on Sundays – a gay night, Black Room. Check the website for details.

Aire
Lesbian

(Sala Diana; Map p254; ☑93 487 83 42; www. grupoarena.com; Carrer de la Diputació 233; Thu free, Fri €5, Sat €6; ⊙11pm-2.30am Thu-Sat; Ⓜ️Passeig de Gràcia) A popular locale for lesbians; here the dance floor is spacious and there is usually a DJ in command of the tunes, which range from hits of the '80s and '90s to Latin and techno. As a rule, only male friends of the girls are allowed entry, although in practice the crowd tends to be fairly mixed.

Arena Classic
Gay

(Map p254; ☑93 487 83 42; www.grupoarena. com; Carrer de la Diputació 233; Fri €6, Sat €12; ⊙2.30-5.30am Fri & Sat; Ⓜ️Passeig de Gràcia) Arena Classic attracts a mixed gay crowd that tends not to get too wild. The dominant sound at this club is handbag, and the vibe joyfully cheesy.

Arena Madre
Gay

(Map p254; ☑93 487 83 42; www.grupoarena. com; Carrer de Balmes 32; Sun-Fri €6, Sat €12; ⊙12.30-5am; Ⓜ️Passeig de Gràcia) Popular with a hot young crowd, Arena Madre is one of the top clubs in town for boys who are seeking boys. Mainly electronic and house, with a striptease show on Monday, handbag on Thursday, and live shows throughout the week. Heteros are welcome but a minority.

🍷 Montjuïc, Poble Sec & Sant Antoni

La Caseta del Migdia   Bar
(📞617 956572; www.lacaseta.org; Mirador del Migdia; ⏰8pm-1am Wed-Fri, from noon Sat & Sun, weekends only in winter; 🚌150) The effort of getting to what is, for all intents and purposes, a simple *chiringuito* (makeshift cafe-bar) is worth it. Stare out to sea over a beer or coffee by day. As sunset approaches the atmosphere changes, as lounge music (from samba to funk) wafts out over the hillside. Drinks aside, you can also order barbecue, fired up on the outdoor grills.

Walk below the walls of the Castell de Montjuïc along the dirt track or follow Passeig del Migdia – watch out for signs for the Mirador del Migdia.

El Rouge   Bar
(Map p256; 📞666 251556; Carrer del Poeta Cabanyes 21; ⏰11pm-2am Mon, 8pm-2am Tue & Thu, 10pm-3am Fri & Sat; 🛜; Ⓜ Poble Sec) Decadence is the word that springs to mind in this bordello-red lounge-cocktail bar, with acid jazz, drum and bass and other sounds drifting along in the background. The walls are laden with heavy-framed paintings, dim lamps and mirrors, and no two chairs are alike. You can sometimes catch DJs, risqué poetry soirées, cabaret shows or even nights of tango dancing.

Bar Calders   Bar
(Map p256; 📞93 329 93 49; Carrer del Parlament 25; ⏰5pm-2am Mon-Fri, 11am-2.30am Sat, 11am-midnight Sun; Ⓜ Sant Antoni) It bills itself as a wine bar, but actually the wine selection at Bar Calders is its weak point. As an all-day cafe and tapas bar, however, it's unbeatable, with a few tables outside on a tiny pedestrian lane, and has become the favoured meeting point for the neighbourhood's boho element.

Bar Olimpia   Bar
(Map p256; 📞606 200800; Carrer d'Aldana 11; ⏰7pm-1am Wed & Thu, to 2.30am Fri & Sat, 6-11pm Sun) This great little neighborhood bar is a little slice of Barcelona history. It was here (and on the surrounding block), where the popular Olimpia Theatre Circus once performed way back in the 1930s. Today the vaguely retro bar draws a diverse crowd, who come for house-made vermouth, snacks (like quesadillas, cheese plates, tuna tartare), and satisfying gin and tonics.

Plataforma   Club
(Map p256; 📞93 329 00 29; Carrer Nou de la Rambla 145; €6-12; ⏰10pm-6am Thu-Sat, 7pm-2am Sun; Ⓜ Paral.lel) With two adjoining if smallish dance spaces, 'Platform' has the sense of a slightly clandestine location in an otherwise quiet residential street. Inside this friendly, straightforward dance dive, far from the glitzy Ibiza look, you'll find popular '80s grooves, timeless rock and occasional nights of live bands, plus drum and bass that attract nostalgics in their 30s and younger partiers.

Pervert Club   Club
(Map p256; Avinguda Francesc Ferrer i Guàrdia 13, Poble Espanyol; €18; ⏰midnight-6am Sat; Ⓜ Espanya) This weekly fete takes place at The One club in Poble Espanyol. Electronic music dominates, and, in spite of the 6am finish, for many this is only the start of the 'evening'. Expect loads of tanned and buff gym bunnies – and plenty of topless eye candy.

Tinta Roja   Bar
(Map p256; 📞93 443 32 43; www.tintaroja.cat; Carrer de la Creu dels Molers 17; ⏰8.30pm-1am Wed, to 2am Thu, to 3am Fri & Sat; Ⓜ Poble Sec) A succession of nooks and crannies, dotted with flea-market finds and dimly lit in violets, reds and yellows, makes Tinta Roja an intimate spot for a drink and the occasional show in the back – with anything from actors to acrobats. This was once a

vaqueria (small dairy farm), where they kept cows out the back and sold fresh milk at the front.

La Terrrazza   Club

(Map p256; ✆687 969825; www.laterrrazza.com; Avinguda de Francesc Ferrer i Guàrdia; €15-20; ⊘12.30am-6am Thu-Sat, closed Oct-Apr; MEspanya) One of the city's top summertime dance locations, La Terrrazza attracts squadrons of beautiful people, locals and foreigners alike, for a full-on night of music and cocktails partly under the stars inside the Poble Espanyol complex.

Metro   Gay

(Map p249; ✆93 323 52 27; www.metrodisco bcn.com; Carrer de Sepúlveda 185; before 2am from €6, after 2am €20; ⊘12.15am-5.30am; MUniversitat) Metro attracts a casual gay crowd with its two dance floors, three bars and very dark room. Keep an eye out for shows and parties, which can range from parades of models to bingo nights (on Thursday nights, with sometimes-interesting prizes), plus the occasional striptease.

To save cash, come before 2am, though you're likely to be drinking all by your lonesome, as Metro doesn't fill up till late.

🍷 Gràcia & Park Güell

Rabipelao   Cocktail Bar

(Map p254; ✆93 182 50 35; www.elrabipelao.com; Carrer del Torrent d'En Vidalet 22; ⊘7pm-2am Mon-Sat, 1-4pm & 7pm-2am Sun; MJoanic, Fontana) An anchor of Gràcia's nightlife, Rabipelao is a celebratory space with a spinning disco ball and DJs spinning driving salsa beats. Patrons aside, there's much to look at here: a silent film plays in one corner beyond the red velvety wallpaper-covered walls and there's a richly hued mural above the bar – not to mention the tropical cocktails (mojitos and caipirinhas) and snacks (*arepas*, ceviche).

There's also a covered patio at the back, and live music from time to time (currently Wednesdays from 8pm).

🍷 Out to the Discoteca

Barcelona's *discotecas* (clubs) are at their best from Thursday to Saturday. Indeed, many open only on these nights. A surprising variety of spots lurk in the old-town labyrinth, ranging from plush former dance halls to grungy subterranean venues that fill to capacity.

Along the waterfront it's another story. At Port Olímpic, sun-scorched crowds of visiting yachties mix it up with tourists and a few locals at noisy, back-to-back dance bars right on the waterfront. The best spots are over on La Barceloneta side.

A sprinkling of well-known clubs is spread over the classy parts of town, in L'Eixample and La Zona Alta. As a rule of thumb they attract a beautiful crowd.

Port Olímpic
IAKOV FILIMONOV/SHUTTERSTOCK ©

Viblioteca   Wine Bar

(Map p254; ✆93 284 42 02; www.viblioteca.com; Carrer de Vallfogona 12; ⊘6pm-1am Mon-Sat, 7pm-midnight Sun; MFontana) If the smell of ripe cheese doesn't rock your boat, this is not the place for you – a glass cabinet piled high with the stuff assaults your olfactory nerves as you walk into this small, white, cleverly designed space. The real speciality at Viblioteca, however, is wine, and you can choose from 150 mostly local labels, many of them available by the glass.

Elephanta   Bar

(Map p254; ✆93 237 69 06; http://elephanta.cat; Carrer del Torrent d'en Vidalet 37; ⊘6pm-1.30am Mon-Wed, to 2.30am Thu-Sat, 5-10pm Sun;

WESTEND61/GETTY IMAGES ©

Ⓜ Joanic, Fontana) This friendly and petite cocktail bar is a fine place to catch up with a friend. It has an old-fashioned vibe, with long plush green banquettes and art-lined walls. The five-seat bar is complemented by old vintage wooden stools.

Gin is the drink of choice, with more than 40 varieties on hand, and the cocktails are deftly mixed (though be patient, these things take time).

Raïm
Bar

(Map p254; Carrer del Progrés 48; ⏰ 9pm-2am Tue-Sat; Ⓜ Diagonal) The walls in Raïm are alive with black-and-white photos of Cubans and Cuba. Weathered old wooden chairs of another epoch huddle around marble tables, while grand old wood-framed mirrors hang from the walls. It draws a friendly, garrulous crowd who pile in for first-rate mojitos and an excellent selection of rums.

El Sabor
Bar

(Map p254; 📱 674 997073; Carrer de Francisco Giner 32; ⏰ 9pm-3am Tue-Sun; Ⓜ Diagonal) Ruled since 1992 by the charismatic

Havana-born Angelito is this home of *ron y son* (rum and sound). A mixed crowd of Cubans and fans of the Caribbean island come to drink mojitos and shake their stuff in this diminutive, good-humoured hang-out. Stop by on Thursdays for a free two-hour salsa lesson (starting at 9.30pm).

La Cigale
Bar

(Map p254; 📱 93 457 58 23; Carrer de Tordera 50; ⏰ 6pm-2am Tue-Sun; Ⓜ Joanic) La Cigale is a very civilised place for a cocktail, with oil paintings on the walls, gilded mirrors and leatherbound volumes scattered about. Prop up the zinc bar, sink into a secondhand lounge chair around a teeny table or head upstairs. Music is chilled, conversation lively, and you're likely to see Charlie Chaplin in action on the silent flat-screen TV (though FC Barça games are also screened). You can also snack on wok-fried dishes and some of the city's best burgers.

Musical Maria
Bar

(Map p254; 📱 93 501 04 60; Carrer de Maria 5; ⏰ 9pm-2.30am; 📶; Ⓜ Diagonal) Even the music hasn't changed since this place got going in the late 1970s. Those longing for rock 'n' roll crowd into this animated bar, listen to old hits and knock back beers. Out the back there's a pool table and the bar serves pretty much all the variants of the local Estrella Damm brew.

Chatelet   Cocktail Bar
(Map p254; ☑93 284 95 90; Carrer de Torrijos 54; ⊘6pm-2am Mon-Fri, noon-2am Sat & Sun; Ⓜ Joanic, Fontana) A popular meeting point in the 'hood, Chatelet has big windows for people-watching and a buzzing art-filled interior that sees a wide cross section of Gràcia society. Blues or old-school American soul plays in the background, while friends chatter over drinks and light fare (hummus, nachos, sandwiches). The cocktails are excellent, and the drink prices fair (with discounts before 10pm).

Alfa   Bar
(Map p254; ☑93 415 18 24; www.alfabar. cat; Carrer Gran de Gràcia 36; ⊘8pm-2.30am Tue-Sat; Ⓜ Diagonal) Aficionados of good old-fashioned rock love this unchanging bar-cum-minidisco, a Gràcia classic. Take up a stool for a drink and chat or head for the no-frills dance area (with 1980s and '90s hits in heavy rotation) just beyond. There's another bar right up the back.

Come on Thursdays for open-mic night (starts at 10pm), or catch up-and-coming local bands on Fridays and Saturdays.

⚐ Camp Nou, Pedralbes & La Zona Alta

El Maravillas   Cocktail Bar
(☑93 360 73 78; Plaça de la Concòrdia 15; ⊘noon-midnight Mon-Thu, to 2am Fri & Sat; Ⓜ Maria Cristina) Overlooking the peaceful Plaça de la Concòrdia, El Maravillas feels like a secret hideaway – especially if you've just arrived from the crowded lanes of the Ciutat Vella (Old City). The glittering bar has just a few tables, with outdoor seating when the weather warms. Creative cocktails, good Spanish red wines and easy-drinking vermouths are the drinks of choice.

Dō Bar   Bar
(☑93 209 18 88; www.do-bcn.com; Carrer de Santaló 30, entrance on l'Avenir; ⊘7pm-1am Mon-Thu, 8am-1am Fri & Sat; ⒭FGC Muntaner) This neighbourhood charmer has a warm and inviting interior, where friends gather over tall wooden tables to enjoy excellent gin and tonics, wines by the glass, craft beer and satisfying small plates (anchovies, mussels, tacos, charcuterie). On warm nights, arrive early for one of the terrace tables out the front.

Mirablau   Bar
(☑93 418 58 79; www.mirablaubcn.com; Plaça del Doctor Andreu; ⊘11am-4.30am Mon-Thu, 10am-4.30am Fri-Sun; ⒭FGC Avinguda Tibidabo) Gaze out over the entire city from this privileged balcony restaurant on the way up to Tibidabo. Wander downstairs to join the folk in the tiny dance space. In summer you can step out on to the even-smaller terrace for a breather.

Bikini   Club
(☑93 322 08 00; www.bikinibcn.com; Avinguda Diagonal 547; €10-25; ⊘midnight-6am Thu-Sat; �🚍6, 7, 33, 34, 63, 67, 68, Ⓜ Entença) This old star of the Barcelona nightlife scene has been keeping the beat since the darkest days of Franco. Every possible kind of music gets a run, from Latin and Brazilian beats to 1980s disco, depending on the night and the space you choose.

The Beer Shop   Bar
(☑93 250 84 28; www.thebeershop.es; Carrer d'Amigó 34; ⊘5-10.30pm Mon, 11am-10.30pm Tue & Wed, to 1am Thu-Sat, 11am-2.30pm Sun; 📶; ⒭FGC Muntaner) Equal parts beer shop and drinking space, this Sant Gervasi spot gathers beer lovers at all hours of the day. If you come to drink (rather than shop), you can grab a table out on the footpath or sit inside chatting with knowledgable staff while sampling a few of the rotating draughts available. Microbrews from Catalonia, England, Germany and the USA ensure wide variety.

Make the most of the experience by going for a tasting flight (six beers for €9).

SHOWTIME

See a flamenco performance,
catch a few bands or dance the night away

Showtime

From high culture to edgy backstreet performances, from opera to death metal, Barcelona teems with venues and stages hosting all manner of entertainment: underground cabaret, comic opera, contemplative drama. Dance companies are thick on the ground, and popular local theatre companies, when not touring the rest of Spain, keep folks strapped to their seats. It's a cultural city par excellence.

In This Section

Tickets & Websites

The easiest way to purchase tickets *(entradas)* for most venues throughout the city is through Ticketea (www.ticketea.com) or Ticketmaster (www.ticketmaster.es).

Guía del Ocio (www.guiadelociobcn.es) has ample listings for all forms of entertainment, as does Time Out (www.timeout.cat).

Good coverage of classical music can be found on www.classictic.com.

CHRISTIAN BERTRAND/SHUTTERSTOCK ©

Hinds, a Madrid-based band, play at the Heliogàbal club (p203)

The Best...

For Jazz

Harlem Jazz Club (p194) Not just jazz, but funk, blues, bossa nova and plenty more.

Jazz Sí Club (p196) Small, lively, cramped and never less than fun.

Jamboree (p194) Basement bar that's seen them all under its vaulted ceiling.

For Live Music

Heliogàbal (p203) A quirky bar where anything goes, from soulful singer-songwriters to pocket opera.

Music Hall (p199) The perfect midsize venue for up-and-coming local and international acts.

Sala Apolo (p200) Cosy booths and a warm red glow give this hugely popular venue something special.

BARTS (p200) The latest contender on the live-music circuit, with superb sound and every mod con.

☆ La Rambla & Barri Gòtic

Gran Teatre del Liceu
Theatre, Live Music

(Map p250; ☏93 485 99 00; www.liceubar celona.com; La Rambla 51-59; ⊙box office 9.30am-8pm Mon-Fri, to 6pm Sat & Sun; Ⓜ Liceu) Barcelona's grand old opera house, re- stored after fire in 1994, is one of the most technologically advanced theatres in the world. To take a seat in the grand audito- rium, returned to all its 19th-century glory but with the very latest in acoustics, is to be transported to another age.

Tickets can cost anything from €10 for a cheap seat behind a pillar to €200 for a well-positioned night at the opera.

L'Ateneu
Classical Music

(Map p250; ☏93 343 61 21; www.ateneubcn.org; Carrer de la Canuda 6; free-€10; Ⓜ Catalunya) This historic cultural centre (with roots dating back 150 years) hosts a range of high-brow fare, from classical recitals to film screenings and literary readings.

Jamboree
Live Music

(Map p250; ☏93 319 17 89; www.masimas.com/ jamboree; Plaça Reial 17; €12-20; ⊙8pm-6am; Ⓜ Liceu) For over half a century, Jambo- ree has been bringing joy to the jivers of Barcelona, with high-calibre acts featuring jazz trios, blues, Afrobeats, Latin sounds and big-band sounds. Two concerts are held most nights (at 8pm and 10pm), after which Jamboree morphs into a DJ-spinning club at midnight. WTF jam sessions are held Mondays (entrance a mere €5).

Buy tickets online to save a few euros.

Harlem Jazz Club
Jazz

(Map p250; ☏93 310 07 55; www.harlemjazz club.es; Carrer de la Comtessa de Sobradiel 8; €6-10; ⊙10.30pm-3am Sun & Tue-Thu, to 5am Fri & Sat; Ⓜ Liceu) This narrow, old-city dive is one of the best spots in town for jazz, as well as funk, Latin, blues and gypsy jazz. It attracts a mixed crowd who maintains a respectful silence during the acts. Most

> *this historic theatre has been transformed into a lavish concert space*

Teatre Principal

concerts start around 10pm. Get in early if you want a seat in front of the stage.

Sidecar Factory Club   Live Music
(Map p250; 93 302 15 86; www.sidecar factoryclub.com; Plaça Reial 7; varies; 7pm-5am Mon-Sat; Liceu) Its entrance is on Plaça Reial, and you can come here for a meal before midnight or a few drinks at ground level (which closes by 3am at the latest), or descend into the red-tinged, brick-vaulted bowels for live music most nights. Just about anything goes here, from UK indie through to country punk, but rock and pop lead the way.

Most shows start around 10pm. DJs take over at 12.30am to keep things going.

Teatre Principal   Live Music
(Map p250; 662 018517; www.teatreprincipal bcn.com; La Rambla 27; concerts €25-50; Café Principal 9.30-11.30pm Mon-Sat, Sala B 8pm & 10pm; Liceu) Following a €6-million renovation, this historic theatre has been transformed into a lavish concert space, though most of it is currently used for one-off events. There are flamenco shows in the atmospheric Sala B, all columns and wood and red velvet banquettes.

Sala Tarantos   Flamenco
(Map p250; 93 304 12 10; www.masimas.com/tarantos; Plaça Reial 17; €15; shows 8.30pm, 9.30pm & 10.30pm; Liceu) Since 1963, this basement locale has been the stage for up-and-coming flamenco groups performing in Barcelona. These days Tarantos has become a mostly tourist-centric affair, with half-hour shows held three times a night. Still, it's a good introduction to flamenco, and not a bad setting for a drink.

Boulevard   DJ
(Map p250; 622 438423; www.boulevard cultureclub.es; La Rambla 27; free to €15, depending on night; 11.45pm-5am Sun-Thu, to 6am Fri & Sat; Drassanes) Boulevard (also known as Dome, depending on the night) is flanked by striptease bars (in the spirit of the lower Rambla's old days), and has undergone countless reincarnations. With three different dance spaces, one of them

🎟 Sardana

On weekends year-round devotees of the folk dance *sardana* gather in front of La Catedral, while a 10-piece band puts everyone in motion. Catalans of all ages come out for the dance, which takes place in a circle with dancers holding hands. Together they move right, back and then left, hopping, raising their arms and generally building momentum as the tempo picks up. All are welcome to join in, though you'll have to watch a few rounds to get the hang of it.

Sardana dancers
GUILLERMO PÉREZ/EYEEM/GETTY IMAGES ©

upstairs, it has a deliciously tacky feel, pumping out anything from 1980s hits to house music (especially on Saturdays in the main room). There's no particular dress code.

☆ El Raval

Filmoteca de Catalunya   Cinema
(Map p250; 93 567 10 70; www.filmoteca.cat; Plaça de Salvador Seguí 1-9; adult/concession €4/3; screenings 5-10pm, ticket office 10am-3pm & 4-9.30pm Tue-Sun; Liceu) After almost a decade in the planning, the Filmoteca de Catalunya – Catalonia's national cinema – moved into this modern 6000-sq-metre building in 2012. It's a glass, metal and concrete beast that hulks in the midst of the most louche part of El Raval, but the building's interior shouts revival, with light and space, wall-to-wall windows, skylights and glass panels that let the sun in.

★ Alfresco Cinema

Outdoor cinema screens are set up in summer in the moat of the Castell de Montjuïc, on the beach and in the Fòrum. Foreign films with subtitles and original soundtracks are marked 'VO' (versió original) in movie listings.

From left: Teatre Principal (p195); Los Vivancos performing at Teatre Grec (p200); Razzmatazz (p198)

In addition to two cinema screens totaling 555 seats, the Filmoteca comprises a film library, a bookshop, a cafe, offices and a dedicated space for exhibitions. This is mainly a film-archive space, though, and is being hailed as the marker of a cultural turning point for its new neighbourhood. The Filmoteca's screenings and exhibitions at the time of writing included themes such as 'The Cinema and The Garden', and 'Popular Comedy'.

Gipsy Lou   Live Music
(Map p249; www.gipsylou.com; Carrer de Ferlandina 55; ⊘8pm-2.30am Sun-Thu, to 3am Sat; ⓂSant Antoni) A louche little bar that packs 'em in for live music, from rumba to pop to flamenco, along with occasional storytelling events, and whatever else Felipe feels like putting on. There are decent bar snacks to keep you going on a long night of pisco sours, the house special.

Jazz Sí Club   Live Music
(Map p249; ☑93 329 00 20; www.tallerde musics.com; Carrer de Requesens 2; cover incl drink €4-10; ⊘8.30-11pm Tue-Sat, 6.30-10pm Sun; ⓂSant Antoni) A cramped little bar

run by the Taller de Músics (Musicians' Workshop) serves as the stage for a varied program of jazz jams through to some good flamenco (Friday and Saturday nights). Thursday night is Cuban night, Tuesday and Sunday are rock, and the rest are devoted to jazz and/or blues sessions. Concerts start around 9pm but the jam sessions can get going earlier.

23 Robadors   Live Music
(Map p250; Carrer d'en Robador 23; cover charge varies; ⊘8pm-3am; ⓂLiceu) On what remains a sleazy Raval street, where streetwalkers, junkies and other misfits hang out in spite of all the work being done to gentrify the area, this narrow little bar has made a name for itself with its shows and live music. Jazz is the name of the game, but you'll also find live poetry, flamenco and plenty more.

Cangrejo   Gay
(Map p250; ☑93 301 29 78; Carrer de Montserrat 9; ⊘11pm-3am Fri & Sat; ⓂDrassanes) This altar to kitsch, a dingy dance hall that has transgressed since the 1920s, is run by the luminous underground cabaret figure of

Carmen Mairena and exudes a gorgeously tacky feel, especially with the midnight drag shows on Friday and Saturday. Due to its popularity with tourists, getting in is all but impossible unless you turn up early.

Teatre Romea
Theatre

(Map p250; ☑93 309 70 04; www.teatreromea. com; Carrer de l'Hospital 51; ticket prices vary; ☺box office 4.30pm until start of show Tue-Fri, from 5.30pm Sat & Sun; Ⓜ Liceu) Just off La Rambla, this 19th-century theatre was resurrected at the end of the 1990s and is one of the city's key stages for quality drama. It usually fills up for a broad range of interesting plays, often classics with a contemporary flavour, in Catalan and Spanish.

Teatre Llantiol
Theatre

(Map p249; ☑93 329 90 09; www.llantiol.com; Carrer de la Riereta 7; ticket prices vary; Ⓜ Sant Antoni) At this charming little cafe-theatre, which has a certain scuffed elegance, all sorts of odd stuff, from concerts and theatre to magic shows, is staged. The specialty, though, is stand-up comedy, which is occasionally in English. Check the website for details.

☆ La Ribera

Palau de la Música Catalana
Classical Music

(Map p254; ☑93 295 72 00; www.palaumusica. cat; Carrer de Palau de la Música 4-6; from €15; ☺box office 9.30am-9pm Mon-Sat, 10am-3pm Sun; Ⓜ Urquinaona) A feast for the eyes, this Modernista confection is also the city's most traditional venue for classical and choral music, although it has a wide-ranging program, including flamenco, pop and – particularly – jazz. Just being here for a performance is an experience. In the foyer, its tiled pillars all a-glitter, sip a pre-concert tipple.

Tablao Nervión
Dance

(Map p250; ☑93 315 21 03; www.restaurante nervion.com; Carrer de la Princesa 2; show incl 1 drink €17, show & set dinner €28; ☺shows 8-10pm Thu-Sat; Ⓜ Jaume I) For admittedly tourist-oriented flamenco, this unassuming bar (shows take place in the basement) is cheaper than most, and has good offerings. Check the website for further details.

La Fura dels Baus

Keep your eyes peeled for any of the eccentric (if not downright crazed) performances of Barcelona's La Fura dels Baus (www.lafura.com) theatre group. It has won worldwide acclaim for its brand of startling, often acrobatic, theatre in which the audience is frequently dragged into the chaos. The company grew out of Barcelona's street-theatre culture of the late 1970s and, although it has grown in technical prowess and received great international acclaim, it has not abandoned the rough-and-ready edge of street performances.

GERARD JULIÉN/GETTY IMAGES ©

☆ Barceloneta & the Waterfront

Razzmatazz Live Music

(📞93 320 82 00; www.salarazzmatazz.com; Carrer de Pamplona 88; €15-40; ⏰9pm-4am; Ⓜ️Marina, Bogatell) Bands from far and wide occasionally create scenes of near hysteria in this, one of the city's classic live-music and clubbing venues. Bands can appear throughout the week (check the website), with different start times. On weekends the live music then gives way to club sounds.

Five different clubs in one huge post-industrial space attract people of all dance persuasions and ages. The main space, the Razz Club, is a haven for the latest international rock and indie acts. The Loft does house and electro, while the Pop Bar offers anything from garage to soul. The

Lolita room is the land of house, hiphop and dubstep, and upstairs in the Rex Room guys and girls sweat it out to experimental sounds. You can save a few euros by purchasing tickets to concerts in advance.

L'Auditori Classical Music

(📞93 247 93 00; www.auditori.org; Carrer de Lepant 150; €7-80; ⏰box office 5-9pm Tue-Fri, 10am-1pm & 5-9pm Sat; Ⓜ️Monumental) Barcelona's modern home for serious music lovers, L'Auditori puts on plenty of orchestral, chamber, religious and other music. The ultramodern building (designed by Rafael Moneo) is home to the Orquestra Simfònica de Barcelona i Nacional de Catalunya.

Teatre Nacional de Catalunya Performing Arts

(📞93 306 57 00; www.tnc.cat; Plaça de les Arts 1; €12-30; ⏰box office 3-8pm Wed-Sat, to 6pm Sun & 1hr before show; Ⓜ️Glòries, Monumental) Ricard Bofill's ultraneoclassical theatre, with its bright, airy foyer, hosts a wide range of performances, including dramas, comedies, musicals and dance performances. Some shows are free.

Sala Monasterio Live Music

(📞616 287197; www.facebook.com/sala.monasterio; Moll de Mestral 30; ⏰9pm-2.30am; Ⓜ️Ciutadella-Vila Olímpica) Overlooking the bobbing masts and slender palm trees of Port Olímpic, this pocket-sized music spot stages an eclectic line-up of live bands, including jazz, *forró* (music from northeastern Brazil), blues jams and rock (usually on Fridays and Saturdays).

Sala Beckett Theatre

(📞93 284 53 12; www.salabeckett.com; Carrer de Pere IV 228; Ⓜ️Poblenou) One of the city's principal alternative theatres, the Sala Beckett does not shy away from challenging theatre, and stages an eclectic mix of local productions and foreign drama. Formerly based in Gràcia, the theatre moved in 2016 to this lovely new space (in the building that formerly housed the Cooperativa Pau i Justícia Poblenou).

Palau de la Música Catalana (p197)

Yelmo Cines Icària — Cinema
(☎902 220922; www.yelmocines.es; Carrer de Salvador Espriú 61; Ⓜ Ciutadella Vila Olímpica) This vast cinema complex screens movies in the original language on 15 screens, making for plenty of choice. Aside from the screens, you'll find several cheerful eateries, bars and the like to keep you occupied before and after the movies.

☆ La Sagrada Família & L'Eixample

Music Hall — Concert Venue
(Map p254; ☎93 238 07 22; www.musichall. es; Rambla de Catalunya 2-4; ticket price varies; ☺7.30pm-midnight; Ⓜ Catalunya) The early-evening incarnation of City Hall, this former theatre is the perfect size for live music, holding a crowd of around 500. The acoustics are great and the layout means everyone gets a good view of the stage.

Mediterráneo — Live Music
(Map p254; ☎93 453 58 45; www.elmedi.net; Carrer de Balmes 129; ☺11pm-3am; Ⓜ Diago-

nal) This jam joint is a great hang-out that attracts a mostly casual student set. Order a beer, enjoy the free nuts and chat at one of the tiny tables while you're waiting for the next act to tune up at the back. Sometimes the young performers are surprisingly good.

Teatre Tívoli — Theatre
(Map p254; ☎93 412 20 63; www.grupbalana. com; Carrer de Casp 8; ticket prices vary; ☺box office noon-8pm; Ⓜ Catalunya) A grand old theatre with three storeys of boxes and a generous stage, the Tívoli has a fairly rapid turnover of drama and musicals, with pieces often not staying on for more than a couple of weeks.

Méliès Cinemes — Cinema
(Map p249; ☎93 451 00 51; www.meliescinemes. com; Carrer de Villarroel 102; tickets €4-7; Ⓜ Urgell) A cosy cinema with two screens, the Méliès specialises in the best of recent releases from Hollywood and Europe.

EMRE TURAN/GETTY IMAGES ©

 **Gig Venues**

Major international bands more often than not play at Razzmatazz (p198), Bikini (p189), Sala Apolo or BARTS, although there are a number of other decent midsize venues. There are also abundant local gigs in places as diverse as **CaixaForum** (Map p256; ☑93 476 86 00; www.fundacio.lacaixa.es; Avinguda de Francesc Ferrer i Guàrdia 6-8; ☎; MEspanya), La Pedrera (p72) and L'Ateneu (p194).

☆ Montjuïc, Poble Sec & Sant Antoni

Sala Apolo   Live Music
(Map p256; ☑93 441 40 01; www.sala-apolo. com; Carrer Nou de la Rambla 113; club €12-18, concerts vary; ◷12.30am-5am Mon-Thu, to 6am Fri & Sat; MParal·lel) This is a fine old theatre, where red velvet dominates and you feel as though you're in a movie-set dancehall scene featuring Eliot Ness. 'Nasty Mondays' and 'Crappy Tuesdays' are aimed at a diehard, we-never-stop-dancing crowd. Earlier in the evening, concerts generally take place, here and in 'La 2', a smaller auditorium downstairs.

Tastes are as eclectic as possible, from local bands and burlesque shows to big-name international acts.

BARTS   Concert Venue
(Barcelona Arts on Stage; Map p256; ☑93 324 84 92; www.barts.cat; Avinguda del Paral·lel 62; €12-40; ◷5pm-midnight Mon-Thu & Sun, to 2am Fri & Sat; MParal·lel) BARTS hasn't been around long, but it has already earned a reputation for its innovative line-up of urban dance troupes, electro swing, psychedelic pop and other eclectic fare. BARTS has a smart design that combines a comfortable midsized auditorium with excellent acoustics.

Gran Bodega Saltó   Live Music
(Map p256; ☑93 441 37 09; www.bodegasalto. net; Carrer de Blesa 36; ◷7pm-2am Mon-

Thu, noon-3am Fri & Sat, noon-midnight Sun; MParal·lel) The ranks of barrels give away the bar's history as a traditional bodega. Now, after a little homemade psychedelic redecoration with odd lamps, figurines and old Chinese beer ads, it's a magnet for an eclectic barfly crowd. The crowd is mixed and friendly, and gets pretty animated on nights when there is live music.

Hiroshima   Live Music, Performing Arts
(Map p256; ☑93 315 54 58; www.hiroshima. cat; Carrer de Vila i Vilà 67; ◷5pm-1am Tue-Thu, to 3am Fri & Sat, noon-1am Sun; MParal·lel) Hiroshima is a creative, new trailblazer in Poble Sec. In a former elevator factory, Hiroshima stages emerging and avant-garde musicians, dancers and performing artists. It has two stages (seating 130 and 250 people, respectively) and a lively ground-floor bar where you can grab a drink after the show. For unconventional fare, this is a good place to look.

Teatre Mercat De Les Flors   Dance
(Map p256; ☑93 256 26 00; mercatflors.cat; Carrer de Lleida 59; €10-22; ◷box office 11am-2pm & 4-7pm Mon-Fri & 1hr before show; ▣55) Next door to the Teatre Lliure, and together with it known as the Ciutat de Teatre (Theatre City), this is a key venue for top local and international contemporary-dance acts. Dance companies perform all over Barcelona. but this spacious modern stage is number one.

Teatre Grec   Theatre
(Map p256; lameva.barcelona.cat/grec; Passeig de Santa Madrona; MEspanya) This lovely amphitheatre on Montjuïc stages one of the city's best festivals, with theatre, dance and music events running throughout the summer. Aside from the Teatre Grec, performances are held all over the city.

Sant Jordi Club   Live Music
(Map p256; ☑93 426 20 89; www.santjordiclub. cat; Passeig Olimpic 5-7; ▣55, 150) With capacity for more than 4500 people, this concert hall, annexed to the Olympic stadium Palau Sant Jordi, is used for big gigs that do not reach the epic proportions of headlining

Sara Baras performs in *Voces* at Teatre Tívoli (p199)

JORDI VIDAL/GETTY IMAGES ©

★ Cultural Information

The Palau de la Virreina (p46) cultural information office has oodles of information on theatre, opera, classical music and more.

📧 Opera & Classical Music

Barcelona is blessed with a fine line-up of theatres for grand performances of classical music, opera and more. The two historic – and iconic – music venues are the Gran Teatre del Liceu (p194) and the Palau de la Música Catalana (p197), while the L'Auditori (p198) is the modern concert hall par excellence and home to the city's orchestra, the Orquestra Simfònica de Barcelona i Nacional de Catalunya (OBC).

The main season for classical music and opera runs from September to June, while in high summer you might find outdoor festivals or performances around town. Check with the tourist office for details.

Fundació Mas I Mas (☑93 319 17 89; www.masimas.com/fundacio; admission €12-15) promotes chamber and classical music, offering concerts in a couple of locations. Classical concerts, usually involving Catalan performers, are held regularly in the Sala Oriol Martorell of l'Auditori (p198), starting at around 8pm. For intense 30-minute sessions of chamber music, see its program of performances at l'Ateneu (p194), a hallowed academic institution-cum-club. These are typically held Fridays, Saturdays and Sundays at 6pm, 7pm and 8pm.

Gran Teatre del Liceu (p194)
IAKOV FILIMONOV/SHUTTERSTOCK ©

international acts. Admission prices and opening times vary with the concerts.

Teatre Lliure Theatre
(Map p256; ☑93 289 27 70; www.teatrelliure.com; Plaça de Margarida Xirgu 1; €15-30; ⊘box office 9am-8pm Mon-Fri, 2hr before show Sat & Sun; MEspanya) Housed in the magnificent former Palau de l'Agricultura building on Montjuïc (opposite the Museu d'Arqueologia) and consisting of two modern theatre spaces (Espai Lliure and Sala Fabià Puigserver), the 'Free Theatre' puts on a variety of quality drama (mostly in Catalan), contemporary dance and music.

Renoir Floridablanca Cinema
(Map p249; ☑91 542 27 02; www.cinesrenoir.com; Carrer de Floridablanca 135; tickets €6-10; MSant Antoni) With seven screens, this is now the last standing in Barcelona of a small chain of art-house cinemas in Spain showing quality flicks. It is handily located just beyond El Raval, so you can be sure that there is no shortage of postfilm entertainment options nearby.

Teatre Victòria Theatre
(Map p256; ☑93 329 91 89; www.teatrevictoria.com; Avinguda del Paral.lel 67; €15-45; ⊘box office 2hr before show; MParal.lel) This modern (and, on the street, rather nondescript-looking) theatre is on what used to be considered Barcelona's version of Broadway. It stages musicals (usually in Catalan), flamenco and contemporary dance.

☆ Gràcia & Park Güell

Soda Acústic Live Music
(Map p254; ☑93 016 55 90; www.facebook.com/sodacustic; Carrer de les Guilleries 6; from €3; ⊘8pm-2.30am Wed-Sun; MFontana) This low-lit modern space stages an eclectic line-up of bands and performing artists. Jazz, Balkan swing, Latin rhythms and plenty of experimental, not easily classifiable musicians all receive their due. The acoustics are excellent. Check its Facebook page for upcoming shows.

Teatreneu   Theatre

(Map p254; ☑93 285 37 12; www.teatreneu.
com; Carrer de Terol 26; ⊙box office 1hr before
show; MFontana, Joanic) This lively theatre
(with a bustling, rambling downstairs bar
facing the street) dares to fool around with
all sorts of material, from monologues to
social comedy. Aside from the main theatre, two cafe-style spaces serve as more
intimate stage settings for small-scale
productions. Films are also shown.

Heliogàbal   Live Music

(Map p254; www.heliogabal.com; Carrer de
Ramón i Cajal 80; ⊙9.30pm-3am Wed-Sat;
MJoanic) This compact bar is a veritable
hive of cultural activity where you never
quite know what to expect. Aside from art
exhibitions and poetry readings, you will
be pleasantly surprised by the eclectic
live-music program. Jazz groups are often
followed by open jam sessions, and experimental music of all colours gets a run.

While many performers are local, international acts also get a look in.

Verdi   Cinema

(Map p254; ☑93 238 79 90; www.cines-verdi.
com; Carrer de Verdi 32; MFontana) A popular
original-language cinema in the heart of
Gràcia, handy to lots of local eateries and
bars for pre- and post-film enjoyment.

☆Camp Nou, Pedralbes & La Zona Alta

Luz de Gas   Live Music

(☑93 209 77 11; www.luzdegas.com; Carrer de
Muntaner 246; up to €20; ⊙Thu-Sat; ☐6, 7,
15, 27, 32, 33, 34, 58, 64, MDiagonal) Several
nights a week this club, set in a grand
former theatre, stages concerts ranging
through rock, soul, salsa, jazz and pop.
From about 2am, the place turns into a club
that attracts a well-dressed crowd with
varying musical tastes, depending on the
night.

Check the website for the latest schedule. Concerts typically cost around €12,
and kick off around 9pm.

Nacho Blanco and Eli Ayala perform at Teatre Grec (p200)

ACTIVE BARCELONA

Sports, spas and everything in between

Active Barcelona

Mediterranean ocean front and a rambling hilly park overlooking the city make fine settings for outdoor activities in Barcelona. For a break from sightseeing, try running, cycling, getting out on the water, or simply pumping fists in the air at a never-dull FC Barça match. Here, football has the aura of religion, and for much of the city's population, support of Barça is an article of faith. There's also another team in town, the unfashionable but solid Espanyol. The city also has successful and popular handball and basketball teams.

In This Section

Sports Seasons

The football season runs from late August to May.

The Spanish basketball season runs from October to June.

Asobal, the Spanish handball league, runs from September to May or early June.

The professional Spanish tennis season is in spring; the big event here is the Barcelona Open in April.

Stand-up paddleboarding (p209), Barceloneta Beach

The Best...

Activities

Castell de Montjuïc (p115) Barcelona's easily accessible mountain offers a scenic setting for running and biking.

Parc de Collserola (p125) The city's best mountain biking.

Camp Nou (p209) See FC Barcelona in action at their home stadium.

Piscines Bernat Picornell (p210) A truly Olympian setting for a swim.

Spas

Rituels d'Orient (p210) A beautiful spa in a historic setting of El Born.

Aire de Barcelona (p210) Indulge yourself in a Moorish fantasy.

Flotarium (p210) Float weightlessly in a salt-filled chamber.

⚐ Tours

My Favourite Things   Tour

(☑637 265405; www.myft.net; tours from €26) Offers tours (with no more than 10 participants) based on numerous themes: street art, shopping, culinary tours, musical journeys and forgotten neighbourhoods are among the offerings. Other activities include flamenco and salsa classes, cooking workshops, and bicycle rides in and out of Barcelona. Some of the more unusual activities cost more and times vary.

Barcelona
Walking Tours   Walking Tour

(Map p254; ☑93 285 38 34; www.barcelonaturisme.com; Plaça de Catalunya 17; Ⓜ Catalunya) The Oficina d'Informació de Turisme de Barcelona organises guided walking tours. One explores the Barri Gòtic (adult/child €16/free; in English 9.30am daily); another follows in Picasso's footsteps (adult/child €22/7, in English 3pm Tuesday, Thursday and Saturday) and winds up at the Museu Picasso; and a third takes in the main jewels of Modernisme (adult/child €16/free, in English 6pm Wednesday and Friday).

Runner Bean Tours   Walking Tour

(Map p249; ☑636 108776; www.runnerbeantours.com; Carrer del Carme 44; ⊗ tours 11am year-round & 4.30pm Apr-Sep; Ⓜ Liceu) Runner Bean Tours comprises several daily thematic tours. It's a pay-what-you-wish tour, with a collection taken at the end for the guide. The Old City tour explores the Roman and medieval history of Barcelona, visiting highlights in the Ciutat Vella. The Gaudí tour takes in the great works of Modernista Barcelona. It involves two hops on the metro.

Barcelona Scooter   Driving Tour

(Map p250; ☑93 221 40 70; www.cooltra.com; Via Laietana 6; tour €50; ⊗ 3.30pm Thu, 10.30am Sat; Ⓜ Jaume I) Run by Cooltra, Barcelona Scooter offers a three-hour tour by scooter around the city, taking in architectural highlights (La Pedrera, La Sagrada Família) and great views (from Montjuïc). Departure is from the Cooltra rental outlet at 3.30pm on Thursdays and 10.30am on Saturdays.

Runners on the Carretera de les Aigües (p211)

MARGARET STEPIEN/LONELY PLANET ©

⚽ Football

Camp Nou   Stadium
(☎902 189900; www.fcbarcelona.com; Carrer d'Arístides Maillol; MPalau Reial) Among Barcelona's most visited sites is the massive stadium of Camp Nou (which means 'New Field' in Catalan), home to the legendary Futbol Club Barcelona. Attending a game amid the roar of the crowds is an unforgettable experience. Football fans who aren't able to see a game can get a taste of all the excitement at the Camp Nou Experience (p70), which includes a tour of the stadium. The season runs from September to May. For information about tickets, see p71.

Estadi RCD Espanyol   Football
(☎93 292 77 00; www.rcdespanyol.com; Avinguda del Baix Llobrega; tickets from €30; ℝFGC Cornellà Riera) Espanyol, based at the 40,500-seat Estadi RCD Espanyol, traditionally plays second fiddle to Barça, although it does so with considerable passion.

🚣 Boating & Water Sports

Molokai SUP Center   Water Sports
(☎93 221 48 68; www.molokaisupcenter.com; Carrer de Meer 39; 2hr lesson €55, SUP rental per hour €15; MBarceloneta) This respected outfit will give you a crash course in stand-up paddleboarding. In addition to the two-hour beginner's class, Molokai can help you improve your technique (in intermediate and advanced lessons, all in two-hour blocks); gear and wetsuit is included. It also hires out SUP boards.

Orsom   Cruise
(☎93 441 05 37; www.barcelona-orsom.com; Moll de les Drassanes; adult/child from €16/11; ⊙May-Oct; MDrassanes) Aboard a large sailing catamaran, Orsom makes the 90-minute journey to Port Olímpic and back. There are three departures per day (four on weekends in July and August), and the last is a jazz cruise, scheduled around sunset. Orsom also runs five daily, 50-minute speedboat tours (adult/child €13/11).

⚽ FC Barcelona

One of the city's best-loved names is FC Barça, which is deeply associated with Catalans and even Catalan nationalism. The team was long a rallying point for Catalans when other aspects of Catalan culture were suppressed. The club openly supported Catalonia's drive towards autonomy in 1918, and in 1921 the club's statutes were drafted in Catalan. The pro-Catalan leanings of the club and its siding with the republic during the Spanish Civil War earned reprisals from the government. Club president Josep Sunyol was murdered by Franco's soldiers in 1936, and the club building was bombed in 1938.

In 1968 club president Narcís de Carreras uttered the now famous words, *'El Barça: més que un club'* ('more than a club'), which became the team's motto – and emphasised its role as an anti-Franco symbol and catalyst for change in the province and beyond. Today FC Barça is one of the world's most admired teams.

**Club Natació
Atlètic-Barcelona**   Swimming
(☎93 221 00 10; www.cnab.cat; Plaça del Mar; day pass adult/child €12.20/7.10; ⊙7am-11pm Mon-Sat, 8am-8pm Sun; ℚ17, 39, 57, 64, MBarceloneta) This athletic club has one indoor and two outdoor pools. Of the latter, one is heated for lap swimming in winter. Admission includes use of the gym and private beach access.

Las Golondrinas   Cruise
(☎93 442 31 06; www.lasgolondrinas.com; Moll de las Drassanes; 40min tour adult/child €7.40/2.80; MDrassanes) Golondrinas offers several popular cruises from its dock in front of Mirador de Colom. The 90-minute catamaran tour (€15) goes out past Barceloneta and the beaches to the Fòrum and back. If you just want a peek at the

🏀🏸 Basketball & Handball

Everyone knows about FC Barcelona's football team, but the club also runs very successful sides in two of Spain's other popular spectator sports, basketball and handball. Both play in the Palau Blaugrana. The handball side, the most notable in the world, has carried all before it in recent years, while the basketballers usually battle it out for the title with...who else but Real Madrid?

area around the port, opt for the 40-minute excursion to the breakwater and back. Both run frequently throughout the day.

Piscines Bernat
Picornell   Swimming
(Map p256; ☑93 423 40 41; www.picornell.cat; Avinguda de l'Estadi 30-38; adult/child €12/8, nudist hours €7/5; ◷6.45am-midnight Mon-Fri, 7am-9pm Sat, 7.30am-4pm Sun; 🚌150) Barcelona's official Olympic pool on Montjuïc. Admission also includes use of fitness room, sauna, jacuzzi, steam bath and track. On Saturdays, between 9pm and 11pm, the pool (with access to sauna and steam bath) is open only to nudists. On Sundays between October and May the indoor pool also opens for nudists only from 4.15pm to 6pm.

🏃 Spas

Rituels d'Orient   Spa
(☑93 419 14 72; www.rituelsdorient.com; Carrer de Loreto 50; baths €29; ◷11am-9pm Sun, Tue & Wed, to 10pm Thu-Sat; MHospital Clínic) Rituels d'Orient offers a setting that resembles a Moroccan fantasy, with window grilles, candle lighting and stone walls. It's a fine setting for luxuriating in a hammam and indulging in a massage or body scrub.

Flotarium   Day Spa
(Map p254; ☑93 217 36 37; www.flotarium.com; Plaça de Narcís Oller 3; 1hr session €40; ◷10am-

9pm Mon-Sat; MDiagonal) Be suspended in zero gravity and feel the stress subside. Each flotarium, like a little space capsule with water, is in a private room, with shower, towels and shampoo, and Epsom salts that allow you to float as if in the Dead Sea.

Aire De Barcelona   Hammam
(☑93 295 57 43; www.airedebarcelona.com; Passeig de Picasso 22; thermal baths & aromatherapy Mon-Thu €31, Fri-Sun €33; ◷10am-10pm Mon-Thu & Sun, 10am-2am Fri & Sat; MArc de Triomf) With low lighting and relaxing perfumes wafting around you, this basement *hammam* (Turkish bath) could be the perfect way to end a day. Hot, warm and cold baths, steam baths and various massage options make for a delicious hour or so. Book ahead and bring a swimming costume.

🏃 Courses

Espai Boisà   Cooking Course
(☑93 192 60 21; http://espaiboisa.com; Ptge Lluís Pellicer 8; MHospital Clínic) 🍴 Run by a young, multilingual Venezuelan-Catalan couple, this first-rate outfit offers cooking courses on various themes and of various lengths. They emphasise organic, seasonal ingredients from local producers that are put to good use in dishes including paella, a range of tapas dishes and *crema catalana* (a Catalan version of crème brûlée).

Swing Maniacs   Dance Classes
(Map p254; ☑93 187 69 85; www.swingmaniacs.com; Carrer l'Església 4; group/private 55min class from €12/40; ◷5pm-midnight Mon-Fri; MJoanic, Fontana) In the last few years, swing dancing has arrived in full force in the Catalan capital, with old-fashioned dance parties happening in far-flung corners of the city every night. To learn the moves, sign up for a class at Swing Maniacs. You can join a drop-in class, and if you don't have a partner, one can be arranged for you. The website lists upcoming events, and Swing Maniacs also hosts its own swing-dancing gatherings (click on School/Tickets for details).

WESTEND61/GETTY IMAGES ©

🚴 Cycling

Barcelona's long, enticing seafront makes a fine setting for a ride; there's a bike lane that's separate from traffic and pedestrians. The city itself has over 180km of bike lanes, including along some major streets. Avid mountain bikers will want to make their way up to the vast Parc de Collserola (p125) with rambling trails on a wooded massif overlooking the city.

Barcelona By Bike Bicycle Tour
(📞671 307325; www.barcelonabybike.com; Carrer de la Marina 13; tours €24; MCiutadella Vila Olímpica) This outfit offers several tours by bicycle, including 'The Original', a three-hour pedal that takes in a bit of Gothic Barcelona, L'Eixample (including Sagrada Família) and the Barceloneta beachfront.

Biciclot Bicycle Rental
(📞93 221 97 78; bikinginbarcelona.net; Passeig Marítim de la Barceloneta 33; bike hire per hour/day €5/€17; ⏲11am-6pm Mon-Fri, 10am-8pm Sat & Sun; MCiutadella Vila Olímpica) Bike rental with a handy seaside location.

> *Barcelona's enticing seafront makes a fine setting for a ride*

Trixi Bicycle Rental
(Map p250; 📞699 984726; www.trixi.com/barcelona; Plaça dels Traginers 4; 30min/1hr/2hr/4hr tour €18/30/50/85; ⏲9am-8pm Mar-Nov; MJaume I) Hires out bicycles, kickbikes and 'trixi-kids' (tricycles with a kind of front-end trolley for transporting young children). It also offers tours, using three-wheeled cycle taxis, which operate around the old town, the waterfront and much of the centre.

🏃 Running

The waterfront esplanade and beaches are perfect for an early-morning run. Or head to Parc de Collserola (p125), which is laced with trails. Among the best is the Carretera de les Aigües, a 9km-long track from Tibidabo to the suburb of Sant Just Desvern, with superb views over the city. More convenient are the gardens of Montjuïc.

REST YOUR HEAD

Top tips for the best accommodation

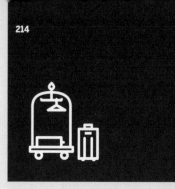

Rest Your Head

Barcelona has an excellent range of accommodation, with high-end luxury hotels, sharp boutique lodgings, and a varied spread of midrange and budget selections. There are also small-scale B&B-style apartment rentals scattered around the city, which are a good-value choice. Wherever you stay it's wise to book well ahead. If you plan to travel around holidays such as Easter, Christmas or New Year's Eve, or in summer, reserve a room three or four months ahead of time.

In This Section

Prices

A 'budget hotel' in Barcelona generally costs up to €75 for a double room during high season. For a modest mid-range option, plan on spending €75 to €200. Luxury options run €200 and higher.

Virtually all accommodation is subject to IVA, a 10% value-added tax. There's also an additional tax of between €0.72 and €2.48 per person per night. These charges are usually included in the quoted rate.

The view from Majestic Hotel and Spa's rooftop pool

Reservations & Check-in

Booking ahead is recommended, especially during peak periods, trade fairs and throughout much of summer.

If you arrive without prebooked lodging, the Plaça de Catalunya's tourist office (p238) can help.

Check-in is around 2pm or 3pm. If arriving earlier, you can usually leave your luggage at reception.

Check-out is generally noon.

Useful Websites

Oh-Barcelona (www.oh-barcelona.com) Good-value selection of hotels, hostels and apartment rentals.

Lonely Planet (www.lonelyplanet.com) Huge range of hotels, hostels, guesthouses, B&Bs and apartments.

Barcelona Bed and Breakfasts (www.barcelonabedandbreakfasts.com) Listings of low-key, oft-overlooked lodging options.

🛏 Accommodation Types

Hotels

Hotels cover a broad range. At the bottom end there is often little to distinguish them from better *pensiones* and *hostales,* and from there they run up the scale to five-star luxury. Some of the better features to look out for include rooftop pools and lounges, views (either of the sea or a cityscape – La Sagrada Família, Montjuïc, Barri Gòtic) and, of course, proximity to the important sights.

Pensiones & Hostales

Depending on the season you can pay as little as €15 to €25 for a dorm bed in a youth hostel. If dorm living is not your thing, but you are still looking for a budget deal, check around the many *pensiones* (small private hotels) and *hostales* (budget hotels). These are family-run, small-scale hotels, often housed in sprawling apartments. Some are fleapits, others immaculately maintained gems.

You're looking at a minimum of around €35/55 for basic *individual/doble* (single/double) rooms, mostly without a private bathroom. (It is occasionally possible to find cheaper rooms, but they may be unappealing.)

Some places, especially at the lower end, offer triples and quads, which can be good value for groups. If you want a double bed (as opposed to two singles), ask for a *llit/cama matrimonial* (Catalan/Spanish). If your budget is especially tight, look at options outside the centre.

Hostels

Barcelona is chock-a-block with back-packer hostels, many of which offer state-of-the-art facilities that shame many midrange hotels. Websites like Hostelworld (www.hostelworld.com) or Hostelbookers (www.hostelbookers.com) are useful resources.

Room & Apartment Rentals

A cosier (and sometimes more cost-effective) alternative to *hostales* and hotels is short-term apartment rental. A plethora of firms organise short lets across town. Typical prices are around €80 to €100 for two people per night.

One of the best options, with hundreds of listings, is Airbnb (www.airbnb.com). In addition to full apartments, the site also lists rooms available, which can be a good way to meet locals and/or other travellers if you don't mind sharing common areas. Prices for a room cost €30 to €60 on average.

Other apartment-rental services include the following:

Aparteasy (www.aparteasy.com)

Barcelona On Line (www.barcelona-on-line.es)

Feel at Home Barcelona.com (www.feelathomebarcelona.com)

Friendly Rentals (www.friendlyrentals.com)

MH Apartments (www.mhapartments.com)

Oh-Barcelona (www.oh-barcelona.com)

Rent a Flat in Barcelona (www.rentaflatinbarcelona.com)

If you want to do a short-term house swap, check out the ads on www.loquo.com. Want to sleep on a local's couch? Try your luck at www.couchsurfing.com or www.hospitality club.org.

🛏 Travellers with Disabilities

Many hotels claim to be equipped for guests with disabilities, but reality frequently disappoints. Check out www.accessible barcelona.com for help with finding genuinely accessible accommodation. The same people also run www.accessible.travel.

Lonely Planet's free Accessible Travel guide can be downloaded here: http://lptravel.to/AccessibleTravel.

Where to Stay

There are good accommodation options in all of Barcelona's central districts, with pros and cons to each location. Choose from historic or seaside districts, or the charming neighbourhoods that are full of restaurants and nightlife.

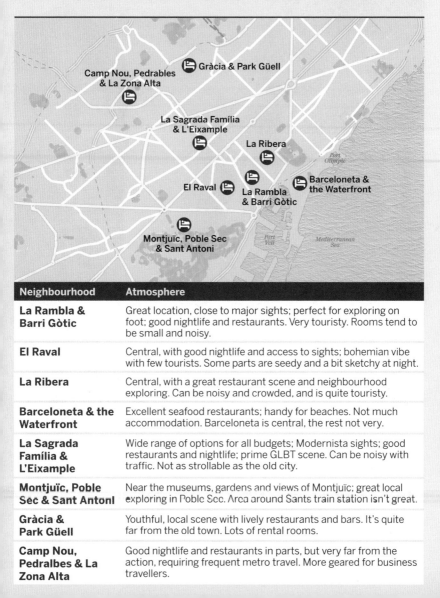

Neighbourhood	Atmosphere
La Rambla & Barri Gòtic	Great location, close to major sights; perfect for exploring on foot; good nightlife and restaurants. Very touristy. Rooms tend to be small and noisy.
El Raval	Central, with good nightlife and access to sights; bohemian vibe with few tourists. Some parts are seedy and a bit sketchy at night.
La Ribera	Central, with a great restaurant scene and neighbourhood exploring. Can be noisy and crowded, and is quite touristy.
Barceloneta & the Waterfront	Excellent seafood restaurants; handy for beaches. Not much accommodation. Barceloneta is central, the rest not very.
La Sagrada Família & L'Eixample	Wide range of options for all budgets; Modernista sights; good restaurants and nightlife; prime GLBT scene. Can be noisy with traffic. Not as strollable as the old city.
Montjuïc, Poble Sec & Sant Antoni	Near the museums, gardens and views of Montjuïc; great local exploring in Poble Sec. Area around Sants train station isn't great.
Gràcia & Park Güell	Youthful, local scene with lively restaurants and bars. It's quite far from the old town. Lots of rental rooms.
Camp Nou, Pedralbes & La Zona Alta	Good nightlife and restaurants in parts, but very far from the action, requiring frequent metro travel. More geared for business travellers.

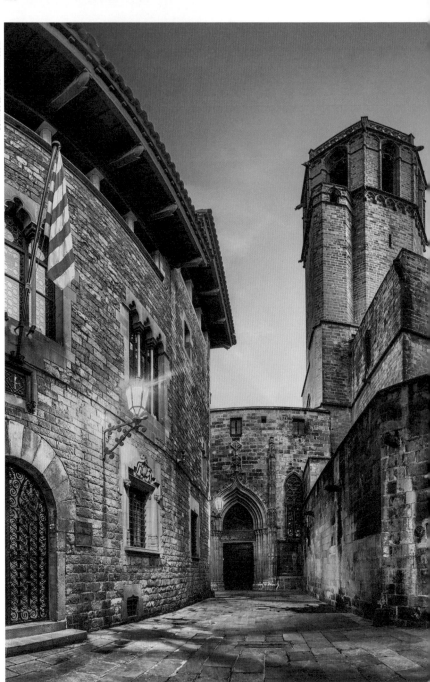

La Catedral (p62)

In Focus

Barcelona Today

Take a stroll through the streets of Barcelona, and you'll likely see some esteladas, *the flag with the lone star that symbolises Catalonia's drive toward independence. Talk of separatism in the city has reached a fever pitch. Of course, there's much more brewing in Barcelona than self-rule. The city's deep commitment to innovation has led to improvements in transport, communications and urban design.*

Above: Barceloneta Beach PETER UNGER / GETTY IMAGES ©

The Nation of Catalonia?

It's a historic moment in Barcelona. The drive toward independence is under way, with the very real possibility that Catalonia could break away from Spain and become a sovereign republic in 2018. With its own language, unique traditions and proud history (at least prior to its conquest by Spain in 1714), Catalonia has always thought of itself as distinct from other parts of the country. But until recently, only a small fringe group sought a permanent and irrevocable break from Madrid.

In the last few years, however, the number of self-proclaimed separatists has skyrocketed. Back in November 2014, Catalonia held a nonbinding referendum, and over 80% of those who voted backed Catalan independence. Spain's Constitutional Court wasted little time in declaring the vote (and all future votes) on independence to be

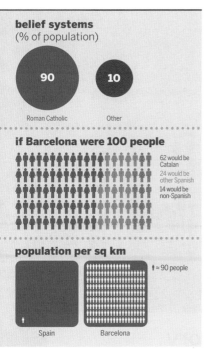

belief systems
(% of population)

90 Roman Catholic

10 Other

if Barcelona were 100 people

62 would be Catalan

24 would be other Spanish

14 would be non-Spanish

population per sq km

♦ ≈ 90 people

Spain

Barcelona

illegal. Then in the following year (September 2015) Catalan nationalists won a majority of the 135-seat regional assembly, which they viewed as an implicit endorsement of secession. A resolution was passed laying out the road map to independence, with legislation under way to draft a Catalan constitution, create a new treasury and design a social security system.

Fuelling the drive is the ongoing economic crisis – Catalonia has long claimed that it pays more in tax revenue than it gets back. According to a 2011 report (released only in 2015), Catalonia did in fact pay €8.5 billion more in taxes than it got back in transfers and investments (Catalan advocates claim the actual figure was above €11 billion).

The repercussions of Catalan independence would be wide-reaching. It could undermine the financial stability of Spain – and cause economic shock waves across the eurozone. How it all shakes out is anybody's guess, but no one is expecting a smooth ride.

City of Innovation

The city that gave birth to Antoni Gaudí and the ingenious creations of Modernisme continues to break new ground in other realms. In particular, Barcelona has become a global model as a Smart City – a place where technology is harnessed to create a more sustainable, efficient and interconnected environment for both residents and visitors alike. Some 120 projects comprise the Smart City initiative, including wide-reaching innovations affecting transport, communications, public and social services, and even tourism.

Shrinking the city's carbon footprint is at the forefront of various new technologies. Self-powered lights installed along one stretch of beach use a combination of solar and wind energy, without needing to tap into the grid. Barcelona has the cleanest fleet of buses in Europe, with a large share of hybrids and natural-gas-powered vehicles (plus anti-pollution filters on its remaining diesel motors).

Speaking of buses, Barcelona has also launched new routes based on the flow of people using the system, creating a new, more intuitive grid that moves vertically, horizontally and diagonally across the city. It has also been expanding its network for electric cars, with 300 existing charging stations and more in the works. Another innovation: smart traffic lights that turn green when emergency vehicles are approaching so they can reach their destination faster.

Fuelling much of the innovation is the 220-hectare district known as 22@ (*vint-i-dos arroba*). This district in El Poblenou has seen enormous growth since its creation back in 2000. Over 90,000 jobs have been created under the 8000 firms at work, largely in the digital, creative and tech industries.

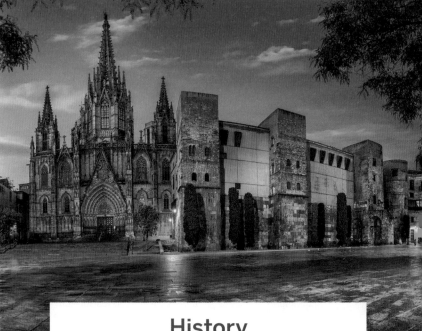

History

Barcelona has seen waves of immigrants and conquerors over its 2000-plus years. Fortunes have risen and fallen, from the golden era of 14th-century princely power to the dark days of civil war and Franco's era. A fierce independent streak has always run through Barcelona, which continues today, with a desire for more autonomy (full independence, say some Catalans) from Spain.

Above left: La Catedral (p62) DOMINGO LEIVA/GETTY IMAGES ©
Above right: Architectural detail, Barri Gòtic SPECTRAL-DESIGN/SHUTTERSTOCK ©

---

15 BC
Caesar Augustus grants the town of Barcino a city title.

AD 415
Visigoths under Athaulf make Barcino their capital. It generally remains so until the 6th century.

718
Barcelona falls to Tariq's mostly Arab and Berber troops on their blitzkrieg march north into France.

Wilfred the Hairy & the Catalan Golden Age

It was the Romans who first etched Barcino onto Europe's map in the 3rd century BC, though the nascent settlement long played second fiddle to the provincial capital in Tarragona. The Visigoths came next, followed by the Moors, whose relatively brief occupation was usurped when the Franks put the city under the control of local counts in 801 as a buffer zone against the still Muslim-dominated caliphate to the south. Eccentrically named Wilfred the Hairy (Count Guifré el Pelós) moulded the entity we now know as Catalonia in the 9th century by wresting control of several neighbouring territories and establishing Barcelona as its key city. The hirsute one founded a dynasty that lasted nearly five centuries and developed almost independently from the Reconquista wars that were playing out in the rest of Iberia. The counts of Barcelona gradually expanded their territory south and, in 1137, Ramon Berenguer IV, the Count of Barcelona, married Petronilla, heir to the throne of neighbouring Aragón. Thus, the combined Crown of Aragón was created.

801	1137	1283
Future Frankish king Louis the Pious wrests Barcelona from Muslims and establishes the Spanish March under local counts.	Count Ramon Berenguer IV is betrothed to the daughter of the king of Aragón, creating a combined state, the Crown of Aragón.	The Corts Catalanes, a legislative council, meets and begins to curtail royal power in favour of nobles and merchants.

Via Sepulcral Romana (p48)

★ **Best Historic Sites**

Museu d'Història de Barcelona (p104)

Museu d'Història de Catalunya (p87)

Museu Marítim (p84)

Via Sepulcral Romana (p48)

Basílica de Santa Maria del Mar (p112)

In the following centuries the kingdom became a flourishing merchant empire, seizing Valencia and the Balearic Islands from the Muslims, and later taking territories as far flung as Sardinia, Sicily and parts of Greece.

The 14th century marked the golden age of Barcelona. Its trading wealth paid for great Gothic buildings: La Catedral, the Capella Reial de Santa Àgata (inside the Museu d'Història de Barcelona) and the churches of Santa Maria del Pi and Santa Maria del Mar were completed during this time. King Pere III (1336–87) later created the breathtaking Reials Drassanes (Royal Shipyards) and extended the city walls yet again to include El Raval.

Marginalisation & Decline

Overstretched, racked by civil disobedience and decimated by the Black Death, Catalonia began to wobble. When the last count of Wilfred the Hairy's dynasty expired without leaving an heir, the Crown of Aragón was passed to a noble of Castilla. Soon these two Spanish kingdoms merged, with Catalonia left as a junior partner. As business shifted from the Mediterranean to the Atlantic after the 'discovery' of the Americas in 1492, Catalans were marginalised from trade.

The region, which had retained some autonomy in the running of its own affairs, was dealt a crushing blow when it supported the wrong side in the War of the Spanish Succession (1702–14). Barcelona, under the auspices of British-backed archduke Charles of Austria, fell after a stubborn siege on 11 September 1714 (now celebrated as National Catalan Day) to the forces of Bourbon king Philip V, who established a unitary Castilian state. Barcelona now faced a long backlash as the new king banned the writing and teaching of Catalan, swept away the remnants of local legal systems and tore down a whole district of medieval Barcelona in order to construct an immense fort (on the site of the present-day Parc de la Ciutadella), the sole purpose of which was to watch over Barcelona's troublemakers.

The Catalan Renaissance

Buoyed by the lifting of the ban on its trade with the Americas in 1778, Barcelona embarked on the road to industrial revolution, based initially on textiles but spreading to wine,

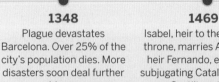

1348	1469	1640–52
Plague devastates Barcelona. Over 25% of the city's population dies. More disasters soon deal further blows.	Isabel, heir to the Castilian throne, marries Aragonese heir Fernando, effectively subjugating Catalonia to the Castilian state.	Catalan peasants declare their independence under French protection. Spain eventually crushes the rebellion.

cork and iron in the mid-19th century. It soon became Spain's leading city. As the economy prospered, Barcelona outgrew its medieval walls, which were demolished in 1854–56. Work on the grid-plan L'Eixample (the Extension) district began soon after. The so-called Renaixença (Renaissance) brought a revival of Catalan culture, as well as political activism. It sowed the seeds of growing political tension in the early 20th century, as demands for autonomy from the central state became more insistent.

Masses & Classes

Adding to the fiery mix was growing discontent among the working class. The grand Catalan merchant-bourgeois families grew richer, displaying their wealth in a slew of whimsical private mansions built with verve and flair by Modernista architects such as Antoni Gaudí. At the same time, the industrial working class, housed in cramped quarters such as Barceloneta and El Raval, and oppressed by poverty and disease, became organised and, on occasion, violent. Spain's neutrality during WWI had boosted Barcelona's economy, and from 1900 to 1930 the population doubled to one million, but the postwar global slump hit the city hard. Waves of strikes, organised principally by the anarchists' Confederación Nacional del Trabajo (CNT; National Labour Confederation), brought tough responses. Left- and right-wing gangs took their ideological conflict to the streets. Tit-for-tat assassinations became common currency and the death toll mounted. When the Second Spanish Republic was created under a left-wing government in 1931, Catalonia declared independence. Later, under pressure, its leaders settled for devolution, which it then lost in 1934, when a right-wing government won power in Madrid. The election of a left-wing popular front in 1936 again sparked Catalan autonomy claims, but also led to the generals' rising that launched the Spanish Civil War (1936–39), from which Franco emerged the victor.

The War Years

The acting capital of Spain for much of the civil war, Barcelona was run by anarchists and the Partido Obrero de Unificación Marxista (POUM; Workers' Marxist Unification Party) Trotskyist militia until mid-1937. Unions took over factories and public services; hotels and mansions became hospitals and schools; everyone wore workers' clothes; bars and cafes were collectivised; trams and taxis were painted red and black (the colours of the

Jewish Barcelona

The narrow Barri Gòtic lanes of El Call were once home to a thriving Jewish population. Catalan Jews worked as merchants, scholars, cartographers and teachers. By the 11th century, as many as 4000 Jews lived in El Call.

As in much of Europe, during the 13th century a wave of anti-Semitism swept through Catalonia. Pogroms followed on from repressive laws; anti-Semitism peaked in 1391 when a frenzied mob tore through El Call, looting and destroying homes and murdering hundreds of Jews. Most of the remaining Jews fled the city.

1869	**1909**	**1936**
L'Eixample (the Extension) district is created. Modernista architects showcase their creations here.	After the call-up of reservists to war in Morocco, *barcelonins* riot. Over 100 are killed in the Setmana Tràgica (Tragic Week).	A military rising begins the Spanish Civil War. General Goded is defeated in Barcelona by left-wing militia, workers and loyalist police.

Anarchists & the Tragic Week

When the political philosophy of anarchism began spreading through Europe, it was embraced by many industrial workers in Barcelona, who embarked on a road to social revolution through violent means.

One anarchist bomb at the Liceu opera house on La Rambla in the 1890s killed 22 people. Anarchists were also blamed for the Setmana Tràgica (Tragic Week) in July 1909 when, following a military call-up for Spanish campaigns in Morocco, rampaging mobs wrecked 70 religious buildings, and workers were shot on the street in reprisal.

anarchists); and one-way streets were ignored as they were seen to be part of the old system. The more radical anarchists were behind the burning of most of the city's churches and the shooting of hundreds of priests, monks and nuns. The anarchists in turn were shunted aside by the communists (directed by Stalin from Moscow) after a bloody internecine battle in Barcelona that left 1500 dead in May 1937.

Later that year the Spanish Republican government fled Valencia and made Barcelona the official capital (the government had left besieged Madrid early in the war). The Republican defeat at the hands of the Nationalists in the Battle of the Ebro in southern Catalonia in the summer of 1938 left Barcelona undefended. It fell to the Nationalists on 25 January 1939, triggering a mass exodus of refugees to France, where most were long interned in makeshift camps. Purges and executions under Franco continued until well into the 1950s. Former Catalan president Lluís Companys was arrested in France by the Gestapo in August 1940, handed over to Franco, and shot on 15 October on Montjuïc, despite international outrage. He is reputed to have died with the words *'Visca Catalunya!'* ('Long live Catalonia!') on his lips.

Recent Times

When the death of Franco was announced in 1975, *barcelonins* took to the streets in celebration. The next five years saw the gradual return of democracy and in 1977 Catalonia was granted regional autonomy.

Politics aside, the big event in post-Franco Barcelona was the successful 1992 Olympic Games, planned under the guidance of the popular Socialist mayor, Pasqual Maragall. The games spurred a burst of public works and brought new life to areas such as Montjuïc, where the major events were held. The once-shabby waterfront was transformed with promenades, beaches, marinas, restaurants, leisure attractions and new housing. After the turn of the millennium, Barcelona continued to invest in urban renewal.

In recent years, soaring unemployment and painful austerity measures – not to mention Catalonia's heavy tax burden – has led to anger and resentment toward Madrid, and fuelled the drive toward independence. Recent polls indicate about half of Catalans support the region becoming a new European state.

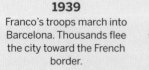

1939
Franco's troops march into Barcelona. Thousands flee the city toward the French border.

1992
Barcelona takes centre stage as it hosts the summer Olympic Games.

2015
Following an election, separatists take control of Catalonia's government. They vow to continue the move toward full secession.

Architecture

Famed for its architectural treasures, Barcelona has striking Gothic cathedrals, fantastical Modernista creations and avant-garde works from more recent days. From the Middle Ages, when Barcelona was the seat of the Catalan empire, to the late 19th century, when it began expanding beyond its medieval confines, to the late 1980s (and continuing today), the city's had three notable and vastly different design eras.

Above: Staircase, La Sagrada Família (p36) NIKADA/GETTY IMAGES ©

Catalan Gothic

Barcelona's first big building boom came at the height of the Middle Ages, when its imposing Gothic churches, mansions and shipyards were raised, together creating what survives to this day as one of the most extensive Gothic quarters in Europe.

Catalan Gothic did not follow the same course as the style typical of northern Europe. Decoration here tends to be more sparing and the most obvious defining characteristic is the triumph of breadth over height. While northern European cathedrals reach for the sky, Catalan Gothic has a tendency to push to the sides, stretching its vaulting design to the limit. Another notable departure from what you might have come to expect of Gothic north of the Pyrenees is the lack of spires and pinnacles.

Facade detail, Casa Amatller (p53)

The Modernistas

The second wave of Catalan creativity, also carried on the wind of boom times, came around the turn of the 20th century. The urban expansion program known as L'Eixample (the Extension), designed to free the choking population from the city's bursting medieval confines, coincided with a blossoming of unfettered thinking in architecture that arrived in the backdraught of the 1888 International Exposition of Barcelona.

A key uniting element of the Modernistas was the sensuous curve, implying movement, lightness and vitality. But as well as modernity, architects often looked to the past for inspiration. Gothic, Islamic and Renaissance design all had something to offer. At its most playful, Modernisme was able to intelligently flout the rule books of these styles and create exciting new cocktails.

Gaudí

Born in Reus to a long line of coppersmiths, Antoni Gaudí was initially trained in metalwork. In childhood he suffered from poor health, including rheumatism, and became an early adopter of a vegetarian diet. He was not a promising student. In 1878, when he obtained his architecture degree the school's headmaster is reputed to have said: 'Who knows if we have given a diploma to a nutcase or a genius. Time will tell.'

As a young man, what most delighted Gaudí was being outdoors. Throughout his work, he sought to emulate the harmony he observed in the natural world, eschewing the straight line and favouring curvaceous forms and more organic shapes.

Gaudí was a devout Catholic and a Catalan nationalist. He lived a simple life, and was not averse to knocking on doors, literally begging for money to help fund construction of the cathedral.

His masterpiece was La Sagrada Família (begun in 1882), and in it you can see the culminating vision of many ideas developed over the years. He died in 1926, struck down by a streetcar while taking his daily walk to the Sant Felip Neri church. Wearing ragged clothes, Gaudí was initially thought to be a beggar and was taken to a nearby hospital where he was left in a pauper's ward. He died two days later. Thousands attended his funeral procession to La Sagrada Família where he was buried in the crypt.

Domènech i Montaner

Although overshadowed by Gaudí, Lluís Domènech i Montaner (1849–1923) was one of the great masters of Modernisme. He was a widely travelled man of prodigious intellect, with knowledge in everything from mineralogy to medieval heraldry, and he was an architectural professor, a prolific writer and a nationalist politician. The question of Catalan identity and how to create a national architecture consumed Domènech i Montaner, who designed more than a dozen large-scale works in his lifetime.

The exuberant, steel-framed Palau de la Música Catalana is one of his masterpieces.

Puig i Cadafalch

Like Domènech i Montaner, Josep Puig i Cadafalch (1867–1956) was a polymath; he was an archaeologist, an expert in Romanesque art and one of Catalonia's most prolific architects. As a politician – and later president of the Mancomunitat de Catalunya (Commonwealth of Catalonia) – he was instrumental in shaping the Catalan nationalist movement.

One of his many Modernista gems is the Casa Amatller, a rather dramatic contrast to Gaudí's Casa Batlló next door. Puig i Cadafalch has designed a house of startling beauty and invention blended with playful Gothic-style sculpture.

Gothic Masterpieces

La Catedral (p62)
Basílica de Santa Maria del Mar (p112)
Església de Santa Maria del Pi (p48)
Saló del Tinell – in the Museu d'Història de Barcelona (p104)
The Drassanes – now the site of the Museu Marítim (p84)

The New Millennium

Barcelona's latest architectural revolution began in the 1980s when, in the run-up to the 1992 Olympics, the city set about its biggest phase of renewal since the heady days of L'Eixample.

In the new millennium, the Diagonal Mar district is characterised by striking modern architecture, including the hovering blue, triangular Edifici Fòrum by Swiss architects Herzog & de Meuron and a 24-storey whitewashed trapezoidal prism that serves as the headquarters for the national telephone company, Telefónica.

Another prominent addition to the city skyline came in 2005. The shimmering, cucumber-shaped Torre Agbar is a product of French architect Jean Nouvel.

Southwest, on the way to the airport, the new Fira M2 trade fair is now marked by red twisting twin landmark towers designed by Japanese star architect and confessed Gaudí fan Toyo Ito.

The heart of La Ribera got a fresh look with its brand-new Mercat de Santa Caterina. The market is quite a sight, with its wavy ceramic roof and tubular skeleton, designed by one of the most promising names in Catalan architecture until his premature death, Enric Miralles. Miralles' Edifici de Gas Natural, a 100m glass tower near the waterfront in Barceloneta, is also extraordinary.

Modern Art

Barcelona is to modern art what Greece is to ruined temples. Three of the figures at the vanguard of 20th-century avant-gardism – Picasso, Miró and Dalí – were either born or spent their formative years here. Their powerful legacy is stamped all over Barcelona in museums and public installations. Today, Catalonia continues to be an incubator for innovative works of contemporary art.

Above: MACBA (Museu d'Art Contemporani de Barcelona; p96) MAREMAGNUM/GETTY IMAGES ©

The Crucial Three

Picasso

It wasn't until the late 19th century that truly great artists began to emerge in Barcelona and its hinterland, led by dandy portraitist Ramón Casas (1866–1932). Casas, an early Modernista, founded a Barcelona bar known as Els Quatre Gats, which became the nucleus for the city's growing art movement, holding numerous shows and expositions. An early host was a young, then unknown, *malagueño* named Pablo Picasso (1881–1973).

Picasso lived sporadically in Barcelona between the innocence-losing ages of 16 and 24, and the city heavily influenced his early painting. This was the period in which he amassed the raw materials for his Blue Period. In 1904, the then-mature Picasso moved to Paris where he found fame, fortune and Cubism, and went on to become one of the greatest artists of the 20th century.

Miró

Continuing the burst of brilliance was the Barcelona-born experimentalist Joan Miró (1893–1983), best remembered for his use of symbolic figures in primary colours.

★ **Best Places to See Modern Art**

Museu Picasso (p76)

Fundació Joan Miró (p58)

Fundació Antoni Tàpies (p53)

MACBA (p96)

Declaring he was going to 'assassinate art', Miró wanted nothing to do with the constricting labels of the era, although he has often been called a pioneering surrealist, Dadaist and automatist. His instantly recognisable style can be seen in public installations throughout the city; halfway along La Rambla, at Plaça de la Boqueria, you can walk all over Miró's *Mosaïc de Miró*. There's also, of course, the Fundació Joan Miró; housed in an extensive gallery atop Montjuïc, this museum has the single largest collection of Miró's work in the world today.

Dalí

Rising on Miró's coat-tails was the extravagant Catalan surrealist and showman, Salvador Dalí (1904–89), from nearby Figueres. He left his single greatest artistic legacy there – the Teatre-Museu Dalí, which he created on the site of an old theatre in central Figueres. Along with housing an awe-inspiring Dalí collection, the building houses the artist's remains – on his death in 1989, he was buried (according to his own wish) in the Teatre-Museu.

A larger-than-life character, Dalí mixed imaginative painting with posing, attention-seeking and shameless self-promotion. Dalí's works and ongoing influences on modern artists are hard to avoid anywhere in the world, especially Barcelona. The city provided a stimulating atmosphere for Dalí, and places like Park Güell, with its surrealist-like aspects, had a powerful effect on him.

Art Goes Informal

Picasso, Miró and Dalí were hard acts to follow. Few envied the task of Catalan Antoni Tàpies in reviving the red hot Modernista flame. An early admirer of Miró, Tàpies soon began pursuing his own esoteric path embracing 'art informal' (a Jackson Pollock–like use of spontaneity) and inventing painting that utilised clay, string and even bits of rubbish. In 1983 Tàpies constructed *Homenatge a Picasso* on Passeig de Picasso; it's essentially a glass cube set in a pond and filled with, well, junk. Tàpies was arguably Spain's greatest living painter before his death in 2012.

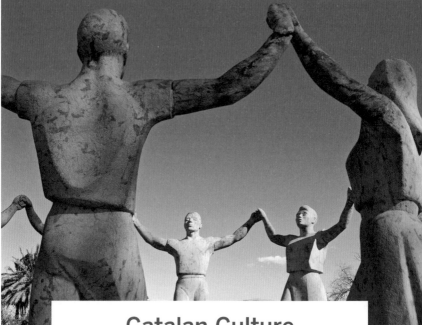

Catalan Culture

The fortunes of Catalonia have risen and fallen over the years, as Barcelona has gone from wealthy mercantile capital to a city of repression under the Franco regime, followed by the boom and bust of more recent years. Despite today's economic challenges, Catalan culture continues to flourish, with a vigorous program of events, traditional music and dance, and abundant civic pride.

Above: *Monumento a la Sardana* by Josep Cañas BRIAN LAWRENCE/GETTY IMAGES ©

Language

In Barcelona, born and bred locals proudly speak Catalan, a Romance language related to French, Spanish (Castilian) and Italian. It was only relatively recently, however, that Catalan was deemed 'legitimate'. Since Barcelona was crushed in the War of the Spanish Succession in 1714, the use of Catalan has been repeatedly banned or at least frowned upon. Franco was the last of Spain's rulers to clamp down on its public use. All that changed in 1980, when the first autonomous regional parliament was assembled and adopted new laws towards *normalització lingüístico* (linguistic normalisation).

Today Catalonia's school system is based on bilingual education, with graduates showing equal skill in using either Catalan or Spanish. Around town, Catalan is the lingua franca: advertising and road signs tend to be in Catalan, while newspapers, magazines and other publications can be found in both languages (though you'll find about twice as many options in Catalan than in Spanish). You'll also find a mix of Catalan and Spanish programming on radio and TV stations.

Music & Dance

Barcelona's vibrant music and dance scene has been shaped by artists both traditional and cutting edge. From Nova Cançó, composed during the dark years of the dictatorship, to the hybridised Catalan rumba, to hands-in-the-air rock ballads of the 1970s and '80s, Barcelona's music evolves constantly. Today's groups continue to push musical boundaries, blending rhythms from all corners of the globe. In the realm of dance, flamenco has a small loyal following, while the old-fashioned folk dance *sardana* continues to attract growing numbers.

Top Albums

- *Techari,* Ojos de Brujo
- *Anells d'Aigua,* Maria del Mar Bonet
- *Verges 50,* Lluís Llach
- *Wild Animals,* Pinker Tones
- *Set Tota la Vida,* Mishima
- *Voràgine,* 08001
- *Rey de la Rumba,* Peret
- *X Anniversarium,* Estopa

Sardana

The Catalan dance par excellence is the *sardana,* the roots of which lie in the far northern Empordà region of Catalonia. Compared with flamenco, it is sober indeed, but not unlike a lot of other Mediterranean folk dances.

The dancers hold hands in a circle and wait for the 10 or so musicians to begin. The performance starts with the piping of the *flabiol,* a little wooden flute. When the other musicians join in, the dancers start – a series of steps to the right, one back and then the same to the left. As the music 'heats up' the steps become more complex, the leaps are higher and the dancers lift their arms. Then they return to the initial steps and continue. If newcomers wish to join in, space is made for them as the dance continues and the whole thing proceeds in a more or less seamless fashion.

Nova Cançó

Curiously, it was probably the Franco repression that most helped foster a vigorous local music scene in Catalonia. In the dark 1950s the Nova Cançó (New Song) movement was born to resist linguistic oppression with music in Catalan (getting air time on the radio was long close to impossible), throwing up stars that in some cases won huge popularity throughout Spain, such as the Valencia-born Raimon.

More specifically loved in Catalonia as a Bob Dylan–style 1960s protest singer-songwriter was Lluís Llach, much of whose music was more or less anti-regime. Joan Manuel Serrat is another legendary figure. His appeal stretches from Barcelona to Buenos Aires. In 1968 he refused to represent Spain at the Eurovision song contest if he were not allowed to sing in Catalan. Accused of being anti-Spanish, he was long banned from performing in Spain.

Born in Mallorca, the talented singer Maria del Mar Bonet arrived in Barcelona in 1967 and embarked on a long and celebrated singing career. She sang in Catalan, and many of her searing and powerful songs were banned by the dictatorship.

Pau Casals (1876–1973) was one of the greatest cellists of the 20th century. Born in Catalonia but living in exile in southern France, he declared he would not play in public as long as the Western democracies continued to tolerate Franco's regime. In 1958 he was a candidate for the Nobel Peace Prize.

Essential Reading

○ *Barcelona* (Robert Hughes, 1992) Witty and passionate study of 2000 years of history.

○ *The Shadow of the Wind* (Carlos Ruiz Zafón, 2001) Page-turning mystery set in post-civil-war Barcelona.

○ *Homage to Catalonia* (George Orwell, 1938) Orwell's classic account of the early days of the Spanish Civil War.

Havaneres

The oldest musical tradition to have survived to some degree in Catalonia is that of the *havaneres* (from Havana) – nostalgic songs and melancholy sea shanties brought back from Cuba by Catalans who lived, sailed and traded there in the 19th century. Even after Spain lost Cuba in 1898, the *havanera* tradition (a mix of European and Cuban rhythms) continued. A magical opportunity to enjoy these songs is the Cantada d'Havaneres (www.havanerescalella.cat), an evening concert held on the Costa Brava in early July. Otherwise, you may stumble across performances elsewhere along the coast or even in Barcelona, but there is no set program.

La Rumba

Back in the 1950s, a new sound mixing flamenco with salsa and other Latin sounds emerged in *gitano* (Roma people) circles in the bars of Gràcia and the Barri Gòtic. One of the founders of rumba Catalana was Antonio González, known as El Pescaílla (married to the flamenco star Lola Flores). Although El Pescaílla was well known in town, the Matarò-born *gitano* Peret later took this eminently Barcelona style to a wider (eventually international) audience.

By the end of the 1970s, however, rumba Catalana was running out of steam. Peret had turned to religion and El Pescaílla lived in Flores' shadow in Madrid. But Buenos Aires–born Javier Patricio 'Gato' Pérez discovered rumba in 1977 and gave it his own personal spin, bringing out several popular records, such as *Atalaya,* until the early 1980s.

After Pérez, it seemed that rumba was dead. Not so fast! New rumba bands, often highly eclectic, have emerged in recent years. Ai Ai Ai, Barrio Negro, El Tío Carlos and La Pegatina are names to look out for. Others mix rumba with styles as diverse as reggae or ragga.

NIKADA/GETTY IMAGES ©

Survival Guide

Directory A–Z

Discount Cards

Articket (www.articketbcn.org) Gives admission to six sites for €30 and is valid for six months. You can pick up the ticket at the tourist offices at Plaça de Catalunya, Plaça de Sant Jaume and Estació Sants train station.

Barcelona Card (www.barcelonacard.com) Handy if you want to see lots in a limited time; costs €34/44/52/58 for two/three/four/five days (about 50% less for children aged four to 12). Includes free transport (and 20% off the Aerobús) and discounted admission prices (up to 30% off) or free entry to many museums and other sights, as well as minor discounts on purchases at a small number of shops, restaurants and bars. Pick up the card at tourist offices or online (buying online saves you 10%).

Ruta del Modernisme (www.rutadelmodernisme.com) This pack costs €12 and is well worth looking into for visiting Modernista sights at discounted rates.

Emergency

The general emergency number is 112.

Electricity

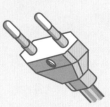

220V/230V/50Hz

Gay & Lesbian Travellers

Barcelona has a vibrant gay and lesbian scene. Despite fierce opposition from the Catholic Church, Spain legalised same-sex marriage in 2005, becoming the fourth country in the world to do so.

As a rule, Barcelona is pretty tolerant, and the sight of gay or lesbian couples arm in arm is generally unlikely to raise eyebrows. Transgenderism, too, is increasingly accepted.

Note that Spain's LGBT capital is the saucily hedonistic Sitges, 35km southwest of Barcelona.

Useful Websites

60by80 (www.60by80.com/barcelona) An excellent website for gay travellers.

Gay Barcelona (www.gaybarcelona.com) A handy listings site for visitors to Barcelona.

Tillate (www.tillate.es) Discover upcoming parties in this nightlife guide to regions around Spain, including Catalonia.

GaySitges (www.gaysitges.com) A specific site dedicated to this LGBT-friendly coastal town.

Insurance

○ A travel-insurance policy to cover theft, loss, medical problems, and cancellation or delays of your travel arrangements is a good idea.

○ European Union residents can access free Spanish healthcare with an EHIC card (http://ehic.europa.eu).

○ Paying for your ticket with a credit card can often provide limited travel-accident insurance, and you may be able to reclaim the payment if the operator doesn't deliver.

○ Worldwide travel insurance is available at www.lonelyplanet.com/travel-insurance. You can buy, extend and claim online anytime – even if you're already on the road.

Internet Access

Wi-fi is widespread. Data packages with a local pay-as-you-go SIM card are reasonable; take an unlocked smartphone and connect.

Money

ATMs

○ Barcelona abounds with banks; many have ATMs.

○ ATMs are also in plentiful supply around Plaça de Catalunya, Plaça de Sant Jaume (in the Barri Gòtic) and La Rambla.

○ Most ATMs allow you to use international debit or credit cards to withdraw money in euros.

○ There is usually a charge (around 1.5% to 2%) on ATM cash withdrawals when abroad.

Credit & Debit Cards

Cards can be used in many hotels, restaurants and shops, although there may be a minimum purchase requirement of €5 or €10.

When paying with a credit card, photo ID is often required, even for chip cards where you're required to enter your PIN (for travellers without chip cards, just indicate that you'll give a signature).

Tipping

Bars It's rare to leave a tip in bars, though a bit of small change is always appreciated.

Restaurants Catalans typically leave 5% or less at restaurants. Leave more for exceptionally good service.

Taxis Optional, but most locals round up to the nearest euro.

Opening Hours

Standard opening hours:

Banks 8.30am to 2pm Monday to Friday; some also 4pm to 7pm Thursday or 9am to 1pm Saturday

Bars 6pm to 2am (to 3am weekends)

Clubs midnight to 6am Thursday to Saturday

Department stores 10am to 10pm Monday to Saturday

Museums and art galleries Vary considerably; generally 10am to 8pm (some shut for lunch around 2pm to 4pm). Many close all day Monday and from 2pm Sunday.

Restaurants 1pm to 4pm and 8.30pm to midnight

Shops 9am or 10am to 1.30pm or 2pm and 4pm or 4.30pm to 8pm or 8.30pm Monday to Saturday

Public Holidays

New Year's Day (Any Nou/Año Nuevo) 1 January

Epiphany/Three Kings' Day (Epifanía or El Dia dels Reis/Día de los Reyes Magos) 6 January

Good Friday (Divendres Sant/ Viernes Santo) March/April

Easter Monday (Dilluns de Pasqua Florida) March/April

Labour Day (Dia del Treball/ Fiesta del Trabajo) 1 May

Day after Pentecost Sunday (Dilluns de Pasqua Granda) May/ June

Feast of St John the Baptist (Dia de Sant Joan/Día de San Juan Bautista) 24 June

Feast of the Assumption (L'Assumpció/La Asunción) 15 August

Catalonia's National Day (Diada Nacional de Catalunya) 11 September

Festes de la Mercè 24 September

Spanish National Day (Festa de la Hispanitat/Día de la Hispanidad) 12 October

All Saints Day (Dia de Tots Sants/Día de Todos los Santos) 1 November

Constitution Day (Día de la Constitución) 6 December

Feast of the Immaculate Conception (La Immaculada Concepció/La Inmaculada Concepción) 8 December

Christmas (Nadal/Navidad) 25 December

Boxing Day/St Stephen's Day (El Dia de Sant Esteve) 26 December

Practicalities

○ **Currency** Euro (€)

○ **Smoking** Banned in restaurants and bars

○ **Major Barcelona newspapers** *La Vanguardia* and *El Periódico* are available in Spanish and Catalan. *El País* publishes an online English supplement (elpais.com/ elpais/inenglish.html).

Taxes & Refunds

Value-added tax (VAT) is also known as IVA (*impuesto sobre el valor añadido;* pronounced 'EE-ba'). The tax is 10% on accommodation and restaurant prices and is usually – but not always – included in quoted prices. On most retail goods the IVA is 21%.

Non-EU residents are entitled to a refund of the 21% IVA on purchases costing more than €90 from any shop, if the goods are taken out of the EU within three months. Ask the shop for a Cashback (or similar) refund form showing the price and IVA paid for each item and identifying the vendor and purchaser, then present the form at the customs booth for IVA refunds when you depart from Spain (or elsewhere in the EU). You will need your passport and a boarding card that shows you are leaving the EU, and your luggage (so do this before checking in bags). The officer will stamp the invoice and you hand it in at a bank at the departure point to receive a reimbursement.

Telephone

Local SIM cards Can be used in unlocked phones. Data packages are the best-value way to stay in touch and make international calls. You'll likely need a passport to register a local SIM.

Making calls To call Barcelona from outside Spain, dial the international access code, followed by the code for Spain (📞34) and the full number (including Barcelona's area code, 📞93). To make an international call from Barcelona, dial the international access code (📞00), country code, area code and number.

Time

Spain is one hour ahead of GMT/UTC during winter, and two hours ahead during daylight savings (the last Sunday in March to the last Sunday in October).

Tourist Information

Several tourist offices operate in Barcelona. A couple of general information telephone numbers worth bearing in mind are 📞010 and 📞012. The first is for Barcelona and the other is for all Catalonia (run by the Generalitat). You sometimes strike English speakers, though for the most part operators are Catalan/Spanish bilingual. In addition to tourist offices, information booths operate at Estació del Nord bus station and at Plaça del Portal de la Pau, at the foot of the Mirador de Colom at the port end of La Rambla. Others set up at various points in the city centre in summer.

Plaça de Catalunya (Map p254; 📞93 285 38 34; www.barcelonaturisme.com; Plaça de Catalunya 17; ⏰9.30am-9.30pm; Ⓜ Catalunya)

Plaça Sant Jaume (Map p250; 📞93 285 38 32; Carrer de la Ciutat 2; ⏰8.30am-8.30pm Mon-Fri, 9am-7pm Sat, 9am-2pm Sun & holidays; Ⓜ Jaume I)

Estació Sants (Plaça dels Països Catalans; ⏰8am-8pm; 🚆 Estació Sants)

El Prat Airport (⏰8.30am-8.30pm)

Palau Robert Regional Tourist Office (Map p254; 📞93 238 80 91; www.palaurobert.gencat.cat; Passeig de Gràcia 107; ⏰10am-8pm Mon-Sat, to 2.30pm Sun; Ⓜ Diagonal) Offers a host of material on Catalonia, audiovisual resources, a bookshop and a branch of Turisme Juvenil de Catalunya (for youth travel).

Travellers with Disabilities

○ Some hotels and public institutions have wheelchair access.

○ All buses in Barcelona are wheelchair accessible and a growing number of metro stations are theoretically wheelchair accessible (generally by lift, although there have been complaints that they are only good for people with prams). Lines 2,

9, 10 and 11 are completely adapted, as are the majority of stops on Line 1. In all, about 80% of stops have been adapted (you can check which ones by looking at a network map at www.tmb.cat/en/transport-accessible).

○ Ticket vending machines in metro stations are adapted for disabled travellers, and have Braille options for those who have a visual impairment.

○ Several taxi companies have adapted vehicles, including **Taxi Amic** (☎93 420 80 88; www.taxi-amic-adaptat.com) and **Gestverd** (☎93 303 09 09; www.gestverd.com).

○ Most street crossings in central Barcelona are wheelchair-friendly.

○ Lonely Planet's free Accessible Travel guide can be downloaded here: http://lptravel.to/AccessibleTravel

Transport

Arriving in Barcelona

After Madrid, Barcelona is Spain's busiest international transport hub. A host of airlines, including many budget carriers, fly directly to Barcelona from around Europe. Most travellers enter Barcelona through El Prat Airport. Some budget airlines, including Ryanair, use Girona-Costa Brava Airport or Reus Airport.

Travelling by train is a pricier but perhaps more romantic way of reaching Catalonia from other European cities. The new TGV takes around seven hours from Paris to Barcelona. Eighteen high-speed Tren de Alta Velocidad Española (AVE) trains between Madrid and Barcelona run daily in each direction, nine of them in under three hours.

Barcelona is well-connected by bus to other parts of Spain, as well as to major European cities.

Flights, cars and tours can be booked online at lonelyplanet.com.

El Prat Airport

Barcelona's **El Prat Airport** (☎902 404704; www.aena.es) lies 17km southwest of Plaça de Catalunya at El Prat de Llobregat. The airport has two main terminal buildings: the new T1 terminal and the older T2, itself divided into three terminal areas (A, B and C).

Bus

Frequent Aerobúses operated by **A1** (☎902 100104; www.aerobusbcn.com; one way/return €5.90/10.20; ⏱6am-1am) make the 35-minute run from Terminal 1 to Plaça de Catalunya (€5.90) from 6am to 1am. The A2 Aerobús from Terminal 2 works to the same hours and follows the same route. Buy tickets on the bus or from agents at the bus stop.

Return departures from Plaça de Catalunya are from 5.30am to 12.30am.

Taxi

A taxi from the airport will cost around €25 and take between 20 and 30 minutes.

Estació Sants

Long-distance trains arrive in **Estació Sants** (Plaça dels Països Catalans; Ⓜ Estació Sants), about 2.5km west of La Rambla. The train station is linked by metro to other parts of the city.

Estació del Nord

Barcelona's long-haul **bus station** (☎902 26 06 06; www.barcelonanord.cat; Carrer d'Ali Bei 80; Ⓜ Arc de Triomf) is located in L'Eixample, about 1.5km northeast of Plaça de Catalunya, and is a short walk from several metro stations.

Girona-Costa Brava Airport

Girona-Costa Brava Airport (www.girona-airport.net) is 12km south of Girona and 92km northeast of Barcelona. The **Barcelona Bus** (☎902 13 00 14; www.barcelonabus.com; Ⓜ Girona) operated by Sagalés is timed with Ryanair flights and goes direct to Barcelona's Estació del Nord (one way/return €16/25, 90 minutes).

Reus Airport

Reus airport ([✆]902 404704; www.aena.es) is 13km west of Tarragona and 108km southwest of Barcelona. Buses operated by **Hispano-Igualadina** ([✆]93 339 73 29; www.igualadina. com; Carrer de Viriat; [M]Estació Sants) are timed with Ryanair flights and go direct to Barcelona's Estació Sants (one way/return €16/25, 90 minutes).

Getting Around

Barcelona has abundant options for getting around

town. The excellent metro can get you most places, with buses and trams filling in the gaps. Taxis are the best option late at night.

Metro & Train

The easy-to-use **Transports Metropolitans de Barcelona** (TMB; [✆]93 298 70 00; www.tmb.net) metro system has 11 numbered and colour-coded lines. It runs from 5am to midnight Sunday to Thursday and holidays, from 5am to 2am on Friday and days immediately preceding holidays, and 24 hours on Saturday.

Ongoing work to expand the metro continues on several lines. Lines 9 and 10

will eventually connect with the airport (2016 at the earliest).

Suburban trains run by the **Ferrocarrils de la Generalitat de Catalunya** (FGC; [✆]900 901515; www. fgc.net) include a couple of useful city lines. All lines heading north from Plaça de Catalunya stop at Carrer de Provença and Gràcia. One of these lines (L7) goes to Tibidabo and another (L6 to Reina Elisenda) has a stop near the Monestir de Pedralbes. Most trains from Plaça de Catalunya continue beyond Barcelona to Sant Cugat, Sabadell and Terrassa. Other FGC lines head west from Plaça d'Espanya, including one for Manresa that is handy for the trip to Montserrat.

Depending on the line, these trains run from about 5am (with only one or two services before 6am) to 11pm or midnight Sunday to Thursday, and from 5am to about 1am on Friday and Saturday.

Bus

Transports Metropolitans de Barcelona buses run along most city routes every few minutes from around 5am or 6.30am to around 10pm or 11pm. Many routes pass through Plaça de Catalunya and/or Plaça de la Universitat. After 11pm a reduced network of yellow *nitbusos* (night buses) runs until 3am or 5am. All *nitbus* routes pass through Plaça de Catalunya and most run every 30 to 45 minutes.

Public Transport Tickets

The metro, FGC trains, *rodalies/cercanías* (Renfe-run local trains) and buses come under one zoned-fare regime. Single-ride tickets on all standard transport within Zone 1 cost €2.15.

Targetes are multitrip transport tickets. They are sold at all city-centre metro stations. The prices given here are for travel in Zone 1. Children under four years of age travel free. Options include the following:

❍ Targeta T-10 (€10.30) – 10 rides (each valid for 1¼ hours) on the metro, buses, FGC trains and *rodalies*. You can change between each transport type.

❍ Targeta T-DIA (€8.40) – unlimited travel on all transport for one day.

❍ Two-/three-/four-/five-day tickets (€14/21/27/32) – unlimited travel on all transport except the Aerobús; buy them at metro stations and tourist offices.

❍ T-Mes (€53) – 30 days unlimited use of all public transport.

❍ Targeta T-50/30 (€43) – 50 trips within 30 days, valid on all transport.

❍ T-Trimestre (€142) – 90 days unlimited use of all public transport.

Climate Change & Travel

Every form of transport that relies on carbon-based fuel generates CO_2, the main cause of human-induced climate change. Modern travel is dependent on aeroplanes, which might use less fuel per kilometre per person than most cars but travel much greater distances. The altitude at which aircraft emit gases (including CO_2) and particles also contributes to their climate change impact. Many websites offer 'carbon calculators' that allow people to estimate the carbon emissions generated by their journey and, for those who wish to do so, to offset the impact of the greenhouse gases emitted with contributions to portfolios of climate-friendly initiatives throughout the world. Lonely Planet offsets the carbon footprint of all staff and author travel.

Taxi

Taxis charge €2.10 flag fall plus meter charges of €1.03 per kilometre (€1.30 from 8pm to 8am and all day on weekends). A further €3.10 is added for all trips to/from the airport, and €1 for luggage bigger than 55cm x 35cm x 35cm. The trip from Estació Sants to Plaça de Catalunya, about 3km, costs about €11. You can flag a taxi down in the streets or call one. Try **Fonotaxi** (93 300 11 00) or **Ràdio Taxi 033** (93 303 30 33).

The call-out charge is €3.40 (€4.20 at night and on weekends). In many taxis it is possible to pay with a credit card and, if you have a local telephone number, you can join the T033 Ràdio taxi service for booking taxis online (www.radiotaxi033.com). You can also book online at www.catalunyataxi.com.

Taxi Amic (93 420 80 88; www.taxi-amic-adaptat.com) is a special taxi service for people with disabilities or difficult situations (such as transport of big objects). Book at least 24 hours in advance if possible.

Bicycle

Over 180km of bike lanes have been laid out across the city, so it's possible to commute on two environmentally friendly wheels. A waterfront path runs northeast from Port Olímpic towards Riu Besòs. Scenic itineraries are mapped for cyclists in the Collserola parkland, and the *ronda verda* is an incomplete 75km cycling path that extends around the city's outskirts. You can cycle a well-signed 22km loop path (part of the *ronda verda*) by following the seaside bike path northeast of Barceloneta.

Cable Car

Several aerial cable cars operate in Barcelona and provide excellent views over the city:

Telefèrico del Puerto (www.telefericodebarcelona.com; Passeig Escullera; one way/return €11/16.50; 11am-7pm Mar-Oct, to 5.30pm Nov-Feb; 17, 39, 64, Barceloneta) Travels between the waterfront southwest of Barceloneta and Montjuïc.

Telefèric de Montjuïc (www.telefericdemontjuic.cat; return adult/child €12/9; 10am-9pm) Two-stage cable car that runs between Estació Parc Montjuïc and the Castell de Montjuïc.

Tram

There are a handful of tram lines in the city. All standard transport passes are valid. A scenic option is the *tramvia blau* (blue tram), which runs up to the foot of Tibidabo.

Language

Catalan and Spanish both have official-language status in Catalonia. In Barcelona, you'll hear as much Spanish as Catalan, so we've provided some Spanish to get you started. Spanish pronunciation is not difficult as most of its sounds are also found in English. You can read our pronunciation guides below as if they were English and you'll be understood just fine. And if you pronounce 'th' in our guides with a lisp and 'kh' as a throaty sound, you'll even sound like a real Spanish person.

To enhance your trip with a phrasebook, visit **lonelyplanet.com**. Lonely Planet iPhone phrasebooks are available through the Apple App store.

Basics

Hello.
Hola. — *o*·la

How are you?
¿Qué tal? — ke tal

I'm fine, thanks.
Bien, gracias. — byen *gra*·thyas

Excuse me. (to get attention)
Disculpe. — dees·*kool*·pe

Yes./No.
Sí./No. — see/no

Thank you.
Gracias. — *gra*·thyas

You're welcome./That's fine.
De nada. — de *na*·da

Goodbye. /See you later.
Adiós./Hasta luego. — a·*dyos/as*·ta *lwe*·go

Do you speak English?
¿Habla inglés? — a·bla een·*gles*

I don't understand.
No entiendo. — no en·*tyen*·do

How much is this?
¿Cuánto cuesta? — *kwan*·to *kwes*·ta

Can you reduce the price a little?
¿Podría bajar un — po·*dree*·a ba·*khar* oon
poco el precio? — *po*·ko el *pre*·thyo

Accommodation

I'd like to make a booking.
Quisiera reservar — kee·*sye*·ra re·ser·*var*
una habitación. — *oo*·na a·bee·ta·*thyon*

How much is it per night?
¿Cuánto cuesta por noche? — *kwan*·to *kwes*·ta por *no*·che

Eating & Drinking

I'd like ..., please.
Quisiera ..., por favor. — kee·*sye*·ra ... por fa·*vor*

That was delicious!
¡Estaba buenísimo! — es·*ta*·ba bwe·*nee*·see·mo

Bring the bill/check, please.
La cuenta, por favor. — la *kwen*·ta por fa·*vor*

I'm allergic to ...
Soy alérgico/a al ... (m/f) — soy a·*ler*·khee·ko/a al ...

I don't eat ...
No como ... — no *ko*·mo ...

chicken	*pollo*	*po*·lyo
fish	*pescado*	pes·*ka*·do
meat	*carne*	*kar*·ne

Emergencies

I'm ill.
Estoy enfermo/a. (m/f) — es·*toy* en·*fer*·mo/a

Help!
¡Socorro! — so·*ko*·ro

Call a doctor!
¡Llame a un médico! — *lya*·me a oon *me*·dee·ko

Call the police!
¡Llame a la policía! — *lya*·me a la po·lee·*thee*·a

Directions

I'm looking for a/an/the ...
Estoy buscando ... — es·*toy* boos·*kan*·do ...

ATM	
un cajero	oon ka·*khe*·ro
automático	ow·to·*ma*·tee·ko
bank	
el banco	el *ban*·ko
... embassy	
la embajada de ...	la em·ba·*kha*·da de ...
market	
el mercado	el mer·*ka*·do
museum	
el museo	el moo·*se*·o
restaurant	
un restaurante	oon res·tow·*ran*·te
toilet	
los servicios	los ser·*vee*·thyos
tourist office	
la oficina de	la o·fee·*thee*·na de
turismo	too·*rees*·mo

Behind the Scenes

Acknowledgements

Climate map data adapted from Peel MC, Finlayson BL & McMahon TA (2007) 'Updated World Map of the Koppen-Geiger Climate Classification', *Hydrology and Earth System Sciences*, 11, 163344

Illustrations p42–3, 116–7 by Javier Zarracina

This Book

This book was curated by Andy Symington and researched and written by Andy Symington, Sally Davies and Regis St Louis. This guidebook was commissioned in Lonely Planet's Melbourne office, and produced by the following:

Destination Editors Jo Cooke, Lorna Parkes, Cliff Wilkinson
Associate Product Director Liz Heynes
Series Designer Katherine Marsh
Cartographic Series Designer Wayne Murphy
Senior Product Editor Catherine Naghten
Product Editor Luna Soo
Senior Cartographer Anthony Phelan
Book Designer Jessica Rose
Cartographers Gabriel Lindquist
Assisting Editors Imogen Bannister, Nigel Chin, Victoria Harrison, Gabrielle Innes, Kristin Odijk, Charlotte Orr, Gabrielle Stefanos, Saralinda Turner, Jeanette Wall
Cover Researcher Naomi Parker
Thanks to James Hardy, Andi Jones, Indra Kilfoyle, Anne Mason, Kate Mathews, Roger McDonald, Campbell McKenzie, Jenna Myers, Claire Naylor, Karyn Noble, Susan Paterson, Kirsten Rawlings, Alison Ridgway, Kathryn Rowan, Dianne Schallmeiner, Lyahna Spencer, Angela Tinson, Stacey Trock

Send Us Your Feedback

We love to hear from travellers – your comments keep us on our toes and help make our books better. Our well-travelled team reads every word on what you loved or loathed about this book. Although we cannot reply individually to postal submissions, we always guarantee that your feedback goes straight to the appropriate authors, in time for the next edition. Each person who sends us information is thanked in the next edition, the most useful submissions are rewarded with a selection of digital PDF chapters.

Visit lonelyplanet.com/contact to submit your updates and suggestions or to ask for help. Our award-winning website also features inspirational travel stories, news and discussions.

Note: We may edit, reproduce and incorporate your comments in Lonely Planet products such as guidebooks, websites and digital products, so let us know if you don't want your comments reproduced or your name acknowledged. For a copy of our privacy policy visit lonelyplanet.com/privacy.

Index

MAREMAGNUM/GETTY IMAGES ©

Barcelona Maps

El Raval & Sant Antoni

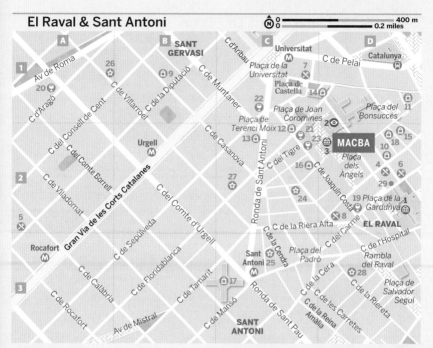

Barri Gòtic, Ciutat Vella & La Ribera

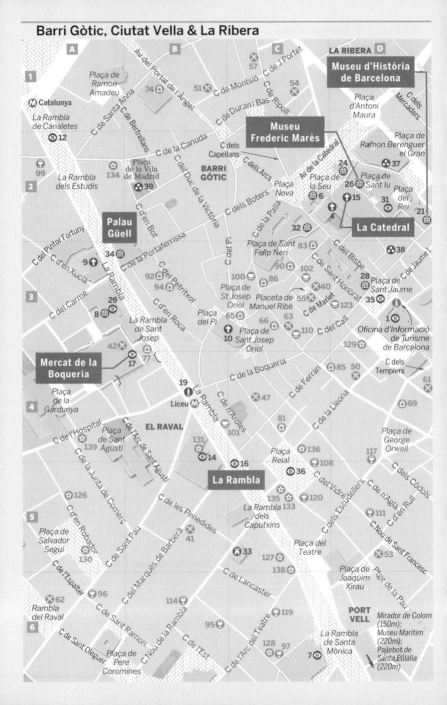

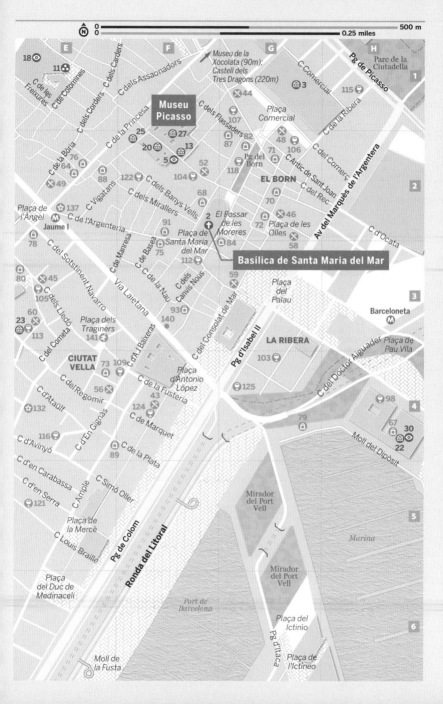

Barri Gòtic, Ciutat Vella & La Ribera

Sights

1 Ajuntament..............................D3
2 Basílica de Santa Maria del Mar.............F2
3 Born Centre de Cultura i Memòria...........G1
4 Capella de Santa Llúcia.....................D2
5 Carrer de Montcada.......................F2
6 Casa de l'Ardiaca........................C2
7 Centre d'Art Santa Mònica...................C6
8 Centre de la Imatge......................A3
9 Església de Betlem.......................A3
10 Església de Santa Maria del Pi.............C3
11 Espai Santa Caterina.....................E1
12 Font de Canaletes.......................A2
13 Fundació Gaspar.........................F2
14 Gran Teatre del Liceu....................B4
15 La Catedral.............................D2
16 La Rambla..............................C5
17 Mercat de la Boqueria....................B4
18 Mercat de Santa Caterina.................E1
19 Mosaïc de Miró..........................B4
20 Museu de Cultures del Món................F2
21 Museu d'Història de Barcelona.............D2
22 Museu d'Història de Catalunya.............H4
23 Museu d'Idees i Invents de
Barcelona..............................E3
24 Museu Diocesà..........................D2
25 Museu Europeu d'Art Modern..............F2
26 Museu Frederic Marès....................D2
27 Museu Picasso..........................F2
28 Palau de la Generalitat..................D3
29 Palau de la Virreina.....................A3
30 Palau de Mar...........................H4
31 Palau del Lloctinent....................D2
32 Palau Episcopal........................C2
33 Palau Güell............................C5
34 Palau Moja.............................A3
35 Plaça de Sant Jaume....................D3
36 Plaça Reial...........................C5
37 Roman Walls...........................D2
38 Temple Romà d'August..................D3
39 Via Sepulcral Romana...................B2

Eating

40 Alcoba Azul............................C3
41 Bar Cañete............................B5
42 Bar Pinotxo...........................A3
43 Belmonte.............................F4
44 Bormuth..............................G1
45 Cafè de l'Acadèmia....................E3
46 Cal Pep..............................G2
47 Can Culleretes.......................C4
48 Casa Delfín..........................G2
49 Cat Bar..............................E2
50 Cerería..............................D4
51 Els Quatre Gats......................B1

52 Euskal Etxea..........................F2
53 Federal..............................D5
54 Koy Shunka..........................C1
55 La Vinateria del Call.................C3
56 Milk.................................E4
57 Onofre..............................C1
58 Paradiso.............................G2
59 Passadís Del Pep.....................G3
60 Pla..................................E3
61 Rasoterra............................D4
62 Suculent.............................A6
63 Xurreria.............................C3

Shopping

64 Arlequí Màscares.......................E2
65 Art & Crafts Market....................C3
66 Artesania Catalunya....................C3
67 Bestiari.............................H4
68 Casa Gispert.........................F2
Cereria Subirà.....................(see 21)
69 Cómplices............................D4
70 Coquette.............................G2
71 Coquette.............................G2
72 Custo Barcelona......................G2
73 Drap Art.............................E4
74 El Corte Inglés......................B1
75 El Magnífico.........................F3
76 El Rei de la Màgia...................E2
77 Escribà..............................B3
78 FC Botiga............................E2
79 Feria de Artesanía del Palau de
Mar..................................G4
80 Formatgeria La Seu...................E3
81 Herboristeria del Rei................C4
82 Hofmann Pastisseria..................G2
83 La Basílica Galeria..................C3
84 La Botifarreria......................G3
85 La Manual Alpargatera................D4
86 L'Arca...............................C3
87 Loisaida.............................G2
88 Nu Sabates...........................E2
Olisoliva..........................(see 18)
89 Papabubble...........................E4
90 Sabater Hermanos.....................C3
91 Sans i Sans..........................F2
92 Torrons Vicens.......................B3
93 Vila Viniteca........................F3
94 Xocoa................................B3

Drinking & Nightlife

95 Bar La Concha........................B6
96 Bar Marsella.........................A6
97 Bar Pastís...........................C6
98 BlackLab.............................H4
99 Boadas...............................A2

L'Eixample & Gràcia

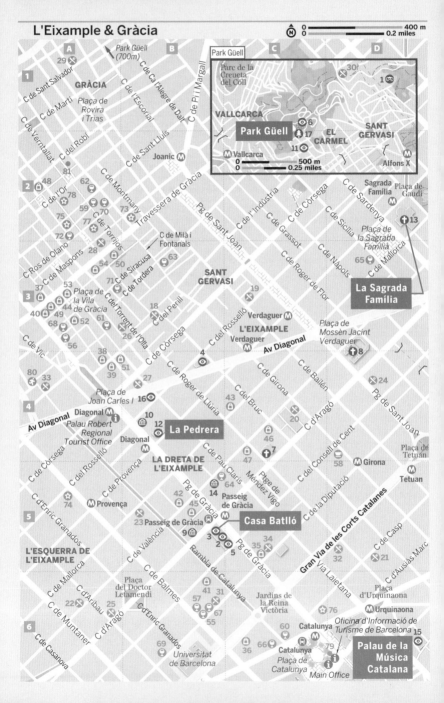

L'Eixample & Gràcia

◎ Sights

1 Bunkers del Carmel.................................D1
2 Casa Amatller... B5
3 Casa Batlló... B5
4 Casa de les Punxes................................. B4
5 Casa Lleó Morera....................................C5
6 Casa-Museu Gaudí.................................C1
7 Església de la Puríssima Concepció I
    Assumpció de Nostra Senyora..........C4
8 Església de les Saleses..........................D4
9 Fundació Antoni Tàpies........................ B5
10 Fundació Suñol......................................B4
11 Gaudí Experience...................................C2
12 La Pedrera.. B4
13 La Sagrada Família.................................D2
14 Museu Egipci... B5
15 Palau de la Música Catalana.................D6
16 Palau del Baró Quadras........................B4
17 Park Güell...C2

◎ Eating

18 Bilbao...B3
19 Can Kenji...C3
20 Casa Amalia..C4
21 Casa Calvet...D5
22 Cata 1.81...A6
23 Cerveseria Catalana.............................. B5
24 Chicha Limoná..D4
25 Cinc Sentits..A6
26 Con Gracia..B3
27 Entrepanes Díaz.....................................B4
28 La Nena...A3
29 La Panxa del Bisbe.................................A1
30 Las Delicias..D1
31 Monvínic...B6
32 Patagonia Beef & Wine D5
33 Roig Robí...A4
34 Tapas 24..C5

◎ Shopping

35 Adolfo Domínguez..................................C5
36 Altaïr..C6
37 Amapola Vegan Shop............................ A3
    Bagués-Masriera ....(see 2)
38 Be..A4
39 Bodega Bonavista...................................A4
40 Cabinet BCN... A3
41 Cacao Sampaka......................................B6
42 Camper..B5

43 Cubiña... C4
44 Doctor Paper Barcelona........................ A3
45 El Bulevard dels Antiquaris.................. B5
46 Flores Navarro..C4
47 Joan Múrria.. C4
48 La Festival...A2
49 Lady Loquita...A3
    Loewe...(see 5)
50 Mercat de l'Abaceria Central................A3
51 Mushi Mushi...A4
52 Nostàlgic...A3
53 Surco...A3
54 Tintin Shop...A3

◎ Drinking & Nightlife

55 Aire... B6
56 Alfa... A3
    Arena Classic.................................(see 55)
57 Arena Madre... B6
58 Cafè del Centre.......................................D4
59 Chatelet..A2
60 City Hall..C6
61 El Sabor...A3
62 Elephanta..A2
63 La Cigale... B3
64 Les Gens Que J'Aime B5
65 Michael Collins Pub...............................D3
66 Milano...C6
67 Monvínic... B6
68 Musical Maria..A3
69 Napar BCN.. B6
70 Rabipelao..A2
71 Raïm..A3
72 Viblioteca...A2

◎ Entertainment

73 Heliogàbal... B2
74 Mediterráneo..A5
    Music Hall....................................... (see 60)
    Palau de la Música Catalana........ (see 15)
75 Soda Acústic... A2
76 Teatre Tívoli..C6
77 Teatreneu..A2
78 Verdi...A2

◎ Activities, Courses & Tours

79 Barcelona Walking Tours D6
80 Flotarium..A4
81 Swing Maniacs..A2

Montjuïc

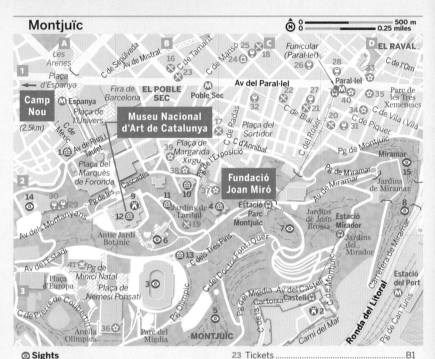

Symbols & Map Key

Look for these symbols to quickly identify listings:

- Sights
- Activities
- Courses
- Tours
- Festivals & Events
- Eating
- Drinking
- Entertainment
- Shopping
- Information & Transport

These symbols and abbreviations give vital information for each listing:

- Sustainable or green recommendation
- FREE No payment required

- Telephone number
- Opening hours
- Parking
- Nonsmoking
- Air-conditioning
- Internet access
- Wi-fi access
- Swimming pool
- Bus
- Ferry
- Tram
- Train
- English-language menu
- Vegetarian selection
- Family-friendly

Find your best experiences with these Great For... icons.

- Budget
- Food & Drink
- Drinking
- Cycling
- Shopping
- Sport
- Art & Culture
- Events
- Photo Op
- Scenery
- Family Travel
- Short Trip
- Detour
- Walking
- Local Life
- History
- Entertainment
- Beaches
- Winter Travel
- Cafe/Coffee
- Nature & Wildlife

Sights

- Beach
- Bird Sanctuary
- Buddhist
- Castle/Palace
- Christian
- Confucian
- Hindu
- Islamic
- Jain
- Jewish
- Monument
- Museum/Gallery/ Historic Building
- Ruin
- Shinto
- Sikh
- Taoist
- Winery/Vineyard
- Zoo/Wildlife Sanctuary
- Other Sight

Points of Interest

- Bodysurfing
- Camping
- Cafe
- Canoeing/Kayaking
- Course/Tour
- Diving
- Drinking & Nightlife
- Eating
- Entertainment
- Sento Hot Baths/ Onsen
- Shopping
- Skiing
- Sleeping
- Snorkelling
- Surfing
- Swimming/Pool
- Walking
- Windsurfing
- Other Activity

Information

- Bank
- Embassy/Consulate
- Hospital/Medical
- Internet
- Police
- Post Office
- Telephone
- Toilet
- Tourist Information
- Other Information

Geographic

- Beach
- Gate
- Hut/Shelter
- Lighthouse
- Lookout
- Mountain/Volcano
- Oasis
- Park
- Pass
- Picnic Area
- Waterfall

Transport

- Airport
- BART station
- Border crossing
- Boston T station
- Bus
- Cable car/Funicular
- Cycling
- Ferry
- Metro/MRT station
- Monorail
- Parking
- Petrol station
- Subway/S-Bahn/ Skytrain station
- Taxi
- Train station/Railway
- Tram
- Tube Station
- Underground/ U-Bahn station
- Other Transport

Our Story

A beat-up old car, a few dollars in the pocket and a sense of adventure. In 1972 that's all Tony and Maureen Wheeler needed for the trip of a lifetime – across Europe and Asia overland to Australia. It took several months, and at the end – broke but inspired – they sat at their kitchen table writing and stapling together their first travel guide, Across Asia on the Cheap. Within a week they'd sold 1500 copies. Lonely Planet was born.

Today, Lonely Planet has offices in Melbourne, London, Oakland, Franklin, Delhi and Beijing, with more than 600 staff and writers. We share Tony's belief that 'a great guidebook should do three things: inform, educate and amuse'.

Our Writers

Andy Symington

Andy hails from Australia but has been living in Spain for 15 years, where, to shatter a couple of stereotypes of the country, he can frequently be found huddled in sub-zero temperatures watching the tragically poor local football team. He has authored and co-authored many Lonely Planet guidebooks and other publications on Spain and elsewhere; in his spare time he walks in the mountains, embarks on epic tapas trails, and co-bosses a rock bar.

Sally Davies

Sally landed in Seville in 1992 with a handful of *pesetas* and five words of Spanish, and, despite a complete inability to communicate, promptly snared a lucrative number handing out leaflets at Expo '92. In 2001 she settled in Barcelona, where she is still incredulous that her daily grind involves researching fine restaurants, wandering about museums and finding ways to convey the beauty of this spectacular city.

Regis St Louis

Regis fell in love with Barcelona a decade ago, after arriving in the city and being awestruck by its wild architecture, culinary creativity and warm-hearted people. Since then he has returned frequently, learning Spanish and a smattering of Catalan, and delving into the endless layers of Barcelona's deep cultural heritage. Favourite memories from his most recent trip include fêting the arrival of three bearded kings during Dia de Reis, catching a surreal circus arts show in a seaside suburb, and exploring far-flung corners of Montjuïc at sunrise. Regis is the author of the two previous editions of *Barcelona*, and he has contributed to *Spain*, *Portugal* and dozens of other Lonely Planet titles. When not on the road, he lives in New Orleans.

EUROPE Unit E, Digital Court, The Digital Hub, Rainsford St, Dublin 8, Ireland

AUSTRALIA Levels 2 & 3 551 Swanston St, Carlton, Victoria 3053
☎ 03 8379 8000,
fax 03 8379 8111

USA 150 Linden Street, Oakland, CA 94607
☎ 510 250 6400,
toll free 800 275 8555,
fax 510 893 8572

UK 240 Blackfriars Road, London SE1 8NW
☎ 020 3771 5100,
fax 020 3771 5101

 twitter.com/lonelyplanet
 facebook.com/lonelyplanet
instagram.com/lonelyplanet
 youtube.com/lonelyplanet
lonelyplanet.com/newsletter